The Christian Education
of Adults

The Christian Education of Adults

Edited by
Gilbert A. Peterson

MOODY PRESS
CHICAGO

Copyright ©1984 by
THE MOODY BIBLE INSTITUTE
OF CHICAGO

Except where indicated otherwise, all Scripture quotations in this book are from the *New American Standard Bible,* ©1960, 1962, 1963, 1968, 1971, 1972, 1973, 1975, and 1977 by The Lockman Foundation, and are used by permission.

Library of Congress Cataloging in Publication Data
Main entry under title:

The Christian education of adults.

    Bibliography: p.
    Includes index.
    1. Christian education of adults—Addresses,
essays, lectures. I. Peterson, Gilbert A., 1935-
BV1488.C46 1985   268'.434   84-27329
ISBN 0-8024-0496-0

    2 3 4 5 6 7 Printing/AF/Year 90 89 88
Printed in the United States of America

We dedicate this volume to our wives—Dolores Peterson, Sandra Downs, Betty O'Byrne, and Karen McCracken—without whose patient encouragement and consistent sacrifice this volume could not have been written. They were willing to give of themselves and both release us from many duties around the home and help us with other responsibilities so that we could give the time necessary to research and write this volume.

Their loving interest, involvement, and support made this book by adults and for adults possible.

Contents

Preface

"The adult learner is a neglected species," observed the noted adult education leader Malcolm Knowles some years ago. In Christian education we have been especially slow to change. Somehow we persist in teaching adults as though they were children, devoid of experience and lacking ability to think and learn for themselves. Church educational programs continue to feed strained food rather than sirloins, to disregard creativity and capability.

This volume is an urgently needed tool. It speaks from historical and psychological perspectives to the practical needs of family life ministry, evangelism, and contemporary issues facing adults of every age. It is excellently devised as a textbook or group study guide. Each chapter climaxes with penetrating study questions, and the concluding resource information for adult ministries is invaluable.

It is a pleasure to recommend this excellent book, written by a choice friend and distinguished colleague, for its educational enrichment. Gilbert Peterson has produced a well-developed and thoroughly researched piece of work that makes a valuable contribution to the literature in this field. He is well qualified as an author not only by virtue of his academic credentials but also because of his years as a journeyman in the laboratory of life. He writes not as an armchair theorist but as a hands-on realist. Anyone concerned with any aspect of adult Christian education will benefit from this superb resource.

HOWARD G. HENDRICKS, Professor
Christian Education Department
Dallas Theological Seminary

PART ONE

ORIENTATION
TO ADULT CHRISTIAN EDUCATION

Gilbert A. Peterson

1

The Ministry of Adult Christian Education

Adult education began when God walked and talked with Adam and Eve in the Garden of Eden. The setting was a perfect garden, planted by God. The Teacher was a perfect teacher, God Himself. The students were perfect though innocent. We can only wonder at the content of those highly personalized lessons; they certainly must have been wide ranging. We do get a small glimpse of the scope of their studies in Genesis 4, where we see Enoch as a builder, Jabal as a herdsman, Jubal as a musician, and Tubal-cain as a metalsmith. God provided a well-rounded educational experience in that first school of adult education.

Of course, Genesis has more important purposes and information for us than just educational history. It is the book of beginnings. It sketches the beginning of the universe, man, sin, and salvation. It does, however, afford us this embryonic view of the beginning of adult education.

ORIGINS OF ADULT EDUCATION

Can you imagine the experience of Adam and Eve walking in the beginning of time with God and being exposed to the great wonders of creation? What a fantastic experience that must have been. In Genesis 2 we read that Adam had the great privilege of naming all the living creatures. He apparently was taught and skilled in many forms of what we have come to call scientific disciplines, such as chemistry, botany, and animal husbandry. He had the responsibility of cultivating the Garden of Eden. This work was not something undesirable or difficult. From his creation, Adam was a brilliant, gifted, and able man taught by God Himself while the pupil was still in an uncorrupted innocent state.

Eve, his wife, was equally skilled and personally taught of God. Together they shared a unique learning experience. Although it had started out as a one-on-one learning situation with God and Adam, it had early turned to the small group with God as the Teacher and Adam and Eve the students. When God the Son came to earth He also took time to instruct individuals as well as small and large groups. In adult education we must learn from the highly personalized teaching approaches of our Creator and utilize the full range of methodological and grouping possibilities.

Parental responsibility in instructing children apparently also began early in the development of mankind. Although the specific instructions to diligently teach the children and youth are not recorded until later, the process must have begun with Cain and Abel. Adam taught Cain what God had taught him about farming and the plant life of God's creation. Adam taught Abel all about the animals that God had created.

We have noted briefly how man's basic knowledge of various facets of life was taught by God to Adam and Eve and was then passed on to their children. Genesis reveals that God's interest in them was greater than simply making them productive and contented. From the beginning, God desired everlasting fellowship with Adam and Eve. For this reason He had revealed Himself to them not only as Creator and Teacher, but as their God and the object of their worship. It was warm, highly personal experience involving regular fellowship.

Chapter 3 of Genesis reveals how Adam and Eve broke that relationship and became separated from God with eternal consequences for them, their future children, and all succeeding generations. Although their sin separated them from God and severely marred the image of God in them, it did not completely obliterate all that God had taught them. They were now incapable, by their own activity, of restoring their relationship with God; they were spiritually dead and were beginning the process of physically dying. They were, however, still possessors of much, if not all, of what God taught them about living on the earth.

God then provided them with new lessons, as the first sacrificial blood was shed upon the earth and God made coats out of the hides of the animals He had slain to cover the effects of sin in their lives. The full lesson is not described in Genesis 3, but the continuing record of Scripture shows Adam and Eve learned that God had now provided for them new spiritual lessons and the way back to fellowship with Him through the shedding of blood and the death of another. One can only wonder at the grace of God and begin to imagine what Adam and Eve told their children about God's great love and forgiveness.

Not all teaching is successful. Adam and Eve chose not to obey one specific area of God's instruction. Cain chose not to obey what both God and his parents had taught him concerning worship, and he became the first murderer. Both of these failed lessons had catastrophic results. Neither, however, became an excuse for not teaching and not learning. The record of Scripture shows that the educational mission of God's people in the Old Testament and in the New Testament was to be sacred and a high priority.

From God's direct contact with individuals He moved to instruct through the family. At times, through the ages, other institutions have arisen and taken the lead in spiritual instruction, but always the family has remained as God's primary focus of concern.

Adults were instructed and were to be instructors as the Scriptures indicate. "He established a testimony in Jacob, and appointed a law in Israel, which He commanded our fathers that they should teach them to their children, that the generation to come might know, even the children yet to be born, that they may arise and tell them to their children" (Ps. 78:5-6).

In addition, there are the most memorable instructions of Deuteronomy 6. Here the nation was taught that families were to bear personal responsibility for teaching spiritual truth in an organized manner by laws and rituals, as well as by their day-by-day living. Family living was permeated with spiritual exercises. From the parchment on the doorposts, reminding everyone entering and leaving that that home belonged to the most High God, to the periodic ceremonies and repeated stories, every act had a spiritual significance and instructive value. This beautiful pattern was to be followed throughout all time. What a powerful impact it could have if instituted again in perhaps new and creative ways.

As the Scriptures indicate, the patriarchs became the next channel through which God would work. The promise to Abraham, Isaac, and Jacob was that the families of the earth would be blessed in and through them (Gen. 12:1-3). While the instruction in the garden to Adam and Eve was designed to maintain fellowship with God, after the Fall the divine purpose in godly education was to both restore the perfect relationship between God and man and then maintain it. In the New Testament this is most clearly seen in Matthew 28:19-20. Here Jesus instructs His disciples, "Go ye therefore, and teach all nations, baptizing them in the name of the Father, and of the Son, and of the Holy Ghost: Teaching them to observe all things whatsoever I have commanded you: and, lo, I am with you alway, even unto the end of the world" (KJV). Verse 19 refers to the restoring evangelizing process and verse 20 to the maintenance of godly living.

After the patriarchs, God next raised up prophets and priests as teachers of His people. God's dramatic object lessons, His spoken words, and His commandments for the performance of rituals to remember their relationship with Him became primary vehicles of godly instruction. In addition, Peter reminds us that "no prophecy was ever made by an act of human will, but men moved by the Holy Spirit spoke from God" (2 Pet. 1:21). God was providing a record of His dealing with His people, instructions for them, and promises for the future.

As time passed, rabbis began to appear on the scene, and the synagogue form as we read of it in the New Testament began to come into being. The rabbi held a very significant place in the whole scheme of Jewish life. He was teacher, reader, lawyer, and scholar. He was a man who was to be respected and given great honor. From the time of Ezra the Scribe, the rabbi became a man of supreme importance who was heard, obeyed, and respected. It was not until approximately one hundred years before Christ, however, that synagogues began to flourish in Palestine. It was into this setting "in the fullness of time" that Jesus came.

Jesus Christ is identified as a teacher in some sixty of the ninety times where He is addressed with a title in John's gospel. Although Christ was far more than just a teacher, it is interesting to note that when it came to His ministry on earth, much more attention is given to what He taught than what He did. The miracles confirmed the message. And Jesus Christ is clearly seen as the Way, the Truth, and the Life. He is Messiah, Savior, Prophet, Priest, and King. As the eternal God-Man, He becomes the one that the families, patriarchs, prophets, priests, and rabbis looked forward to and whom the apostles and believers today look back to. He is the focal point of all biblical education.

Jesus Christ selected twelve men whom He would instruct and disciple during His brief earthly ministry. These disciples ("taught ones") became apostles ("sent ones"). Having received the Word of God, they preached the Word of God in the synagogues of the Jews and in other places throughout the known world. As the Word of God was proclaimed throughout all the regions, scores came to know Christ as Lord and Savior, and the testimony of unbelieving Jews at Thessalonica was that "these men who have upset the world have come here also" (Acts 17:6). The message they taught and the manner of their living challenged and changed people. With the birth of the New Testament church, again certain specialized areas of service were identified, such as those of evangelists and pastor-teachers. The purpose still was "for the equipping of the saints for the work of service, to the building up of the body of Christ; until we all attain to the unity of the faith, and of the knowledge of the Son of God, to a mature man, to the measure of the stature which belongs to the fulness of Christ" (Eph. 4:12-13).

The Bible is a book written by adults for an adult audience, its purpose being to make the adult audience spiritually mature. The educational ministry of the local church today must place a high priority on its ministry with and to adults.

ADULT EDUCATION

In our present world adult education has aroused renewed interest and continues to be the largest segment of the American educational scene. Today more adults are involved in some type of formal learning situation in America than all the children and youth enrolled in our public and private school systems. Some learn for fun, others for profit. Popular courses on golf, auto mechanics, and food preparation stand side-by-side with courses in literature, computer programming, and Oriental philosophy. Adult education is coming of age and growing rapidly.

Many factors have brought about this renaissance in adult learning. Today there are more adults than we have had in any prior time. The sheer increase in numbers of people creates an opportunity that calls forth new and innovative ways of providing solutions to growing needs.

There are adults today who are past traditional college age but are returning to school in search of an education they bypassed earlier in life. Some have had enough experience to really know what they need, and they bring eagerness for learning and healthy maturity to the learning situation.

Adults are also distinctive individuals. They have passed the youth stage, where conformity plays such a large part, and most have developed special and distinct personalities. Their work and social experience, heredity, age, prior education, and a host of other socio-religious-economic factors make for a highly heterogeneous group. Their desires and interests vary greatly, and new vistas of learning opportunities open up before them.

Single adults are more numerous today, and here too a myriad of learning opportunities and motivations present themselves. The temporarily single man or woman, the widowed single, the divorced single, the single who has chosen a life without a marriage partner—all have needs and interests that deserve and demand our attention.

Married adults looking for answers to practical marriage and child rearing questions search out books, magazines, seminars, and study/support groups. Courses have become available in churches and colleges to meet this growing need.

Older adults, who have seen so much take place in their lifetimes and want to stay alert, growing, interested, and useful, form a large and growing group in North America. There are, of course, special needs and concerns in this sub-group of adults, but "gray power" is a factor to be reckoned with in all areas of life, education included.

Concern for adult education is not new. It began with two adults, Adam and Eve, continued with adults in Egypt, Greece, the Hebrew nation, and Rome, and has continued in the church. The Christian education of children and youth, a relatively recent development, is very important. It should be noted, however, that the great spiritual revivals and revitalizations that have taken place over the centuries have been sparked by the Holy Spirit in the hearts and lives of adults who then ministered to the children and youth.

Although the future of society and the church is with its young, the life of society and the church today, as well as the direction for tomorrow, lies in the hands of today's adults. We must courageously strive for the upgrading, promotion, and the proper development of the educational programs and opportunities for today's adult learners. Learning is fun, exciting, and fulfilling. To make it dull, boring, and routine is sinful.

ADULT CHRISTIAN EDUCATION

This book will present adult Christian education as the greatest educational challenge facing the church today. It is necessary to reflect on where we have been; without a sense of history we lose a great heritage. Often in Scripture God's people are told to recall lessons given in the past. We too shall look back and see what has been accomplished so that we can profit from the past.

It is also valuable to look carefully at what is now occurring, so that a clear view of present reality can keep us focused on relevant issues at hand. Dynamic things have been happening in adult Christian education across the United States and Canada. This, combined with what has been happening in Third World Countries in Theological Education by Extension, and the implications of this new dimension for all of adult education are exciting to consider.

It is important that future possibilities be explored as well. Only as we look thoughtfully into the future and candidly project where we want to go can we ever expect to develop by design rather than by drift.

Projecting the future is risky business, especially if one tries too hard to specify programs and procedures. We shall therefore confine our projections to anticipated needs, working principles, and vital goals.

ADULT MINISTRIES

"Where will we ever find the leaders we need?" This is a common question in churches the world over. The answer in most cases is, "Grow your own!" A very important focal point for adult Christian education is the recruitment, training, and utilization of your adult leaders. Some leaders will transfer in from other churches. Some you can hire and need to do so. The majority, however, you will need to cultivate yourself: you must identify their potential, give them learning experiences to help them gain knowledge and confidence, and carefully involve them in the day-to-day, week-by-week ministry of the church. Teachers, ushers, board members, youth leaders, secretaries, bus drivers, and a host of others are needed weekly to carry on the proper ministry of your church. Few churches have waiting lists of prepared, willing workers.

Family Life Education signals another sensitive need area in local churches. With the pressures of an unfriendly society upon it, the family is coming under increased attack, and the local church (a collection of committed families) must provide the context and resources needed to face those challenges. In Old Testament times, a family found its significance in terms of its relationship with other families in great tribes; today, the Christian family can be strengthened by its relationship with other families in the church. That will not just happen, however—it must be cultivated.

Older adults are also proving to be a source of increased concern to contemporary Christian educators. Their numbers are increasing, as are their needs. Some are cared for in the homes of their children, but increasing numbers are being institutionalized; and for them Christian education or even Christian activities are often limited to the visits of occasional church groups. Some have lost the capacity for productive activity, but a great majority want to continue learning and can continue learning; yet little is available for them in Christian education.

The task before us is large and rewarding. Revitalizing the life of the adult Christian education program of the local church is our goal. Providing satisfying, involving, practical, and productive learning opportunities is indeed possible. The resources are at our fingertips. Let us resolve to use them for the glory of God and the good of our brethren.

THE NEW ADULT WORLD

Adults today are living in a brand-new world, much changed from the world of 1950. As the world approaches the turn of the century, the rapidity of change is increasing, and the significance of this change must be understood by the informed evangelical Christian education leader.

Some of those forces that need to be dealt with are: America's transformation from a youth-oriented society to an adult-oriented society; the computer revolution; the influx of women into the job market and the dramatic rise in the number of working mothers (from 18.4 percent in 1950 to 57.2 percent in 1983, according to the United States Department of Labor); the growth of minority groups in size and influence; the educational boom, with 23 million Americans involved in continuing education programs (almost twice the number involved fifteen years ago); and the medical miracles that have increased longevity and the quality of life.

AN ADULT-ORIENTED SOCIETY

One of the slogans of the sixties and early seventies was "Don't trust anyone over thirty." Things have changed, and as the following chart indicates, the under-twenty group has been declining while the forty and older group has been increasing.

These shifts affect our social, economic, political, and spiritual landscape. Industry is rethinking its use of older adults. The entertainment world is concentrating on meeting more of the needs and desires of adults. There is a possibility that tax funds may begin to shift from schools toward long-term health care.

It has been further noted that young people entering the work force after 1990 can look forward to less competition from their peers than their older brothers and sisters had. On the other side of it, industry's use of older people for longer periods of time and in part-time capacities will also likely increase. The overall picture may be a blessing of talent and experience available to the church and to the world that has never been there before.

THE COMPUTER EXPLOSION

Today the computer and the technology of the computer affect the lives of everyone in one way or another. Computers design products, construct products, control flow and production of products, and are used as major communication and control mechanisms in the service

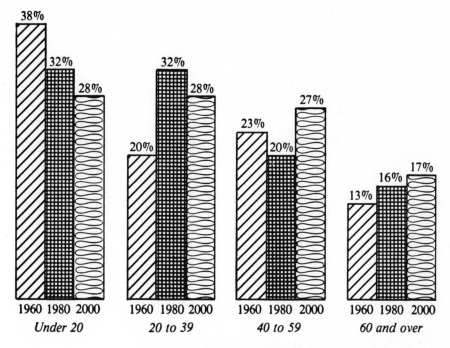

Data: U.S. Dept. of Commerce[1]

industries. We talk today about plastic money, automated bank-teller machines, direct cash transfers to pay for products at local stores, and a host of other tasks uniquely suited to computer capabilities and potentials.

In the area of education, the computer is reshaping approaches to learning. In this early phase of computer involvement in education, there is much confusion as to what role the computer should take, but the question of whether the computer will be involved in education is not being even considered. Christian educators need to consider carefully the role of the computer in their ministry. The widespread use of computers and machinery can accelerate the rapid decline of interpersonal human relationships already rampant in high-density population areas. People need people. The computer will never replace the innermost need of the individual for a right relationship with God and its attendant blessing of right relationships with other people.

1. "Ten Forces Reshaping America," *U. S. News and World Report,* 19 March 1984, p. 41.

THE NEW ROLE OF WOMEN

Dramatic changes have occurred in the last twenty to thirty years as to the role of women. Not only are women more numerous in the work place, and not only has the number of working mothers increased dramatically, but women now hold jobs in just about all the major types of industries and occupations available. Women outnumber men in college by 52 percent to 48 percent as of 1984; one-third of all United States law students are women; and although the total numbers are not great in the area of politics, the number of women elected to legislatures has increased by 300 percent from 1972 to 1984, for a total of 993 state legislators. Women hold the edge in voting-age population, and the number of women scientists and engineers with doctoral degrees has more than doubled in the past ten years. They still represent only 12 percent of the total but are on the increase. Finally, women outlive men by more than seven years at the present time; in the area of spiritual ministry, this dramatic trend demands specific attention, creative programs, and Spirit-guided development.[2] The impact of the change in women's roles, opportunities, and influence in terms of church ministry and spiritual outreach is dealt with in later chapters.

THE POTENTIAL OF MINORITIES

The American public is now accustomed to seeing the worlds of entertainment, sports, business, and politics populated with significant leadership from minority groups. Language has changed, and although bigotry and racism obviously have not been eradicated, there has been a significant change in the patterns and developments of racial groups and interracial relationships within the United States. Today, blacks, Orientals, Hispanics, Vietnamese, Laotians, and others are residents and leaders of neighborhoods and groups where there are significant white populations. Latin Americans will soon replace blacks as the largest minority. Some attitudes, programs, and policies have changed among fundamentalists and evangelicals, but there still remains a dramatic need for developing relationships and cooperation in ministry and resource developments between white and non-white Christians. This can be one of the most significant challenges of the late eighties and nineties.

2. "10 Forces Reshaping America," pp. 46–48.

EDUCATIONAL EXPANSION

A very interesting phenomenon is developing in the area of education and jobs in America. The United States Bureau of Labor Statistics predicts that the biggest growth in jobs will be among those requiring either little or highly specialized education. And so more youths and adults are involved in educational enterprises today than ever before in the history of America. This is true not only numerically but also on a percentage basis. Schools traditionally given to liberal arts curricula have added to their programs majors in what are called "marketable job skills," such as analytical thinking, computer programming, teacher education, and business. At the present time, colleges are turning out more graduates than the job market can accommodate, and one of the problems is that the job skills that they come out with will be outmoded in a short period of time.

With this emphasis on only those skills that will earn money, thinking in the type of education that will develop character is far more needed than most people realize. Again, the Christian educator must be alert to the potential and need for proper educational programs and must work hard at clarifying values and objectives. Christian educators must also take into consideration the tremendous impact that technology is having in education today with computers and communications forces leading the way. Education is a prime concern for all Americans but of particular concern to Christians, since the Bible focuses so much on knowing, believing, and behaving in a godly way.

MEDICAL ADVANCES

Statistics regarding longevity indicate that people in our nation today are able to live longer, fuller, and more active lives. Childhood diseases are being virtually eliminated; people who died just twenty and thirty years ago from the failure of various organs are now able to live longer and often normal lives through implants, pacemakers, various kinds of drugs, and diet control. One of the effects of all this has been an increasingly older population.

There has also been the dramatic reduction of infant mortality. If it were not for the high rate of infanticide through abortion, the nation would be experiencing a significant baby boom.

There are moral, ethical, and spiritual questions that need answers in today's world. The Christian educator must be involved. We have learned how to keep alive the very old, sick, and feeble, as well as infants that are born terribly deformed. The questions are: Should we do so, and for how long? And who is to decide whether, and when, to pull the plug? Those questions bring us as Christian educators into the theological realms of the sovereignty of God, the sanctity of life, and human responsibility. We are moving into an exciting age that will demand the best from every Christian educator. We need scholars who will research and, with Spirit-directed wisdom, come up with systematic answers to pressing questions. We need practitioners who will apply those answers to the everyday lives of believers in the church. We need other Christians who will dedicate themselves to influencing for God a society that is moving in a godless direction. We need effective witnesses to lead people to Jesus Christ.

The challenge of adult Christian education is so enormous that one is tempted to shrink from the task. If it were not for the tremendous biblical truth that we are partners together with the Lord in this process, it would be impossible.

Adult education began in the Garden of Eden, but it did not end there. We can only reflect on the excitement, the content, and the impact upon Adam and Eve that God had in that direct contact. The foundation of all learning for human beings was laid in those days. By the entrance of sin and the subsequent fall of Adam and Eve and all of creation, satanic influence took control. As the Scriptures abundantly declare, however, God did not give up. He has patiently and persistently presented Himself down through the ages to mankind in direct revelation, culminating in the written Word of God.

Throughout the Scriptures we are confronted with the importance of education and learning. The culmination of this in the person and work of Jesus Christ, who was identified as a teacher, is most significant. We all recognize that the Scriptures were written by adults to adults and that the leadership of the church of Jesus Christ is indeed in the hands of adults. We face practical questions that demand practical answers, answers based upon absolute and eternal principle.

We also face tremendous challenges as the society in which we live changes, and a variety of technical, human, and interpersonal forces play upon us. It is our prayer that in the reading of this book you will not only be challenged by the scope and potential of adult ministry in the local church, but that you will be changed and called to be involved as a worker together with the Lord in bringing men and women to direct confrontation with God in intelligent and meaningful ways, so that they will know Him as Lord and serve Him with all their being. People can be changed for the glory of God. Revival and a maturing Christian church is desperately needed in this age; to that end, this book has been written.

1. Read Genesis 1 through 4 and identify the type of learning that took place in the early days of God's interaction with man as well as the types of professions, or categories of learning, that are represented in these early experiences in Scripture.

2. Study John, chapter 4, and note the progression of Jesus' informal teaching of the woman at the well. Outline the progression of this teaching experience from initial contact to a life response.

3. Survey one year's worth of periodicals, such as *Change, The Learning Connection, Moody Monthly, Pastoral Psychology, Psychology Today, The Christian Herald, Today's Education,* and similar publications. Identify the major issues being discussed that directly affect the Christian education of adults.

4. Write a paragraph that finishes the sentence "I believe that Christian education of adults is important because . . . " Save this particular paragraph and review it after you have finished reading this book; note those changes that have occurred in your thinking.

5. Survey the local church you attend and identify those programs that are specifically designed for adults, noting their purpose, objectives, and program development.

2

The Historical Development
of Adult Learning

As indicated in the previous chapter, adult Christian education is deeply rooted in both the New Testament and the Old Testament. Adult education began in the Garden of Eden and throughout the ages, with the intensity changing from time to time, there has been a great concern for the education of adults.

The Old Testament is a record of God's calling out a people for His name and through them providing the Redeemer, the Savior. Throughout progression from verbal communication in the Garden to the written record, continuing to the development of ceremonies and rituals and on to the present era with its multi-media and word processing concepts, the biblical education of adults has been a priority with God. It has had a rather erratic pattern through the ages but is coming into its own in the latter part of the 1980s and on into the early 1990s.

Ingrained in the very essence of the relationship between God and Israel was the concept of teaching and learning. Learning was not simply a cognitive process but was a total, involving experience that resulted in changed behavior. Israel was to be instructed in living a holy life before a holy God. They were taught by the Lord and were to be consistent communicators of His truth, not only to their children but also to the stranger that came within their gate (Deut. 31:12). In addition to the historical record of God's dealing with His people (Genesis, Exodus, Numbers), we find His careful instruction regarding such things as food habits, sexual behavior, sickness, purification, sacrifices, feasts, offerings, and redemptions (Leviticus, Deuteronomy). These instructions were designed to help the adults live according to God's design, teach their offspring to follow the Lord, and witness by the distinctiveness of their lives to the nations around them.

Even the location that God chose for them on the face of the earth had teaching significance. In *A Promised Land for a Chosen People*,[1] Gordon Ceperley notes the multiple references in the Scriptures to the good land that God had prepared for His people. Of all the places on the face of the earth, Palestine was selected by the Lord as a place uniquely suited to learning. The four topographical areas of Palestine indicated in Deuteronomy 1:6-8 and in Numbers 13:29 are: the Negev, or rocky barren wilderness; the mountainous area of the north; the sea coast along the Mediterranean; and the Jordan Valley. Ceperley shows that in the Negev, God was trying to teach His people faith, diligence, and hospitality. In the mountains, He was attempting to teach them gratitude, humility, and confidence. In the coastal plain, He was trying to teach them the way of witness. And in the Jordan Valley, He was attempting to teach them understanding, trust, and unity in the midst of diversity. As Ceperley says, "Size, serene beauty, and mineral resources become trivial in the light of God's eternal purposes. Ultimately, the concern of God is for people rather than places; souls rather than scenes; and behavior rather than physical beauty."[2] Physical environment is a powerful teacher. Sometimes Israel learned well from their surroundings, as is evident in David's expression in Psalm 121:1-2; sometimes they failed, as is evident in their failure to occupy the coastal plain and witness to the nations.

In addition to speaking to His people through the environment and topographical surroundings, God also gave instructions for rituals and ceremonies in order that they might remember their relationship with Him and what He had done for them. Like today, however, sometimes the rituals became ends in themselves, and God had to speak to His people through prophets, judges, and scribes. He called them back to repentance and to reality.

> Hear the Word of the Lord, you rulers of Sodom; give ear unto the instruction of our God, you people of Gomorrah. "What are your multiplied sacrifices to Me?" says the Lord. "I have had enough of burnt offerings of rams,

1. Gordon G. Ceperley (W. Collingswood, N.J.: Friends of Israel Gospel Ministry, 1978).
2. Ibid., p. 69.

and the fat of fed cattle. And I take no pleasure in the blood of bulls, lambs, or goats. . . . Wash yourselves, make yourselves clean; remove the evil of your deeds from My sight. Cease to do evil, learn to do good; seek justice, reprove the ruthless; defend the orphan, plead for the widow. Come now, and let us reason together," says the Lord. "Though your sins are as scarlet, they will be as white as snow; though they are red like crimson, they will be like wool. If you consent and obey, you will eat the best of the land; but if you refuse and rebel, you will be devoured by the sword." Truly, the mouth of the Lord has spoken. (Isa. 1:10–11, 16–20)

Here we see a very prominent Old Testament teaching: the spiritual nature and significance of all learning. The sacred and the secular were not separated. All life and all learning had spiritual direction. There were no concepts like "art for art's sake."

Parents took on a major role in the learning process, and the community would gather to memorize what God had said in Scripture. This they did not only by rote recall but also by singing. Children were then instructed through learning the Scripture hymns and through an extensive question-and-answer process (Deut. 6:20–25). The revelation of God was in written form; thus, much emphasis was laid on the art of reading. Although the Old Testament does not contain references to formal schooling, we note from the New Testament record (Matt. 21:23; Mark 14:49; Luke 20:1; John 18:20) that there was instruction in the law given in the Temple area in the outer court. We note also that Ezra, the priest, was called "a scribe skilled in the law of Moses" (Ezra 7:6).

During the so-called silent years, the four hundred years between the Old and New Testaments, there apparently developed a great number of schools for youth throughout Israel. Family influence seemed to diminish, and foreign influences caused disintegration. A bright light for Judaism was Rabbi Joshua ben Gamala, who about 64 B.C. instituted reforms. He established a system wherein every province and town would have teachers to whom children should be brought at the age of six or seven years of age for instruction in the Torah.[3]

Central in Jewish instruction throughout the years since the time of Christ has been the *Schema,* or *Principle of Jewish Prayer,* beginning with the verses from Deuteronomy 6, and the *Daily Prayer Book,* or *Siddur,* one of the greatest documents of devotional literature. The roots of much adult Christian education go back to the principles and practices of

3. Nathan Drazin, *History of Jewish Education from 1515 B.C.E. to 200 C.E.* (Baltimore: John Hopkins, 1940), p. 37.

ancient Judaism. Primary methods often used were lecture, question and answer, and group discussions.[4]

The principal method of instruction continuing to Jesus' day was the interlocutory, or the question-and-answer process. The Jewish method emphasized the pupil's questions. It was the teacher's role to listen and the pupil's part to question. The ability of the Hebrew teacher was gauged by the ability of the pupil to ask intelligent and penetrating questions. The concept was grounded in the conviction that a person could not ask intelligent questions unless he had mastered the subject.

The catechetical method, which developed in the early New Testament church, was a modification of the interlocutory method. Again, it was a question-and-answer process, but developed primarily for the purpose of being able to give consistent, biblical answers to those who questioned the Christian faith.

EARLY NEW TESTAMENT ADULT EDUCATION

Just as Adam and Eve were directly instructed by God in the Garden of Eden, so the disciples were directly instructed by God the Son during the earthly ministry of our Savior. The Old Testament looks forward to the coming of Messiah, and the New Testament looks back and proclaims Him the Savior of mankind. At the time of Christ's coming, the Jewish nation had substituted a very formal and legalistic regimen for the free, open, and spiritual life taught in the Law, Prophets, and Writings. The extra-biblical Talmud, with its detailing of every aspect of life, was having greater influence on the minds and behavior of God's people than was the Torah of Moses.

When Jesus came, He spoke with authority and not as the many teachers of His day. "Never did a man speak the way this man speaks" was the comment of His enemies. Jesus used teaching as the chief means of training His disciples for the work of the ministry. Although Jesus at one point called attention to children as an illustration of faith, His ministry was primarily directed towards adults. The manner of Jesus' teaching was more informal than formal, and more conversational than discursive. The emphasis that Jesus put on effective teaching can even be seen in His last words to His disciples, where He instructed them to carry the message of the gospel to all nations and all peoples, and to instruct in such a manner that men would act in accordance with the way they had been taught.

4. *Universal Jewish Encyclopedia*, "Education: Early Jewish History" (New York: Universal Jewish Encyclopedia Co., 1948).

It was on the Day of Pentecost that Peter began to teach in detail the truth concerning Jesus Christ. Later the apostle Paul called himself a teacher, and became the most outstanding teacher of the early New Testament church. His ministry was directed toward small groups of adults, normally meeting in homes for discussion. His writings were directed toward adult believers with the intent of giving them additional knowledge and understanding of the truths concerning Jesus Christ and the living of a Christlike life. Paul's training in a rabbinical school shows in his ability to organize and present God's truth: The Holy Spirit so directed him that what he wrote was not only without error but was essential for Christian life and growth.

The setting for much of the instruction in the early New Testament church, as far as the apostles were concerned, was the synagogue. The general purpose of the synagogue was for the study and teaching of the law rather than for worship. Normally the worship times were reserved for the Temple area. This provided, therefore, a natural setting, since synagogues were to be found in all towns and villages in Palestine and in many other cities where there were sufficient numbers of Jewish population to support them. At the age of twelve, a Jewish boy became a "son of the law" (*Bar Mitzvah*) and was, therefore, admitted to the synagogue and considered able to both hear the teaching and answer questions. We can see in Luke 2:46 that it was very natural, therefore, for our Savior to be found with the educators and theologians in the Temple area in Jerusalem engaged in such dialogue. The early New Testament church picked up the concept since the first members were Hebrews and well-oriented to the process. Synagogue teaching was quite informal and carried on in a manner similar to that which Jesus had done.

In the first and second centuries, however, catechumenal schools were established to give a more systematic and complete preparation of converts before admitting them to church membership. The word *catechumen* comes from a Greek word meaning literally to "pound into the ear." Adults were first admitted to hear the reading of Scripture and an explanation. There was some elementary instruction with regard to doctrine at this first level. The second level was for those who had advanced and demonstrated in their lives that they were serious in their following of Christ. The third level was for those who had received intensive instruction in preparation for baptism and membership. Eavey identifies these three levels as hearers, kneelers, and the chosen.[5]

5. C. B. Eavey, *History of Christian Education* (Chicago: Moody, 1964), p. 85.

The primary method of the catechumenal school was the question-and-answer, or catechetical, method. It was far more than what is normally thought of today when that term is used. It involved dialogue wherein both students and teachers asked and answered questions, with the teacher as the primary guide in the process. This particular form of adult Christian education originated during the first and second centuries, and was practiced until approximately A.D. 450.

Following the period of the catechumenal schools came the development of the catechetical schools. In all probability, these grew out of the catechumenal school concepts of the early New Testament church, but the focus of attention was now shifted from teaching lay adult Christians their Christian life responsibilities to the training and equipping of clergy to meet the intellectual challenges coming to them from the pagan world. It was Clement and Origen who brought this phase of adult education in the early church to its zenith. Although catechetical schools were not originally intended to be only for clergy instruction, that was the direction they took, and became the forerunner of the later cathedral schools of the fifth and sixth centuries. As Eavey so clearly says,

> The episcopal and cathedral schools intensify the tendency begun in the catechetical schools to take less and less interest in the instruction of all Christians and to form a special priestly class. In time, the result was an intellectual aristocracy in the church, with much ignorance among the masses. As the church grew in worldly prominence, it lost spiritual life through failure to continue to perform the duty imposed upon it by its Lord in the Great Commission. Man does not live by truth he discovers through his own thinking, but by truth he learns through coming to know the Scriptures. As Greek learning came in, the Bible went out; as the Bible went out, spiritual life declined. When thorough instruction in the Word of God ceased, vital piety was by church orthodoxy and barren formalism.[6]

What began in the early New Testament church as a passion for teaching adult believers the Scriptures and Christian living, declined as Hellenistic influence grew in the church.

In the Middle Ages (from approximately 500 to A.D. 1300) there was a great barrenness among both laymen and clergy, with the only teaching being done by the clergy. And even that was extremely limited. The influences of the Greeks and Romans in the development of cathedral schools had placed great emphasis on the "seven liberal arts" (grammar, rhetoric, logic, mathematics, geometry, astronomy, and music). In addi-

6. Ibid., p. 90.

tion to these liberal arts were added the study of theology, the canon and civil law, ethics, and the Scriptures. Little attention, however, was paid to the education of the masses in the truth of God's Word.

It was during this period that two very diverse systems of educational thought developed. The first was Scholasticism, which was closely connected with the rise of universities and was an outgrowth of the cathedral school concept. The second, Scholasticism's antithesis, was the concentration on emotions of the Mystics. It was in Thomas Aquinas that Scholasticism found its most articulate teacher and writer. Among the Mystics, names like Bernard of Clairveaux, Hugo, and Thomas á Kempis became familiar. While Scholasticism emphasized reason, Mysticism emphasized spiritual union with God.

A third group came into being, the Waldenses, who later became a seedbed for the Reformation. They are generally considered to be the most evangelical of the groups that existed during the medieval period. Their emphasis was on preaching and teaching the Bible as their rule and guide for faith and life. Persecuted, they survived and passed their truth on to the Lollards (of whom John Wycliffe was the leader) and the Hussites (of whom John Huss was the leader). Their primary concern was getting the Scriptures into the language of the people. They emphasized the doctrines of purity in living, the authority of Scripture, and loving one's neighbor. Although they emphasized personal reading of the Scriptures, they were not well taught in biblical and theological doctrine.

The Reformation, which started as a movement to correct the excesses of the Roman church, was a major turning point in Christian education history. The authority of the Bible, and the right of individual conscience to make decisions regarding living the Christian life because the individual believer is a priest himself before the Lord, stood in opposition to Roman Catholic doctrine. If everyone was to be under the authority of the Word and a believer-priest before the Lord, then everyone needed education; and although this education developed in different ways under men like Luther, Melanchthon, Zwingli, and Calvin, many characteristics were similar. Elementary school education became important; books became important; reading, writing, and language were developed at the secondary and what was later to be the college level. The final goal was to be universal Christian education. This was sought through not only the translation of the Bible into the language of the people but also the revival of biblical and doctrinal preaching, together with teaching the Bible in the family.

Early American Christian Education

The colonists imported Christian education to America on the very first ships to arrive. The first settlers were, in the main, those who had left Europe for personal religious freedom. As Protestants, they were concerned that the Scriptures guide their daily practice. Therefore they built their entire societal structure on a foundation of education that was essentially Christian. With the twin forces of education for all and education in the Scriptures came a third force, a part of what is often called today the "work ethic": the idea that ignorance produced idleness, and that idleness was the worst of sins.

In the development of education in America, the first emphasis was not on adult education. Survival was the first priority, and apprenticeship was the tool for the development of vocational training of children and youth. Malcolm Knowles writes,

> The first permanent institutional form of education to be created was the university. Sixteen years after the Puritans landed in Massachusetts, in 1636, they founded Harvard College. Harvard certainly had nothing to do with adult education at that time, being primarily a school for training ministers at what would now be considered the secondary level. But it was the beginning of an institutional form that has grown to an important position in adult education.[7]

Other schools of higher education came into being in the years that followed, including William and Mary College, Virginia (1696); Yale, Connecticut (1701); Princeton, New Jersey (1747); King's College (now Columbia University), New York City (1754); and the University of Pennsylvania, Pennsylvania (1755).

Following quickly was a system of public schools not initiated by, but fostered by, the Massachusetts Law of 1642, which instructed local town governments to establish instruction for children; and by the time of the American Revolution, town schools were common.

It was the church, however, that was the single most important place for intellectual growth and development during the colonial period. In addition to Sunday sermons, there were often mid-week lectures on a variety of subjects, and although the broad program that is now available for adults in churches and communities was not in place at that time, the ground was being prepared. Knowles writes, "The church was

7. Malcolm S. Knowles, *History of the Adult Education Movement in the United States* (Huntington, N.Y.: Robert E. Krieger, 1977), p. 5.

probably the most influential institutional force for the education of adults in the first two centuries of our national life."[8]

The Christian education of adults through the church did not begin in the Sunday school. The Sunday school movement was transplanted from England to the United States in the late 1700s, and in 1824 the American Sunday School Union (now American Missionary Fellowship) was founded. The emphasis was on the education of children in biblical truth. Adults were important in the process through their role as teachers, and methods for training them began to develop.

> Founded on the shores of Chautauqua Lake in Western New York in the summer of 1874, Chautauqua Institution was initially conceived as a pan-denominational normal school for Sunday School teachers. This was the sole purpose in the minds of its founders, Dr. John Vincent, Secretary of the Methodist Sunday School Union, and Louis Miller, a businessman and church layman. The idea of a summer education program proved so popular that the Chautauqua began to attract participants other than Sunday School teachers and began broadening its program to include every aspect of culture.[9]

That broadening continued. Correspondence courses were developed for adults. The YMCA began in Boston in 1851, concentrating on young men with its program of prayer meetings, Bible studies, and classes on commercial subjects, languages, public affairs, and other areas. The adult education movement from the middle 1800s to the early 1900s was marked by a multiplication of programs and adult education institutions. Correspondence schools, summer schools, evening schools, libraries, recreation and learning centers, voluntary associations, and vocational training programs were but some of the major developments.

Adult Christian Education: 1920 to the Present

From the 1920s to the present the Bible has remained the focus of most adult educational programs in Protestant and evangelical churches. Weekday courses have addressed areas such as marriage, family development, music, and even drama. Specialization has tended to take place, with larger churches having not only directors of Christian education, but also directors of adult work or ministers of adult education. It has been said that free society requires an enlightened citizen. It is even more importantly true that biblical Christianity requires enlight-

8. Ibid., p. 9.
9. Ibid., pp. 36–37.

ened believers. Adult Christian education in the church must be biblically grounded and closely related to the needs of each adult learner.

Need orientation has marked the direction and development of adult Christian education in the twentieth century. The term that has come to mean the most is *lifelong learning*. This is the concept that education is a process beginning at birth and ending at death, and that the participant is active and involved throughout the process.

> Lifelong learning includes, but is not limited to, adult basic education, continuing education, independent study, agricultural education, business education and labor education, occupational education and job training programs, parent education, postsecondary education, pre-retirement and education for older and retired people, remedial education, special educational programs for groups or for individuals with special needs, and also educational activities designed to upgrade occupational and professional skills, to assist business, public agencies, and other organizations in the use of innovation and research results, and to serve family needs and personal development.[10]

Lifelong learning is an all-encompassing experience and quite in keeping with the biblical concept of education. It is exciting today to consider the renewed interest in learning on the part of adults.

It is exciting to consider the new attitude on the part of people in general, and leaders in particular, toward the need to develop a well-grounded and well-designed adult educational program. It is also exciting to note that educators of adults are beginning to concentrate on the end result of education rather than attempting to develop a rigid pattern of educational conformity. There are still many critics about who emphasize the failures in adult education programs, and their arguments are seductive. They often gain support because they focus on one or two genuine problem areas rather than taking a comprehensive and cohesive look at the total educational program for adults. The decade before us calls for new enthusiasm, new commitment, new ideas, and new approaches that will allow the church to show the lasting value that Christian education of adults can have.

New dimensions and directions have come in more recent years, and they are exciting to behold. They include: intergenerational learning; renewed and reinvigorated camping and conference programming; short-term learning experiences, such as seminars; the opening of the postsecondary experiences for adults at all ages; and even the opportunity for ministry through missions at home and abroad for adults of all ages.

10. Higher Education Act of 1965, Title I, Part B, Section 132.

Adults want self-directed learning experiences, practical education based on solid theoretical frameworks, and the freedom to move in and out of the learning experience as determined by their physical, financial, social, and educational needs. We are in a new day and a new era, and it is an exciting one. Flexibility and innovativeness will mark adult Christian education during the years that are ahead.

Underscoring this is the research done by Joan Cronin in her attempt to develop guidelines for people who are working in the field of adult Christian education. Paraphrasing her eleven points, we find the following: (1) The adult Christian educator must respect and support adults in the learning process and assist them in their self-directed learning. (2) The adult Christian educator must be aware of the cultural, socio-economic, ethnic, religious, and educational background of the learner. (3)The adult Christian educator must allow adults to participate in the planning of their learning process and the setting of their learning goals. (4) The adult Christian educator should provide a wide variety of learning opportunities that are related to the variety of needs the adult learner has. (5) The adult Christian educator should recognize that adults need encouragement and support as they learn to develop toward those goals or experiences that are before them. (6) The adult Christian educator should recognize that adults learn well when they are with peers and especially working in groups, and learning approaches should reflect this. (7) The adult Christian educator must understand that adults need to see immediate results and progress. Realism and flexibility are essentials here. (8) The adult Christian educator must recognize that adults have formed habit patterns and are often slow to change or accept new approaches and ideas. (9) Adult Christian educators should be aware of the fact that adults are living in a time of dramatic change and are looking for deeper and newer faith experiences. (10) Adult Christian educators should plan a wide variety of spiritual exercises such as prayer, Bible reading, meditation, and witnessing into their total adult Christian education curriculum. (11) Adult Christian educators should assist adults in evaluating themselves according to the goals that have been established either by themselves or by a program.[11]

In keeping with these concepts, let us turn our attention to five newer approaches that are being used in church and church-related organizations today.

---

11. Joan Cronin, "Implications for Adult Religious Education," in *Faith Development in the Adult Life Cycle,* ed. Kenneth Stokes (New York: W. H. Sadlier, 1982), pp. 294–95.

INTERGENERATIONAL EDUCATIONAL EXPERIENCES

In his excellent book *Family Ministry,* Charles Sell deals with the intergenerational experience as it relates to adult Christian education. He discusses groups, as small as seven or eight persons or as large as more than twenty families, as mini-churches wherein individuals or families can participate in a closeness and a bond of unity that is unique. He says:

> Herein is their strength. They are not designed just for one thing like construction, business, or recreation. Rather, they are groups dedicated to all that is meant by being a church. Yet they do not replace the larger church body. They support the larger group as well as receive its support. Freedom from divisiveness or cliquishness is maintained by semi-annual or annual rotation of members; or by the growth, division, or turnover within the groups themselves.[12]

The intergenerational experience is called by various names in various areas. In the United States, we talk about small groups; overseas they can be "koinonia" groups, which have to do with community or community fellowship; when developed in Christian schools overseas, they are often called "caring groups." The benefits of the intergenerational experience are more often affective than cognitive. They have to do with development of care, concern, understanding, affirmation, and general support. Reactions to intergenerational experiences are somewhat mixed, because the idea is somewhat new. Having grandmothers and primaries, teenagers and tots all together can provide a dramatic new opportunity for the local church that has been programmed over the years to think only in terms of separate age groups for learning, fellowship, and training experiences. Intergenerational learning will not take the place of separate age and separate group learning experiences but can be a significant supplement to it.

FAMILY CAMPING

During the first fifty to sixty years of this century the Bible conference developed. Biblical camps and conferences dotted the landscape from coast to coast. Their traditional format contained morning Bible studies, followed by afternoon recreation, and then evening rallies or services. Some weeks were set aside for youth, others for children's

---

12. Charles Sell, *Family Ministry* (Grand Rapids: Zondervan, 1981), p. 231.

ministry. Everyone ate in the common dining hall, and the conference center became a Christian summer recreational experience.

A newer move has been underway in the last twenty years, known as *family camping.* This is a move away from the hotel or motel-like accommodations of the Bible conference toward either primitive tent or tent-trailer camping. The important difference is that the family is staying together, having its meals together, and having its recreation and leisure times together.

Family camps of this nature are often now associated with Bible conferences, so that the family can have options regarding its meals, Bible study, prayer, and worship. Charles Sell, in arguing for the value of family camping as opposed to conference orientation, indicates that there are many benefits that family camping can provide. He identifies them as having fun together, learning relational dynamics, understanding the changing relational dynamics, sharing with other generations, increasing family identity, developing spiritual dynamics, and providing inter-family contact.[13]

SHORT-TERM SEMINARS

The late sixties introduced us to another form of adult education. This was the short-term seminar, running from one day to a week. The most familiar and popular has been Bill Gothard's Institute on Basic Youth Conflicts. Another has been the "Walk Thru the Bible" series. Gospel Light Publications' International Center for Learning has a short-term seminar designed to provide teacher and Sunday school leader training in a condensed program. Concentrated learning in a short period of time, with a sharp focus, using multiple methodological approaches has proved to be both interesting and effective.

One reason this approach has slowed down in the mid-eighties is economic. Many Christians believe that the experiences they are getting through the seminars should be provided for them through the local church without cost. The time, effort, talent, and cost that goes into the development of a seminar, however, is extensive, and Christians will need to become more increasingly realistic with regard to the cost of the educational programs that they require.

POSTSECONDARY EDUCATION

From the late fifties until the late seventies, many young people who would normally have gone to college bypassed the college route. This

13. Ibid., pp. 255-56.

was partly due to their anti-"establishment" attitude, but also because they did not see the need for postsecondary education. One of the new trends in colleges and Bible colleges during the eighties is the return of these people to the classroom. Many work in businesses and have families, and come with renewed interest and concern for a quality education. Many are being called by God to ministry and service and want to be adequately prepared for what God would have them do. This is putting a special pressure upon Bible colleges, Christian liberal arts colleges, and Bible institutes to adapt to the changing needs and expectations of older students. This is a healthy pressure and one that is extremely productive. God is calling out a new group of Christian leaders, and schools must be willing to make the adaptation that is necessary to give them the kind of education that is best for them.

MISSIONS

The same kind of thing that is happening in postsecondary education is happening in the area of home and foreign missions. Many adults are being called by God to this kind of service later in life than formerly, and mission boards have had to change their strategy and their age limitations to meet this ongoing movement. Further, the opportunities for the utilization of very diverse and specialized skills, both at home and abroad, are coming into play. People with computer backgrounds, printing, aviation, medical, and other skills are now being sought by mission boards to meet the growing needs of the fields. Adult Christian educators are thrilled and challenged by this new movement, which utilizes the talent of not only the thirty-to-fifty age group, but the fifty-and-older age group as well.

ADULT CHRISTIAN EDUCATION ON THE MOVE

Looking back shows us the pattern of days gone by in adult Christian education. Much can be learned as we reflect on the historical and cultural developments under our forefathers. A look at our present is more difficult, since the present passes so rapidly. It is difficult to determine trends. We must do our best to make adult Christian education the best it has ever been. The purpose of this volume is to not only look back, but to look ahead; and that with enthusiasm and commitment. We have several needs that should be addressed. They are as follows:

THE NEEDS OF GENERAL ADULT CHRISTIAN EDUCATION

A biblically-based theology of adult education. There are many books that purport to be a theology that are a philosophy, and some that purport to be a Christian theology that are not biblically-based. This need is before us in adult education.

A biblically-based adult educational philosophy. Many books address the methodological approach to adults or special adult problems and concerns such as the family, but none that gives us a firmly rooted approach to adult educational philosophy.

A biblically consistent spiritual, social, cultural, economic, and physical program for adults. For the broad scene of adult Christian education, there is a need for principles that cover all ages and varying kinds of educational approaches.

THE NEEDS OF THE LOCAL CHURCH

A clear statement of the purpose of adult education in the local church. This can provide the framework for a renewed commitment on the part of the church toward adult education.

A clear statement of the goals and objectives toward which adult education is moving in the local church so that we can measure our results.

A clear statement of the programs and methodological approaches that will be used to accomplish our targets in line with our purpose. As churches during the fifties and sixties hired many as youth directors, churches are now seeing the need for ministers of adult education as well.

The adult Christian scene is exciting and expanding rapidly. The need for clear thinking based on past experience and biblical mandates will provide us with the framework for future ministry.

1. Using a Bible concordance and a Bible dictionary, trace the biblical statements about the family from Genesis to Revelation. Identify a minimum of five things that God requires of the family that is to honor Him.

2. Compare and contrast the catechumenal and the catechetical schools of thought. List the similarities and differences.

3. Choose one organization, such as the YWCA or a newer organization such as Christian Service Brigade, and trace its development from its inception to the present, noting its philosophy, program, and changes from its founding days.

4. Write a brief essay defending the thesis "Lifelong learning has its roots in the Scriptures of the Old and New Testaments."

5. Write to a series of mission boards and ask them about their requirements and needs for missionaries. Inquire what changes they have made over the last twenty years in these areas, and summarize your results in a chart showing past and present mission expectations.

3

Adult Christian Education
in Perspective

Is there an underlying pattern or a set of principles upon which an effective ministry to and with adults can be constructed? In order to arrive at the answer to this most vital question, we must spend some time in both the library of philosophy and in the garden of culture. As we study these two areas of man's experience, we will seek to evaluate the information gathered in the light of spiritual truth.

Every person has biases and preferences, and these are the natural extension of an individual's *faith perspective*. If a person has faith in the innate goodness of mankind, then certain basic beliefs will logically follow. If, on the other hand, a person believes that men have sinned and have followed in the footsteps of Adam and Eve, then a very different set of beliefs will follow. Every person who is rational exercises faith. The key is where the faith is placed.

Many authors, for the sake of presenting their viewpoint in the most powerful manner possible, will polarize the issues, putting their viewpoint in the most favorable light. Some typical polarizations used in education are democracy versus authoritarianism, liberalism versus conservatism, dynamic experience versus static experience, modern versus old-fashioned, humane versus mechanistic, and relative value versus absolute value. Questions in education such as, "Are teachers to be the transmitters and conservators of history and culture, or are they to be social and cultural critics and agents of change?" are posed. Some teachers and writers clearly set forth their assumptions and perspectives, whereas others do not. It is important that Christian educators be able to think their way through the various authors they read, determining the assumptions that are made, the logic of the arguments that are developed, and the validity of the facts presented. Philosophy's goal is to help establish a framework in which that kind of thinking is made possible.

Some dichotomies or polarizations are helpful in that they tend to set apart and define basic differences. Some polarizations, however, confuse the issues by over-simplifying complex concerns and diverse perspectives; in so doing, they miss or at least cloud major issues. For example, to say that one person is Calvinistic and another person is Arminian does not settle very many issues. It may show direction of thought and some fundamental differences in hermeneutical approach, but it certainly does not explain the great variety of theological nuances that are possible within a system or between systems.

In opening the philosophic library we will find a framework for thinking. In the garden of culture, we will walk among various cultural elements and attempt to define and integrate them into our experience. Since philosophy tends to upset people, many people shy away from it or make jokes to excuse themselves from its demands. Philosophy, they say, is like a blind man in a dark room, looking for a black cat that is not there. Philosophy does examine the root questions of what we believe and why we believe that way. Forcing a person to examine and evaluate beliefs can be upsetting; but as one wise teacher many years ago said, no one has truly believed until they have first examined. Faith for the Christian is not blind belief, but rather the resting of the soul in the *sufficiency of the evidence*. Not all Christians are at the same level of maturity, and thus the sufficiency of the evidence for a less mature person will be different than the sufficiency of the evidence for a more mature person. In either case, however, the Christian position is that there is evidence.

In considering culture, we shall attempt to identify some significant elements and trends in contemporary North America. Here, too, the process can cause a person some discomfort, since we tend to view things from the standpoint of our past experience and personal learning, as well as our present attitude and disposition.

PHILOSOPHIC FUNDAMENTALS

The word *philosophy* is derived from two Greek words, *philia* and *sophia*. *Philia* has to do with a fond affection, or a brotherly love; *sophia* refers to wisdom. The term therefore means the love of wisdom. Over the twenty-four centuries since the term was first coined. it has come to mean many things. For the sake of our study, we will consider our philosophizing to be the integration of the variety of experiences and facts that we confront into a unified and consistent pattern or picture. When God said through the prophet Isaiah, "Come now, and let us reason together" (Isa. 1:18), He was indicating that there is a rational, logical, integrated, and coherent way of thinking, and that biblical living was not merely a matter of experience, but a matter of proper thinking as well. We understand that until we reach heaven we will continue to see "in a mirror dimly" (1 Cor. 13:12), but it is still our responsibility to attempt to see into that mirror.

The role of science in relation to philosophy also needs a word of clarification. Warren Young put it well when he said,

> Philosophy endeavors to relate and integrate the information which the various sciences are able to discover. Sciences, particularly the physical science, are analytical in approach, while philosophy is synoptic. The sciences are concerned with the discovery and investigation of factual data, while philosophy is concerned with the meaning and significance of that data. In general, the scientist is the discoverer, while the philosopher is an interpreter.[1]

If it is the role of science to uncover facts, then it is our role as educators and philosophers to help integrate those facts into a coherent and consistent pattern.

VALUES

In order to understand how people think and why they think the way they do, which is one of the tasks of philosophy, it is also helpful to understand what they have done in days gone by. For this reason, history and philosophy are often tied together. The history of education and of Christian education helps one understand how present-day problems, theories, policies, and practices came into being; philosophy assists in deciding what education ought to be doing. Without an understanding of these areas, the Christian educator is at a loss. Education is not just a matter of teaching, curriculum, administration, and leadership. No educator, especially a Christian educator, can do a proper job unless he has an integrated view of the educational process.

1. Warren C. Young, *A Christian Approach to Philosophy* (Grand Rapids: Baker, 1954), p. 26.

One of the goals of a teacher or administrator, especially in Christian education, is to help people change the way they think and live. The Scriptures teach that we are to be conformed to the Person and teachings of Jesus Christ our Lord. That involves change. The influence a teacher or leader has on others is an expression of the value system that they hold; so those values are too important to be left to chance discovery. They should be systematically studied and evaluated. It is not the intent of this chapter to cover in such a short space what is dealt with in volumes on the history and philosophy of education and Christian education, but simply to stress the importance of those studies and to set forth certain areas that need critical consideration.

KEY ISSUES FOR CHRISTIAN EDUCATORS

Most curricular programs in colleges and seminaries require Christian education students to take courses in history and philosophy of education, and often the value of such studies is questioned. There are a number of key issues that will help the Christian educator both with understandings, attitude development, skill development, and a basic appreciation for their discipline. Christian educators should be able to give clear, fact-filled, biblically integrated, and rationally consistent responses when asked concerning the seven major concerns of the philosophy of Christian education.

First, one should be able to state *the purpose of Christian education* in a clear and cogent manner. This should include the aims of education, why they have been developed, how they are evaluated, and what groupings they form. Another aspect of this should be a clear statement of what it means to be an educated person.

Second, discerning *the relationship between educational institutions and other institutions in society* is also important. The relationships between the Sunday school and the church, between the Christian day school and the church, between the Christian college and the Christian day school, between national youth organizations and the local church, all need definition and clarification.

A third concern is *the identification of key issues* in the total educational process. What is the nature of the learner, especially the adult learner? How is the learning process carried on? What is the proper function of the teacher, the school, the church, the home? Being able to identify the problems, concepts, and principles in each of these areas is important.

A fourth issue is *the ability of the Christian educator to distinguish between competing philosophies of education.* Too often simplistic, sloganeering responses mean that the underlying issues and implications of competing systems are not clearly understood or communicated. Terms take on different meanings over the course of years, or are used with specific definitions by certain authors or schools of thought. An interesting study to highlight this would be the use of the word *humanism* over the past fifty years. The use of this term in a philosophic, educational, psychological, and colloquial sense will prove illuminating.

A fifth concern is *the place of education in contemporary culture.* To understand this, contemporary educational approaches, schools, and organizational forms must be understood.

A sixth issue for educators is *the ability to analyze problems in a systematic and reflective manner.* To be able to see specific educational problems in the light of the whole educational scene and to be able to penetrate them to their philosophical base is a task of the educator.

Seventh and last among the issues that an educator should be able to grapple with in an intelligent and coherent manner is *the evaluation of the outcomes of the educational process.* We need to secure a greater awareness of what is actually happening as the process of education takes place. The role of competencies, the role of values, the relationship between attitude, skill, and knowledge acquisition, and similar issues need greater definition.

CHRISTIAN CONSIDERATIONS

A number of evangelical writers over the years have contributed to a clearer understanding of the philosophy of Christian education. Frank E. Gaebelein in 1951 wrote *Christian Education in a Democracy* (Oxford: Oxford U.), a source book for Christian educators ever since. Mark Fakkema in 1952 wrote *Christian Philosophy: Its Educational Implications* (Chicago: National Association of Christian Schools, 1952), stressing a bibliocentric approach to educational process and emphasizing both moral discipline and theistic teaching. Then in 1958, Lois E. LeBar contributed *Education That Is Christian* (Westwood, N.J.: Revell), in which she explored key implications for Christian education drawn from a study of the life of Christ and other significant portions of Scripture. In 1975, Lawrence O. Richards wrote *A Theology of Christian Education* (Grand Rapids: Zondervan) in an attempt to build an educational model on philosophical and theological grounds. Since that time, a large number of volumes have appeared in Christian education that touch on a Christian philosophy of education from either a leadership or a local church perspective.

Gaebelein may have said it best when he wrote concerning the foundation of Christian education:

What is the factor that distinguishes a Christian philosophy of education from other religious philosophies, such as Judaism or a theistic view based on Greek thought? It is this one thing—the centrality of Jesus Christ. Christianity is an ethical religion, yet ethics is not its center; its center is a Person, and in a holy unique sense, every Christian is organically united to his Lord. To be a Christian is nothing less than to be "in Christ" through personal rebirth into the family of the redeemed through faith in the finished work of the Saviour. It is not following Christ that makes Christians, but a transforming relationship through personal surrender to Him. Then, as a consequence of that crucial experience, comes obedient following in His steps and membership in the church. But the point cannot be too strongly made that Christianity *is* Christ. Christ is the eternal Son of God, "Very God of Very God; Begotten not made," as the ancient creed so truly says. Therefore, He is for men the ultimate manifestation of Deity. As such, He is the goal of philosophy, for He is Himself that truth and final reality which philosophy seeks.[2]

Gaebelein goes on to discuss the idea of a Christian school, and sets forth six criteria for a Christian educational institution. These could also be applied to a Christian educational leader. To paraphrase these six criteria and make them applicable to an educator of Christian adults, they would be as follows:

(1) The educator of Christian adults must have a completely Christian philosophy of education.

(2) He must be thoroughly committed to a distinctive Christian philosophy. This Christian philosophy is not something that is merely conceived in the mind, but lived out in the life. As Gaebelein indicates, the Bible is truth to be practiced, not simply truth to be acknowledged.

(3) He must have the written and living Word of God as the effective focus and integrating force for everything that he teaches.

(4) While recognizing his evangelistic responsibility toward the unbelievers who may be a part of the church or educational process, the educator of Christian adults has a primary responsibility to see that believers are growing in their Christian faith.

(5) He must recognize that there is a substantial core of essential biblical truth that believers need to know and fundamental experiences, such as witnessing and worship, that believers need to practice. To this, of course, is added other specific felt needs and interest areas.

(6) He must practice what he preaches. Truth taught should be truth lived; acknowledging the Lord in *all* our ways, while true for all believ-

2. Frank E. Gaebelein, *Christian Education in a Democracy* (New York: Oxford U., 1951), p. 25.

ers, is especially true for the educator of Christian adults. We must not
be timid in our day with regard to a consistent, aggressive, and thoroughly Christian educational approach. Whether as institutions or individuals, our thought processes and expressions of those processes must
be Christian in every way.

INFLUENCES OF CULTURE

It is not difficult to ignore culture in the process of educating adults
in the midst of the twentieth century—it is impossible. We are told over
and over again in Scripture that we are to be in the world, but not of it.
The system of this world embraces such diverse areas as economics,
politics, technological developments, and sociological implications; and
it is more important for the Christian to comprehend the total scene
than it is for the non-Christian.

Gene Getz put it well when, in commenting about the Christian's
need for cultural discernment, he said, "Christians, more than any other
group, should face the need to understand culture. This is an imperative.
First, so that we might effectively penetrate our society with the gospel
of Jesus Christ; and second, so that we may be truly Christian in the
midst of a culture that is increasingly becoming antagonistic to our
biblical presuppositions."[3]

Getz then goes on to discuss the issue by pointing out that there is a
deep-rooted institutionalism, a departure from the biblical principles
upon which America was founded, and a pluralistic society that is
producing pluralistic thinking in our culture. This, he indicates, has
weakened us politically, morally, and spiritually.[4]

Just what is this thing called culture? An early, and still working,
definition for many educators was given by Edward B. Tyler in 1871:
"Culture . . . is that complex whole which includes knowledge, belief,
art, morals, law, customs, and other capabilities and habits acquired by
man as a member of society."[5] Another definition, suggested by Kroeber
and Kluckhohn, suggests that culture is a "set of attributes and products of human societies and therewith of mankind, which are extraso-
matic and transmissable by mechanisms other than biological heredity,
and are essentially lacking in sub-human species as they are characteristic of the human species as it is aggregated in society."[6]

3. Gene A. Getz, *Sharpening the Focus of the Church* (Chicago: Moody, 1974), p. 213.
4. Ibid., p. 227.
5. Edward B. Tyler, *Primitive Culture,* 5th ed. (London: J. Murray, 1929), p. 1.
6. A. L. Kroeber, and Kluckhohn, Clyde. *Culture: A Critical Review of Concepts and Definitions*
(Massachusetts: Peabody Museum, 1952), p. 145.

We see that there are many cultures existing on the earth, and some quite diverse. We have also come to understand that within cultures there are sub-cultures, or smaller groups having distinctive patterns of thought, behavior, and beliefs. There is what could be called American culture. Within American culture there are sub-cultures, such as a New England culture, and even a Deep South culture. Within the New England and Southern subcultures, there is the possibility of even further subcultures.

In earlier days, peoples from other lands and cultures often made the assumption that American culture was Christian, largely due to missionaries and others who not only shared their beliefs and the Word of God with other peoples, but also led them to establish patterns and procedures that paralleled the North American way of doing things. This produced a confusion in the minds of many as to what a Christian really was. Many thought that to be an American was to be a Christian. But Getz points out,

> Today it is a different story. In some instances, there is a "great gulf" between the person who is a "Christian" and the person who is simply an "American." Again this is a blessing in disguise. It used to be that it was difficult to explain to people why believing "born in America" was not equal to "being a Christian." But today this is no problem. Most people clearly see the difference and again, this provides us with unlimited opportunities in evangelism."[7]

For an excellent discussion of the implications of culture for church ministry, chapters 18 and 19 of Getz's book *Sharpening the Focus of the Church,* (Chicago: Moody, 1974) will prove extremely valuable.

From a non-Christian point of view, a volume that proves extremely stimulating in thinking through the social and cultural factors involved in education is Morris P. Hunt's *Foundations of Education: Social and Cultural Perspectives* (New York: Holt, Rinehart & Winston, 1975). Hunt, who identifies himself as being "reared a Christian idealist; as a late teenager converted to a stubborn Comtist positivism; as a university student, veered sharply toward a Deweyan scientific-humanism; as an adult, developed a major commitment to a liberal-democratic mode of human relations and a relativistic world view reflecting the convergence of the Peirce-James-Dewey philosophical tradition and a Lewinian cognitive field psychology, upon which is superimposed a certain warmth

7. Getz, *Sharpening the Focus of the Church,* p. 234.

toward existentialism,"[8] presents a very aggressive inquiry, though somewhat biased, into the role of religion, church, and education in the whole cultural scene.

His chapter dealing with religion is a mixture of some very clearly presented facts and some persuasively argued fantasy. At one point, for example, he argues,

> It is a historical fact that most Americans call themselves Christians, but we have two broad categories of Christianity—at least in this century. We have had fundamentalists and modernists and their views on many issues are light-years apart. Yet each group can make a case for calling itself Christian.
>
> As for the operational beliefs of Americans, and their overt behavior, Christian fundamentalists are particularly inconsistent in that they tend to be conservative in an extreme or radical, not a classical, sense, and support mostly causes which are anti-humanitarian, anti-libertarian, and anti-democratic.
>
> On the other hand, since World War II, the more liberal, modernist denominations have moved into a pattern of somewhat militant support for liberal causes. If New Testament teachings imply some sort of "social gospel," then the modernist churches have moved a considerable distance toward achieving it and can be viewed as perhaps consistently Christian.[9]

At another point the same author, who has made a case for the fact that middle Americans make up the core of fundamentalist churches and are of a law-and-order orientation, argues that the hard hats during the sixties and seventies who attacked gatherings of youths as a method of resolving the disputes that occurred during that period of time were acting in a fundamentalist manner. Fundamentalists, he argues, favor punishment, whereas liberals favor rehabilitation. In support of his arguments, he charges fundamentalists with racism, self-interest, and antiquated conservatism.

In a very interesting discussion on sin and morality, Hunt asks the question,

> What is sinful and what is immoral? Our cultural answers to this question are formally rooted in Christian belief. Since Christ had nothing to say about most acts that contemporary fundamentalists call sin, our religious answers to what sin is are based, at best, on heresay evidence.

8. Morris P. Hunt, *Foundations of Education: Social and Cultural Perspectives* (New York: Holt, Rinehart & Winston, 1975), p. ix.
9. Ibid., p. 305.

First, there are the orthodox beliefs about sex . . . perhaps most at issue in the seventies are what Christian fundamentalists refer to as "perversions" (i.e., any sexual practice you don't agree with) and sex out of wedlock, commonly practiced by a large proportion of both youth and adults.

Second, there are the vices. We know of no Biblical injunctions against consuming alcohol in moderation, smoking pot, betting on horses, using tobacco, or loafing in the sun. Yet these, and dozens of other behaviors, are condemned by fundamentalists and are taught as being sinful, immoral, and leading to hell in many of our public schools.[10]

Even the study questions in the text contain the same kind of innuendo and biased information. An example is, "Do you consider the Hebraic-Christian Bible literally true, that is factual? If so, how do you define fact? If the Bible is a narration of fact, why can't such facts be used as evidence in a court?"[11]

It is because of issues like the ones just presented that Christian educators, and especially those who are concerned with the education of adults, must first understand the tremendous influence that culture is having on the minds of people, and secondly, be able to separate the opinions people express from the facts upon which the opinions are based. A clear understanding of the doctrine of the inspiration, authority, and inerrancy of Scripture is necessary, since writers like Hunt will say that the teachings of Christ and the writings of Paul are at odds one with another, or that some of the teachings of Christ are normative for us if we agree with them and others are not, or even that Paul was simply writing personal opinions. These issues need clear and definitive answers.

We must come to grips with what Theodore Brameld defines as some of the characteristics of a "schizophrenic age," referring to conflicts such as self-interest versus social interest, inequality versus equality, nationalism versus internationalism, absolutism versus experimentalism, man against himself versus man for himself, technology versus humanism, and abundance versus want. Brameld then describes three major educational belief systems: education as cultural transition; essentialism: education as cultural conservation; and perennialism: education as cultural regression.[12] We probably need a fourth, which we might call biblicism: education as cultural and personal transformation. North American cultural values have drifted significantly apart from

10. Ibid., p. 312.
11. Ibid., p. 312.
12. Theodore Brameld, *Philosophies of Education in Cultural Perspective* (New York: Holt, Rinehart & Winston, 1955), pp. 3–16.

biblical values. The biblical teaching of the Christian educator is not simply to conserve, regress, or provide for transition, but rather to bring an individual into conformity with Jesus Christ. As that person then lives Christ in a consistent and committed manner, society and culture are affected and transformed. In the world, but not of it; wise as snakes, harmless as doves; sheep among wolves. There is to be a difference between a regenerated believer (and regenerated believers living and working together in fellowship), and the unregenerate individual (and the unregenerate society) in need of God's truth. This is our task, and it must be our commitment.

This chapter has sought to raise in the minds of Christian leaders questions that demand thorough and well-documented answers. It is not enough to repeat clichés. The prepared Christian leader of adults must have answers to the philosophical and cultural questions of our day that affect our educational process and our spiritual endeavor. We must both require and give clear, consistent, and rational definitions to the terms we use. We must both require and give documented reasons for the hope that is within us. We must both require and give complete and coherent answers to the fundamental questions of philosophy and culture. We must enter into the battle for the minds and souls of men fully confident that the Lord is with us and there is none greater.

1. Define philosophy in terms of Christian education of adults.
2. Define culture in terms of Christian education of adults.
3. Belief, in the biblical sense, means to embrace a truth, concept, or practice in such a manner that one's mental process and manner of life are under the discipline of that truth. Describe the difference between a "preference" and a "belief," and give two illustrations from adult Christian education where these differences can be seen.
4. Trace the usage of the term *humanism* over the past fifty years and identify several areas where this concept has influenced Christian education.
5. In what ways can adult Christian education have the written Word of God as its focus and integrating force in teaching on the subject of the "citizenship responsibilities of today's Christian"?
6. What areas of present-day American culture are most problematical to Bible-believing Christians?

4

The Needs and Nature of Adults

Adulthood is the longest span of a person's life, generally more than twice as long as childhood and youth put together. With people living longer, the number of adults living in the United States, as well as in other areas of the world, is greatly increasing. Adults are becoming more numerous than any of the other age groups and make up the overwhelming majority of the multitudes that are still unreached by our local churches. If we are to win the large number of unconverted adults to Christ and see that they grow in grace and in the knowledge of our Savior, it will take both better understanding on our part and greater effort.

In studying any age group, we often speak of the "average" or "normal" person. But of course, no two people are exactly alike. There are more than four billion people in the world today, and all of them are different. They do have similarities, and when we try to put the similarities together we can talk about averages or norms. But when we look at people as individuals, we see the vast differences that are there.

Look around your local church. Bill is thirty-five, single, and a lonely man, unable to find his place in life. Linda was divorced a couple of years ago and is raising two daughters. You know from her comments in class and her general behavior that she is timid and reluctant to reach out to people. Sue is twenty-four years old, healthy, prosperous, and a most popular young lady. She has an exciting job, enjoys her work, and lives to the fullest. John is thirty and has just been promoted in his job. He is a happy-go-lucky young man but also has a very serious side. Anna has just suffered a serious illness in her sixties. Your heart goes out to her as you reflect on her circumstances. Margaret, too, has great needs. She is in her early forties but has recently been widowed after the long illness of her husband. The strain of caring for him—and now his absence—has left her broken-hearted. They never had children, and both her parents have died. She, too, is very lonely. At fifty-one Sam is a successful businessman. From his actions and from his work in the church, he appears to be quite satisfied with life. You know from his comments in class and in church business meetings, however, that he is closed-minded and more interested in giving opinions than in really learning. No two adults are alike. Each has specific needs; each has developed a specific type of personality; and each has something to learn and something to contribute.

THE WORLD OF ADULTS

Adults live in a world today that is rapidly changing. It is not so much the fact of change that poses a threat, but rather it is the speed of change. We no longer have time to adapt to the major changes that occur within our lifetimes. We must, as individuals and as families, learn to cope with a myriad of the social, ethical, political, educational, physical, technical, and scientific changes that constantly invade our daily living.

As clearly stated by Theodore Hesburgh and others, "The changing nature of our society requires virtually all citizens to gain new skills and intellectual orientations throughout their lives. Formal education of youth and young adults, once thought of as a vaccine that would prevent ignorance in later life, is now recognized as inadequate by itself to give people all the educational guidance that they will need to last a life-time."[1]

Change marks the life of adults today, and whether we live in the cities or the suburbs, we are all affected by it.

Change finds its way into our lives in different ways. We are a nation of nomads. Thirty percent of the American public changes its residence every year; and as we can tell from various commercials, the extended family keeps in contact by telephone or tape recorder, if it maintains contact at all.

1. Theodore Hesburgh, Paul A. Miller, and Clifton R. Wharton, Jr., *Patterns for Lifelong Learning* (San Francisco: Jossey-Bass, 1974), p. 3.

Isolation and loneliness are increasingly common psychological disorders. Apartment complexes, condominiums, and other multi-residence arrangements with security protection only seem to heighten man's isolation and feelings of being alone in the midst of a crowd. Although cities have been with us for more than five thousand years, the megapolis is less than a half century old but is growing rapidly.

Changes in the area of scientific developments stagger us as we project ourselves into the decade ahead. Laser communication, cloning, transplants of vital organs, and bio-feedback are no longer new words in the adult vocabulary brought to us originally by the entertainment media; they now describe present realities.

The increase in the volume of information has been phenomenal. Man has been a collector and disseminator of knowledge since creation. It is reported that in the sixteenth century in Europe, 1000 books were produced per year. In the United States alone in 1965, the number was 365,000. In 1985, it is estimated that one-half million books will be produced in the United States alone—and this is only one information medium. Data that is being gathered by orbiting satellites is difficult to comprehend. It has been estimated that less than 5 percent of this mass of data can actually be filtered and utilized.

Leisure time has taken on new meaning for today's adult world. The fifty- and sixty-hour work week of old has been cut back to forty hours, and a thirty to thirty-five-hour work week may become the pattern. That change has produced an increase in the amount of leisure time and opportunities for adults. Many students of adulthood and adult educators see a problem in profitable use of this increased leisure time. Making off hours and retirement days satisfying and productive has taken on a new priority. As life spans increase, it is not the lengthening of years that presents the problem but rather the use of those years. More attention must be given to adults. As J. R. Kidd states,

> We have hundreds of studies about the child; the child of one week, the child of two weeks, the child of six months. There are also innumerable books about personality changes in children, about health, intellectual development, and hundreds of other aspects. We also have scores of studies about the various phases of adolescence. In recent years, there have been an increasing number of studies of older people, particularly those of advanced years. For the middle years, there is a handful of highly specialized reports, but there is practically nothing which deals with the full-life development of man in a comprehensive way, at least as it affects learning. It is almost as if we assumed that all of adulthood was identical; that it progressed at the same pace, in the same directions, on the same plane.[2]

2. J. R. Kidd, *How Adults Learn* (New York: Association, 1959), p. 40.

MATURITY

One of the major tasks of adult education, and particularly adult Christian education, is to teach us how to live a full, productive life in which health and wealth are not overlooked, but are seen as of less importance than one's relationship with God and our fellow man. Maturation means the development of the individual toward being a complete person in terms of spiritual, physical, social, emotional, cultural, and vocational objectives. Maturity is a process that involves having a meaningful destination and well-directed, well-disciplined, responsible actions designed to take a person to that destination. The purpose of adult Christian education is to cause people to mature to become responsible, self-directing, profitable and satisfied people. As Paul Bergevin states, "We as adults need to know. We need to act intelligently on what we know. We need to learn to discipline ourselves, to accept responsibility for, and have something to say about the forces that shape us."[3] Growing in grace and in the knowledge of the Savior; selfless commitment to the development of others; thinking, creating, problem-solving; truly understanding that it is not ourselves, but Christ living through us that makes the difference; this is what Christian maturity is all about.

ADULT LEARNER NEEDS

With the concept of maturity in mind, the next concern for the educator is to identify the needs of adult learners. William Adams suggests that there are only two universal basic human needs: omnipotence and omniscience. By omnipotence, Adams means the desire for unlimited power to control one's life, health, and destiny. Omniscience refers to the need for intimate and ultimate knowledge of things, circumstances, and relationships.[4]

A more practical way of defining needs, especially in the educational realm, is what Bergevin calls the sympotomatic, felt, and real educational needs.[5] A symptomatic need is one that an individual considers fundamental, but is actually tangential. For example, an absence of sufficient teachers in the Sunday school may lead one to believe that what is needed is an effective recruiting program, whereas in reality what is probably needed is an effective leadership training program; simply securing untrained leaders to put in positions will only magnify the problem.

3. Paul Bergevin, *A Philosophy for Adult Education* (New York: Seabury, 1967), p. 9.
4. William A. Adams, *The Experience of Teaching and Learning* (Washington: Psychological Press, 1980), pp. 26–29.
5. Bergevin, pp.144–46.

The felt need is one that the individual considers to be absolutely necessary to his own well-being or the well-being of others. At times, felt needs can be real needs; but often, again, they are tangential to the actual need. There have been students over the years who have felt that they needed more degrees in order to secure proper positions in churches or schools, since they felt inferior. The felt need was strong and tended to cloud the real need, which was for better skills in relating to people and in communicating.

A real need in the educational sense is something that an adult actually lacks and can acquire through a learning experience. The adult educator must be sensitive to and helpful in identifying and assisting adults in the meeting of their real needs.

Turning our attention to some of the real needs that all adults face, we note that there are physical needs, security needs, significance needs, accomplishment needs, and creativity needs.

PHYSICAL NEEDS

The physical needs are the most easily identified; everyone recognizes the needs for sleep, food, water, and exercise. With some adults, caring for the body and physical needs is an obsession. Our youth-oriented society with its emphasis on appearance and vigor has elevated physical needs to the number one priority in many individuals' lives. But there is also the other extreme, where the bodies that God has given us are not only neglected, but abused. Maintaining a healthy balance in the identification and meeting of physical needs must be a concern for adult Christian education.

SECURITY

Everyone wants to feel safe. This is true not just in the realm of the physical but also in the psychological and social realms as well. We want to be accepted by those around us, and so the vast majority of people will tend toward the middle range in dress, activities, and behavior. There is safety in being part of the great majority. There is also security in belonging. We belong to organizations, we belong to our families, and we belong to various sub-groups within the society. This security through belonging helps us to feel accepted and approved. Another means to gaining security is the acquisition of properties and safety devices such as insurance policies and laws that protect us. The Scriptures teach that although these are props on every side that are needed from a human perspective, our greatest security is to be found in a right relationship with God through Christ Jesus, and this must be at the forefront of our Christian education of adults ministries.

SIGNIFICANCE

Another need common to adults is the need to be appreciated and receive the admiration of others. Signals of significance from others answer the question for adults, What am I worth? and have far-reaching implications for personality development. Significance is a motive for service and a strong driving force that seeks satisfaction.

ACCOMPLISHMENT

Much management literature today shows that certain needs in life are maintenance-oriented, particularly in the physical and economic realms. The higher realm is in the area of recognition and achievement. A person is more highly motivated when he is convinced that he is growing in knowledge, social relationships, skills, attitudes, and accomplishments in his vocational and spiritual life. A vital principle built into all of creation is growth. Where growth is not occurring, death soon follows. Even in the later years of adulthood, it is those who maintain a healthy growing experience that not only survive, but flourish.

CREATIVITY

The Scriptures teach that we are made in the image of God, and one of the most evident characteristics that God has built into the universe is His creativity. We do need safety and a feeling of significance; we must feel we are accomplishing something; and we have to take care of our physical needs. But probably the highest driving force we have is the need for new experiences, the development of new friendships and vital new relationships. Experiences that were once fresh can become routine; practices that pioneered a new path become ritual; and knowledge once exciting becomes routine. God is a God of creativity, and a great need for those of the household of faith is to continue to grow in the creative way.

ADULT DEVELOPMENT

For many there is no longer a mystery concerning the way children and youth grow and develop. Studies have been conducted on literally millions of children, and the data developed from conception to approximately age twenty amounts to a good-sized mountain. Moving to the twenty-year-old and onward, however, there is no vast array of data.

Robert Havighurst says, "Middle age is an unknown territory to the social scientist. Although he thoroughly is familiar with the length and breadth and depth of childhood and adolescence, and he has made intensive explorations into the domain of old age, his knowledge of middle age is limited to a small amount of highly specialized knowledge gained from marriage counselors, psychiatrists, and social workers, about small and non-representative groups of middle-aged people."[6]

We do know that people develop physically at a rapid rate during the first three years of life, and then have a second major growth spurt from approximately age twelve to sixteen. We further know that between the ages of sixteen and twenty the final physical maturation process is accomplished, with the skeletal, major muscle structures, and nervous system developed to their approximate capacity. It is from this point on that we will look at the adult world of life and growth. For the sake of convenience, we will divide adulthood into four periods of time: young adulthood (18–34), younger middle adulthood (35–49), older middle adulthood (50–64), and older adulthood (65 and up).

YOUNG ADULTHOOD

In younger adulthood (18–34), individuals have unique needs. Through the period of adolescence they grappled with the concept of identity. How well they fared in coming to grips with that issue will have a bearing on the rest of their adult lives.

During young adulthood the emphasis and crisis will be in the area of interpersonal relationships and intimacy with others. This intimacy for some will take the form of marriage and the establishment of a home. For others, it will take the form of close personal friendships that will be long lasting. This intimacy is the opening of one's self to another without fear of reprisal or being hurt. It is a most critical time of life, a fragile time of life. The influence of friends at this juncture is of greatest importance—second only to adolescence. Young adults are trying to come to grips with their relationships to the opposite sex and to marriage. They are developing self-support, starting their careers, and learning how to handle their physical and emotional development, which is peaking.

As the chart on page 11 shows, there will be a sharp increase in the number of young adults in the days ahead. It has been estimated that 75 percent to 80 percent of adults are living in urban areas, mostly for

6. Robert J. Havighurst, *Social Roles of the Middle-Age Person* (Chicago: Center for the Study of Liberal Education for Adults, 1953), p. 4.

career and educational purposes. The city and its environs, however, can be a lonely place for the young adult. Young adults also have a variety of subcultures within their age group. These include the collegian, vocational, athletic, and non-conformist subcultures. Each of these groupings brings together young adults of common interests, common needs, and common potentialities. It should also be noted that while most of these young people are living in urban areas, approximately 70 percent of Protestant churches are located in town and country areas. This leaves in many cities a great void of spiritual care for this vital age group.

MIDDLE ADULTHOOD

The middle-aged group can be divided into two groups: the younger middle-aged, from 35 to 49, and the older middle-aged, from 50 to 64. This is the least written about, least studied, and probably neediest group of all. They are not too young and not too old. Many stereotypes have been developed with regard to middle age. The older, as well as younger, middle-age persons are responsible for paying bills, raising children, solving problems, and providing leadership in the home, church, and community. Although all ages have basic needs, as indicated earlier, the primary needs of the middle-aged adults are affection, security, and achievement. Over half the divorced men and women today are between the ages of thirty and thirty-five. Therefore, the end of young adulthood and the beginning of middle adulthood present some very critical concerns. These concerns span physical, mental, emotional, social, and spiritual areas. Physically, the younger middle adult is reaching a time in life where stamina and strength are continuing with very little noticeable decline. At the latter stages of the younger middle adult age and moving into the older middle adult age, however, there is a slow declining strength and energy level. Most often the older middle adult is not willing to admit this and sometimes will press beyond the limit in order to prove himself. Obvious physical characteristics are the gaining of weight and the receding of the hairline for men and the loss of that girlish figure for the women.

Mentally, there is continued alertness. Irving Lorge concludes from his research that although there is a decline in the rate of learning as age progresses, intellectual power itself does not change from age twenty to age sixty. The decline, he indicates, is based solely on reaction times and seeing and hearing skills.[7] As in the physical realm with middle

7. Irving Lorge, *Review of Educational Research: XI,* December 1941; XIV, December 1944; XVII, December 1947; XX, June 1950.

adults, problems are not due to natural degeneration, but neglect of skills. Attitudes toward learning, growth, and life are vitally important.

Socially, the group of friends will grow smaller and the activities will grow quieter as the middle adult ages. During younger middle age, the children go through adolescence and prepare for marriage. During older middle age, the children who once brought life to the home move out and establish their own homes, and the "empty nest" factor becomes important. All these changes call for adjustments on the part of the middle-aged adult.

Emotionally too, middle age can be a time of many changes. In younger middle adulthood, careers are peaking. Involvements outside the home, at work and at church, produce special pressures. There is an increasing concern with bodily health, friendships, and changes in jobs and friends. With one out of five families in the United States moving every year, there is a great deal of shifting of friends, neighbors, and responsibilities.

Vocationally, the middle adult, both younger and older, often receives a relative degree of satisfaction and success and is progressing according to a defined or generally felt life plan. But the direct opposite can also be true. There can be general frustration and anxiety about life and work, and many career changes can take place—but not without stress. It is a time when values are tested regarding job, family, friends, spiritual life, and even the meaning of success. It is a time when Christian education in relationship to the adult must be carried on in a creative, personal, and relevant way if the actual needs of the middle adult are to be met.

OLDER ADULTHOOD

The older adult in today's culture is presented with some special challenges and special insights. Things have changed dramatically in the last twenty to thirty years. A whole new set of insights is available to us, and more studies have been conducted to help with the process of the education of the older adult.

The life expectancy is now approximately seventy years for men and seventy-eight for women. Further, it has been estimated that over half of the people who have ever lived past the age of sixty-five are alive today. Approximately one-tenth of our population is over sixty-five and this segment is increasing at the rate of about 820 per day.

The mobility of today's population also affects older adults. It is true that children today are more likely to have living grandparents, but they probably will see those grandparents only on special occasions. A long distance phone call is better than no contact at all, but it is a poor substitute for a grandmother being able to hold her grandchildren on her lap.

Older adults are not participating in the work force to the extent that they have in the past. Early retirement, normal retirement at sixty-five, and government programs such as Social Security and Medicare have brought a degree of independence to older citizens. Although government programs are in jeopardy, they still have provided some minimal support for a great number of Americans.

Another phenomenon that faces older adults is the prediction that in the near future 60 percent of all retired people will have either a parent or a close relative older than themselves for whose care they will be at least partially responsible. This will have not only an economic impact upon older adults but will present a unique challenge to the church, which has been called by her Lord to do good unto all men, and especially to believers.

Physically, the older adult is normally in a period of decline and is faced with possible illness and disability. As age progresses, cell tissues become drier and do not grow as rapidly as in earlier years of life; therefore, even healing takes longer. The body cells also are less elastic, and so there is a decrease in the speed, intensity, and endurance of the chemical neuromuscular system. Vision and hearing often decline, and the internal organs of the body lose some of their effectiveness. Legs are not so steady as they used to be, and stamina generally decreases. In Ecclesiastes 12:1–8, we are given a graphic picture of the physical decline that the older person often suffers.

Mentally, older adults, although still able to learn, have greater difficulty remembering. Their speed of reaction decreases, and often in a classroom situation their inability to turn pages and hear directions causes them to remain passive. People who have difficulty seeing are clearly identified, but people who have difficulty hearing will often cover up their declining ability. Their hearing loss makes them feel left out, isolated, and even cut off from others, and thus physical and mental characteristics are clearly linked and vitally interdependent.

Socially, older adults are keenly aware of the fact that many of their close friends are also aged or have died, leaving them more alone than they would like to be. They are conscious that younger people have taken their places in work areas as well as in the leadership of the church. Some even resent such "usurping" of their positions and responsibilities.

Emotionally, it can be a time of loneliness and frustration over having the ability and the alertness to know what is going on but the inability to keep up with younger people. Many adjustments are necessary: retirement, bodily changes, loss of mates, different housing arrangements, differing roles in leadership, vocation, social responsibilities, and the inevitable fact of death.

Older adults are also conscious of the fact that when younger people die, there is a great sense of loss; but when death comes to an older person, the feeling of loss is much less severe. This, in many older adults, can often cause despair. Also, death has become more impersonal than it used to be. Over half of all deaths occur now in nursing homes, hospitals, and similar institutions. That removes much of the personal sense of responsibility and loss that earlier generations had when the care of the elderly and sick was more often confined to the home than to institutions.

In the spiritual realm, older adults are often the "pillars of the church." Their ability to pray, the experience that they have had in walking with the Lord, and their habit of faithful attendance at church are a tremendous challenge to the rest of the church family. In the spiritual realm, we need to give them opportunities to contribute and so help them feel useful. The Christian life is a process, not a package. The older adult has not "arrived" but is in the process of continuing to grow and develop, and trust becomes even more important to him.

Adults, even older adults, present a wide spectrum in terms of spiritual development. Some have come to know Christ at a later age, although this number is relatively small. Some have known Him earlier but have not grown. Yet most adult Christians want to be competent in their understanding and use of the Scriptures. They need to know what the Bible says, what it means, and how it relates to them. Adults also want to know what they believe and why they believe it. Many are looking for something worth committing their lives to, or, in the case of the very elderly, leaving their possessions to.

Another concern most adults have is the role of the church in their personal lives, their families, their communities, and the world at large. They want to know where they stand as individuals and as a group in God's great plan for the ages. One great encouragement in our age is the opportunity for senior adults to serve Christ even in missionary and Christian organizations world-wide.

Adults are also looking for answers to questions that arise in daily life regarding all aspects of life, with special emphasis on practical matters. Effective teachers know the Word, know their students, and design their teaching with specific learning objectives in mind.

Adults are a very diverse group of people who have real needs and vital potentials. Middle adulthood is one of the most neglected age groups in society and in the church. As things are presently going in the world, the middle- and older-age-adult population will be expanding at an ever increasing rate for another twenty to fifty years. Meeting the needs and providing creative ways by which Christian adults can maximize their potential is a present major challenge for Christian educators.

1. Visit an adult Sunday school class and describe the similarities and differences in the people there.

2. Interview at least two adults in each of the four different age groups (18-34; 35-49; 50-64; 65 and up) for a total of eight interviews, and compare your findings with the descriptions of adult needs given in this chapter.

3. Choose one of the four different adult age groups and plan a social or educational activity that will meet some of the needs identified in the text.

4. Evaluate the adult program of your local church and identify its strengths and weaknesses as it relates to the adult nature and needs.

5. Prepare an annotated bibliography of at least five books or periodicals that are "must" reading for an adult Christian educator in the area of the nature and needs of adults.

PART TWO

TEACHING ADULTS

Perry G. Downs

5

The Evangelization of Adults

Perhaps the greatest privilege and the greatest responsibility for us as believers is the ministry of evangelization. To us has been entrusted the great message of the gospel, the good news that God has offered to mankind reconciliation through His Son, the Lord Jesus Christ. But with this wonderful news also comes the awesome responsibility of bearing the message. The apostle Paul put it this way: "All this is from God, who reconciled us to himself through Christ and gave us the ministry of reconciliation: that God was reconciling the world to himself in Christ, not counting men's sins against them. And He has committed to us the message of reconciliation" (2 Cor. 5:18-19, NIV).

In order to better understand the importance of evangelism we need to remind ourselves of the fact that mankind is in a terrible plight before a holy God. By nature, man is a sinner, an object of God's wrath, and destined to spend eternity in hell separated from the grace of God. As believers, we need to be careful that we have a balanced viewpoint on the character of God, which includes both His goodness and His sternness (Rom. 11:22). We love to focus on the grace of God, but we must not forget the wrath and justice of God that calls for the judgment of sin and of the sinner. Prompted by this fear of the Lord and by a genuine love for people, it is our great privilege to tell the good news of God's offer of reconciliation through His Son, our Lord Jesus Christ.

PERRY G. DOWNS is professor of Christian education at Trinity Evangelical Divinity School, Deerfield, Illinois.

This chapter focuses upon the evangelization of adults in the context of Christian education. The emphasis will be on ways of winning adults to Christ in the Christian education of the church. A well-developed Christian education program for adults will probably attract many people to the church, some of whom may not be believers. Therefore, through sensitivity and the motivation arising from the knowledge that the justice of God is a reality, we should seek to present these people with the message of reconciliation.

THE MESSAGE OF THE GOSPEL

The place to begin a study of the evangelization of adults is first to remind ourselves again of the true message of the gospel. At a time when evangelicals pride themselves in their allegiance to the Scriptures, it is alarming to discover how biblically vague many of the messages proclaimed by the evangelicals really are. The gospel as presented by some evangelicals has been changed, misinterpreted, and removed from its biblical mooring, so that a conglomeration of popular theology and wishful thinking has replaced the true biblical message.

The gospel begins with the character of God. Until a person understands who God is and what his condition is before this God, he is not ready to receive or even understand the good news of the cross of Christ. Therefore, like Paul as he preached to the Athenians (Acts 17:24–31), we must begin the gospel message with the fact of God's authority over mankind by virtue of His creative acts, and the truth of man's absolute dependence upon God. The gospel begins with the idea of man's complete and total dependence upon God as creator and with God's authority over His creatures. Until this is understood, man's complete need of salvation will not be evident.

The second point of the gospel message focuses on sin. The gospel points out that "all have sinned and fall short of the glory of God" (Rom. 3:23). Man must understand his predicament before God as a sinner who is worthy only of God's condemnation and as a vile offender against God's holy ways.

We must be careful at this point not to confuse sin with the psychological or sociological idea of imperfection. Sin is more than simply a frustrating weakness in an individual. Sin is a theological concept, and it focuses on man's total unworthiness before God. Until a person sees himself as totally helpless before a holy God, he is not ready to respond in faith to the gift of salvation through the Lord Jesus Christ. Until a person recognizes that he is alienated from God, he is not ready to receive the good news of the possibility of reconciliation with God.

The third part of the gospel message is the story of Christ, the Son of God incarnate, the perfect sacrifice for sin, the risen Lord of all, and the perfect Savior. The good news is that God has sent His Son to be the perfect and acceptable sacrifice for sin and that He has raised His Son from the dead and declared Him to be Lord of all.

As the message of Christ is proclaimed, we must be careful not to separate the idea of the atonement from the person of Christ Himself. Those who proclaim a message of Jesus as the incarnate Son of God, but fail to mention the absolute necessity of His atoning work on the cross, remove from Him the glory of His obedience even unto death (Phil. 2:8). But, on the other hand, to preach only the death of Christ and not preach faith in Him as risen Lord is to remove from Christ His rightful authority and glory as the King of kings and Lord of lords. A message that invites people to "believe that Christ died for you" without a true invitation to believe in Jesus separates the atonement from the person of Christ and thus changes the gospel message. The biblical message is "Believe in the Lord Jesus, and you shall be saved" (Acts 16:31). This message includes both the atonement and the person of the Lord Jesus Christ.

The fourth point of the gospel message is the invitation to faith and repentance. Because of the holiness of God and the sinfulness of man, and because of the death of the Lord Jesus Christ on our behalf, we can invite people to have faith in the Lord Jesus Christ as their Savior, to repent from their lives of sin, and to follow Him in obedience. In presenting the message of faith, we must be sure to help our people understand that faith in the biblical sense is more than holding a creed or system of belief. Faith is a way of trusting in a person so completely that one's life is changed by that trust. Moreover, repentance must be understood as more than sorrow for sin; it is a willingness to turn from sin and to live in obedience to Christ.

As we invite people to believe in Jesus, we must be sufficiently honest with them to explain that this faith or belief will be very costly. Our Lord Himself said, "If anyone comes to Me, and does not hate his own father and mother and wife and children and brothers and sisters, yes, and even his own life, he cannot be My disciple. Whoever does not carry his own cross and come after Me cannot be My disciple" (Luke 14:26–27). Dr. J. I. Packer observes:

> In our own presentation of Christ's gospel, therefore, we need to lay a similar stress on the cost of following Christ and make sinners face it soberly before we urge them to respond to the message of free forgiveness. In common honesty, we must not conceal the fact that free forgiveness in

one sense will cost everything; or else our evangelizing becomes a sort of confidence trick. And where there is no clear knowledge, and hence no realistic recognition of the real claims that Christ makes, there can be no repentance, and therefore no salvation.[1]

As we speak of the evangelization of adults, we must begin by understanding the gospel message. Weak evangelization results in weak Christians. A weak gospel message will produce Christians who are not committed to the Lord, who have no true desire for obedience. However, when the gospel message with its full ramifications is presented, as God draws people to Himself, their salvation will bring about a marked change in them so that they will truly be "new creatures in Christ."

EVANGELIZATION AND CHRISTIAN EDUCATION

In its purest sense Christian education begins where evangelism ends. Christian education is the instruction by the church of believers, to aid them in their spiritual growth and development. However, both historically and logically, Christian education and evangelism go hand-in-hand. The fact is that when a church has an effective educational program, it will draw into its ranks a variety of people, some of whom may not be Christian. Therefore, the practice of evangelization within the context of the Christian education ministry is both warranted and reasonable.

As we observe the ministry of the apostle Paul with unbelievers, it quickly becomes evident that one of his primary methods of evangelization was that of teaching! In Colossians 1:28 Paul says, "We proclaim Him, admonishing every man and teaching every man with all wisdom, that we may present every man complete in Christ." Again, in 2 Timothy 1:11 Paul states, "And of this gospel I was appointed a herald and an apostle and a teacher" (NIV). The intertwining of teaching and preaching in the ministry of Paul was clearly his evangelistic method.

The gospel is a rather simple story with profound implications. The careful evangelization of adults requires systematic teaching of the message so that the truth of the gospel may be understood. Especially for adults, with their increased ability to think and reason clearly, the teaching of the gospel is an effective means of reaching them. The gospel message is reasonable and logical in its development and lends itself naturally to a careful explanation of its major points. Therefore, the

---

1. J. I. Packer, *Evangelism and the Sovereignty of God* (Downers Grove, Ill.: InterVarsity, 1961), p. 73.

educational program of the church is a highly appropriate place to practice consciously the evangelization of adults.

In the Key Biscayne Presbyterian Church in Miami, Florida, Pastor Steve Brown conducts an adult education class for agnostics only. In this class, adults who are questioning and searching are invited to come to present their concerns to the pastor. By means of a careful and reasoned answering of their concerns and by means of a well-developed and logical presentation of the gospel, this pastor has seen numerous people find faith in Christ through this class. Although not every church would be sufficiently staffed to hold a separate class such as this, presentation of the gospel through the teaching ministry of the church is an extremely effective means to evangelize adults.

An important concern here is that the unbeliever must experience the reality of the gospel as well as understand it. When an unbeliever comes into the context of the Christian church, he must be aware of the fact that he is among the people of God, and that there is a lived reality to their faith. David Watson states:

> Nothing is more meaningful in a church to an outsider than a loving, caring community and one which is obviously in love with God and offering real worship. It is reality, not rearrangement that will win the pagan and the agnostic.[2]

It is highly appropriate to think in terms of evangelization through the Christian education program of the church. But if we do consider inviting or attracting unbelievers to our church, we must be sure that what they experience will, in fact, be a true representation of the gospel. We must be sure that the message that is taught is biblically accurate and that the reality of the faith is experienced in our people. We must remember that Jesus gave the world the right to judge Christians on the basis of their love when He stated, "By this all men will know that you are My disciples, if you have love for one another" (John 13:35). As we consider using our Christian education programs as a means of evangelism, let us be sure that our teachers understand the theology of the gospel and that our people are living the reality of the gospel.

EVANGELISM APPROACHES

Traditionally, evangelism has been carried out in one of three ways: mass evangelism, confrontation evangelism, and relational evangelism.

2. David Watson, *I Believe in Evangelism* (Grand Rapids: Eerdmans, 1976), p. 142.

Each of these approaches is valid and has been used by God to bring people to Himself.

Mass evangelism means evangelistic meeting with a professional evangelist speaking to a crowd. The function of the laity is to bring friends to hear the gospel as it is proclaimed by the evangelist.

Confrontation evangelism means personal evangelism whereby individuals are purposefully contacted and confronted with their need of salvation. (The term "confrontational" does not imply a negative contact but rather an intentional contact calling for a decision.) In this approach to evangelization, the function of lay persons is normally to be involved either singly or in pairs door-to-door, in shopping malls, and so on.

Relational, or friendship, evangelism is no less intentional than the other two but is more comfortable for some people because it functions along the lines of normal human relationships. The approach to evangelization calls upon the lay person to build a friendship with an unsaved person and then through the basis of that friendship share the gospel. Because many adults wish to evangelize but feel uncomfortable in confrontational evangelism, relational evangelism can be very helpful in overcoming uneasiness.

PRINCIPLES OF FRIENDSHIP EVANGELISM

THE VALIDITY OF OUR LIVES

If we intend to win adults to Christ by means of friendship, or relational evangelism, we must begin by understanding that our lives must be an accurate reflection of the good news we proclaim. We must first *be good news* before we tell the good news.

A living epistle of the gospel of Christ should be characterized by love, joy, peace, patience, kindness, goodness, faithfulness, gentleness, and self-control (Gal. 5:22). This does not mean that we must be perfect in each of these categories, but rather that we should be growing in these areas, so that the truth of the gospel may be seen in our lives. In effect, believers are called to be a second incarnation of the gospel by being living examples of the power of God.

It is important to remember that as we attempt to build relationships with people to win them to the Lord, we are called upon to be examples not of perfection but rather of the process of redemption. What needs to be seen is the process of God at work in us, changing us to be conformed to the image of His Son. It is the process of redemption, not the ultimate outcome of perfection, that should be seen in the life of the believer.

The point is that our lives are the starting places for relational evangelism. As we become friends with other adults to bring them into the Body of Christ, the first contact with the power and love of God will be in our lives. Therefore the validity of our own lives is an essential characteristic of relational evangelism. The responsibility of the church to nurture its people effectively so that they will be growing to maturity is an essential characteristic of a church that would win others to Jesus Christ. Joe Aldrich makes the pithy observation that "God is not in the business of putting healthy babies in sick incubators."[3] We need healthy churches to produce healthy believers for relational evangelism.

BEING A FRIEND OF SINNERS

Many people have the mistaken idea that being separated from the world means being separated from sinners! We are warned, "Do not love the world, nor the things in the world" (1 John 2:15a). But the world (its system and values) is not the same as individual people.

The Pharisees accused our Lord of being "a friend of tax-gatherers and sinners" (Luke 7:34). For them this was an accusation, but our Lord observed that "wisdom is vindicated by all her children" (Luke 7:35). The truth was that our Lord was much more effective in reaching the multitudes than the Pharisees were. Rather than separating Himself from sinful people, He became their friend so that by His love they would understand His message.

The principle is the same for those of us who want to win adults to Christ through our friendships. The place to begin is to establish friendships with those outside the bonds of Christ. If all our activities and time are spent with believers (a serious problem in an active Christian community), the potential for friendships with those outside the faith is greatly hindered. Therefore, an effective strategy for winning adults to Christ is to encourage our church members to become friends with the unsaved, so that through their friendships they might successfully evangelize. Consciously planning social activities and various outreach programs into the community can greatly help our people to establish friendships with those outside of Christ. Rather than insulating our people from the world, we should be willing to send them out into the world to proclaim the gospel.

The friendship approach requires sincere motivation. If we establish friendships in a manipulative way so that we can somehow coerce people into the kingdom of God, we will have violated their trust and will

3. Joseph C. Aldrich, *Lifestyle Evangelism* (Portland: Multnomah, 1981), pp. 102-3.

perhaps do more damage than good, because adults are insightful and sensitive. We must be sure that we value them simply because they are people for whom Christ died and must establish friendships that genuinely seek good for the other person. Our relationships cannot grow out of a need to fulfill a "program" but rather should grow from a heart of love that desires to know other people and to help them to know the Savior as well.

SPEAKING THE GOSPEL

A potential danger with relational evangelism is that people never come to the place where they actually communicate the gospel to those whom they befriend. Not only should we seek to establish friendships, but we must also speak the gospel in words that can be understood. Therefore, as we encourage our people to establish friendships with unbelievers, we must also be sure that they understand the gospel message and have a sincere desire to explain to others the good news of God's grace and the way of salvation.

The key to speaking the gospel is naturalness. If a relationship with God and rejoicing over His grace is a natural part of the life of the believer, the most normal thing in the world would be to speak to his friend about this aspect of his life. Rather than attempting to establish contrived times when we can "slip in the gospel," we should be sensitive to those times of deep conversation to discuss those things that really matter. In a very natural context of good friendships, it is normal to talk of those matters that are the deeper concerns of our lives. It is in these normal relational times that the believer can share the gospel in words that accurately portray the message of Christ. The opening portion of this chapter discussed those matters briefly.

The point is that to establish a relationship is not sufficient. Although it is the foundation, the culmination comes when we speak to others specifically of the good news of Christ. We must not only be good news, we must also speak the good news.

THE CONTEXT OF THE CHURCH

What is the relationship of the church to friendship evangelism? The church can provide an important context in which the process of evangelization can take place. As our people establish friendships with other adults, it would be a very natural and normal thing for them to invite those people to visit our church. If the church is important in their lives, it would be normal for them to want to share this important aspect of their experience with unbelievers. Thus, the church becomes involved in this process of friendship evangelism.

The adult education program in the church is a good place to bring unbelievers for their first exposure to the Christian community. The combined realities of the Word of God's being taught in a life-related way and the experience of warm Christian fellowship can be effective in helping people to see and understand the reality of the gospel. As people come into the context of the church and hear the Word of God and experience the reality of the people of God in community together, they can understand the gospel more fully.

This does not imply that the teacher must be prepared to present an evangelistic lesson. Because relational evangelism is an ongoing process, there is plenty of time for the people to hear the entire gospel message. The normal process of teaching Scripture and relating it to needs and experiences of believers will be used by God to speak to unbelievers. Moreover, seeing believers relating to one another in love can greatly help people to see the validity of the gospel.

If the church is to be a context for a friendship evangelism, there must indeed be reality within the church itself. If there is pettiness, division, and lack of true commitment, the context for evangelization is marred. But a mature and healthy group of believers who are relating to one another in love and seeking to honor God in their lives can be extremely attractive to the unsaved world. Again, it is not perfection that the church must demonstrate, but the grace of God in the process of redemption in their midst.

BUILDING BRIDGES TO ADULTS

Several guidelines can help us to reach into the adult community for evangelistic purposes. These guidelines are intended to allow us to cooperate with God as He draws people to Himself for salvation. When we realize that He desires people to be saved, and that He is operating in their lives to bring them to Himself, we are more free to work in natural ways to build bridges to adults so that we can bring to them the good news of salvation.

1. PROGRAM TO MEET REAL NEEDS

As the church establishes its strategy for adult education, a strong consideration should be the needs of adults. By offering programs that will speak to the real life needs of adults, the church can provide a context into which its people may easily invite their friends. Providing seminars on such relevant issues as parenting, understanding adolescents, divorce recovery, or communication in marriage will cause the church to be a very natural context for outreach into the community. When those topics are handled in a distinctly Christian manner, people can be provided with immediate help and can also hear the gospel as it relates to those very real human needs. Therefore, Christian education programs need not be evangelistic in the confrontational sense, but rather should be Christian so that evangelism is a natural by-product.

By means of a sensitive awareness to the needs and interests of the community, a creative adult department in the church can offer programs that help adults in the church to bring their unsaved friends into contact with the functioning Body. Not only do these programs strengthen the community, but they offer effective opportunities for creative evangelism. Because adults are need-oriented in their learning, Christian and non-Christian alike will respond to a seminar that addresses a genuine life need. The gospel message can be communicated as a natural part of the Christian perspective on the issue being addressed.

David Watson observes that the church "must understand and seek to meet the real needs of real people, or else it will soon become moribund and fossilized."[4]

2. UNDERSTAND AND VALUE OTHER PEOPLE

In building bridges to adults, we must be sure that we value and understand people outside the Christian community. We must avoid the assumption that because we are Christians we are inherently more insightful or valuable than unbelievers. As we develop true love for those outside the faith, our attitude should change so that we will, in fact, value and appreciate others.

Jim Petersen observes, "Going into the world requires change. It implies participation in people's lives. It means to think, to feel, to understand, and to take seriously the values of those we seek to win."[5] One of the more remarkable things about our Lord's earthly ministry is that He listened intently to people. Rather than always trying to speak to others, we should be careful to take time to listen. By listening to people, we show that we are interested in them as people and that we value their perspective.

4. Watson, p. 15.
5. Jim Petersen, *Evangelism as Lifestyle* (Colorado Springs: Navpress, 1980), p. 95.

The attempt to understand and value other people does not mean that we will then change our understanding of the truth. The gospel itself is not negotiable. But to understand and listen to other people so that we can bring the gospel to them in a way that is relevant and meaningful to them is a valid objective. Therefore, we need to train our people to look at other people as human beings, not as "prospects" or "souls to be won." An important foundation for our bridge to other people is the foundation of integrity, which shows that the person is valued for who he is.

3. AVOID CULTURAL BARRIERS

Joe Aldrich contends that "the greatest barriers to successful evangelism are not theological, they are cultural. Many of our culturally determined patterns of life keep people from Jesus Christ!"[6]

An ongoing difficulty for Christians of all ages is to separate the gospel from culture. The twentieth-century United States is not exempt from this problem. We have established certain cultural patterns in our practice of Christianity that are not rooted in Scripture. Such practices as 11:00 A.M. Sunday morning worship services, dressing in a formal manner for church, and the adoption of certain unique terminology ("receive Jesus as your personal Savior") are not wrong in themselves but can provide cultural barriers to evangelism. For example, the eleven o'clock time for the morning worship service grew out of an agricultural society where milking the cows and caring for the farm livestock demanded seven-day-a-week attention. The chores had to be done before the family could go to church. The pattern is so well established that we often assume that there is a chapter and verse in Scripture to support it.

Because the gospel already makes strong demands on our lives, we dare not add to those demands by establishing a subculture into which we require people to fit. It is more helpful to become aware of the things we do as Christians that are meaningful to us, but that are not rooted in Scripture. As we become aware of those practices, we should determine whether these are actually barriers or helps to the process of evangelization.

Our goal should be to help our people to be comfortable in relating to those outside the Christian community. If we can establish a pattern of relationships and Christian life-style that is formed in our relationship with God rather than in the Christian subculture, we will be well on the way to avoiding cultural barriers to evangelization.

6. Aldrich, p. 40.

The key to avoiding cultural barriers is naturalness. If we can help our people to feel at ease as they live their lives in an open and honest way, Christ *will* be seen in them, and we will have done a great deal to help them avoid cultural barriers to evangelism. Many unbelievers are uncomfortable around Christians because the Christians tend to be "religious." What is needed is for believers to learn to be more authentic and less religious, so that the cultural barriers can be removed.

4. DEVELOP LOVE FOR THE LORD

Ultimately, the strongest and most effective bridge to an adult or to any other person will be our genuine love for that individual. The reason many evangelistic efforts are futile is that they are not prompted by a genuine love for people. Guilt or pride often cause Christians to perceive unbelievers as conquests to be made, rather than as objects of God's love and of their love. As a result of this kind of impure motivation, outreach efforts become impersonal, mechanical, shallow, and devoid of true Christian compassion. They ultimately become moribund, and rightly so.

Evangelistic efforts that are rooted in authentic love for people and are motivated by concern for their good will be understood by unbelievers to be different from their other involvements with people. The reality of unconditional love offered by the Christian to his friend can be a strong bridge to the unbeliever. Their first contact with the reality of the love of God for them will be in the form of the love that their Christian friend demonstrates.

Clearly, the ultimate source of this kind of love must be the love of the Father for us. The apostle John reminds us, "Let us love one another, for love is from God" (1 John 4:7). Notice that the source of love is the Father, but that *we* are responsible to love one another. We learn to love by staying close to the source of love, deciding to be loving people, and asking God to help us to love the people around us. Love is both a spiritual discipline and a choice that we make.

The marvelous outcome of evangelism that is motivated by love is naturalness. Rather than being nervous about our "evangelistic technique," when we are relating to people in love we are free to focus on them and their needs, and we need not be concerned about our performance. We can ask what they need and offer the gift of ourselves and of our Lord out of love for them, which only seeks their good. This may be the strongest argument for the gospel that many adults have ever encountered.

The evangelization of adults must begin with a clear understanding of the gospel message. That message must establish the need for salvation and the good news of the offer of salvation through faith in Christ. Faith must be expressed in a desire for obedience in order to be effectual.

Because the gospel message has profound implications, it is appropriate to think in terms of teaching the gospel in our adult education programs. However, when an unbeliever becomes involved with our churches, he should experience a uniquely Christian community that is characterized by love for all people, so that he will know the reality of the message by means of what he experiences.

For many believers, the most comfortable form of evangelism is through relationships. This requires that our lives be a valid reflection of God's work in us, that we must be friends of sinners, that we must be careful to speak the gospel as well as live it, and that the church should provide an appropriate context for continued proclamation of the reality of the Christian faith.

The church can help build bridges to adults in the community by offering programs that are of interest and help to those outside the church. Moreover, individual believers must value other people, avoid unnecessary cultural barriers to evangelism, and develop a God-given love to those outside the faith.

FOR FURTHER STUDY

1. Examine several evangelistic sermons in the book of Acts to determine the context in which the gospel message was proclaimed. Sample passages are: Acts 2:14–36; 7:2–53; 17:22–34.

2. Using a concordance, look up the word *teach* in the New Testament and see how often it is used in relation to evangelization. What are the implications of this to modern practices of evangelism?

3. Think about the normal contacts adults have with unbelievers and develop a list of strategies for developing friendships from these contacts.

4. Survey the gospel of Mark to see the pattern of Jesus' relationship with sinners. In what ways was He a "friend of sinners," and how did He maintain His own purity in the midst of these contacts?

5. What are potential cultural barriers to evangelism, and how can we avoid them?

6. Develop a list of programming ideas that could serve as bridges to the unbelievers in your community. Next, rank them in terms of potential effectiveness as you perceive it. Finally, develop a brief plan of action as to how the best idea could be brought into existence.

6

The Adult Educational Process

As the American population grows older, the church has the opportunity for significant educational ministry to adults. But the success of the church's educational efforts will rest to a large degree upon its sensitivity to the fact that adults as learners are different from children as learners. And this difference in learning approaches means that there must be a different approach to teaching adults. The worst mistake that could possibly be made would be to approach the education of adults in the same manner as the education of children.

Educators speak of *andragogy,* the art and science of helping adults learn, and *pedagogy,* helping children learn. The two terms should not be understood as opposites but rather as descriptions of the differences between the teaching of children and the teaching of adults. The chart on the next page shows the primary difference between andragogy and pedagogy.

ADULTS AS LEARNERS

Four primary observations may be made regarding adults as learners.

1. ADULTS WANT TO LEARN

Adults, by their nature, are learners. Learning is a very common aspect of adult life and a foundational desire. Malcolm Knowles observes

Pedagogy	Andragogy
The learner	
Dependent	Interdependent
The goal	
Acquire knowledge	Solve problem
The process	
Teacher-directed	Self-directed
Teacher determines need	Student determines need
Authority oriented	Mutually respectful
Formal	Informal

that "learning is indeed a natural, normal, organic part of living. . . . Adults do indeed want to and do indeed pursue learning."[1]

In an important study conducted for the Ontario Institute for Studies in Education, researcher Alan Tough studied adult learning procedures to discover what adults were learning, why they were learning, and how they obtained help for the learning they desired. One of the more remarkable findings Tough reported was that "almost everyone undertakes at least one or two major learning efforts a year, and some individuals undertake as many as fifteen or twenty."[2]

The proliferation of adult continuing education programs in high schools and colleges bears out this observation. Either through formal or informal educational processes, it is clear that adults are interested in education and want to learn.

2. MOTIVATION FOR LEARNING

Why do adults want to learn? Rather than an innate wish to improve themselves or to be more educated simply for the sake of education, studies indicate that the motivation for learning is usually practical. It appears that three fundamental issues motivate the adult learner.

First, Knowles observes that "clearly pleasure and self-esteem were critical elements in the motivation of Tough's subjects."[3] Adults learn partly because it gives them pleasure and helps them to feel better about themselves. A sense of pride and achievement is a critical factor in motivating adults to learn.

1. Malcolm Knowles, "Adult Learning Process: Pedagogy and Andragogy," *Religious Education* 72 (March–April 1977), p. 205.
2. Alan Tough, reported in Malcolm Knowles, *The Adult Learner: A Neglected Species* (Houston: Gulf, 1975), p. 36.
3. Knowles, p. 37.

It should be noted that although Scripture speaks of pride as a grievous sin (Prov. 8:13; 1 John 2:16), there is also an appropriate pride and self-esteem that is necessary for all people to hold. For example, Paul spoke proudly of the church at Thessalonica (2 Thess. 1:4). This healthy and appropriate pride is not arrogance but is the positive self-esteem that is necessary for a well-developed personality. Therefore the desire for pleasure and self-esteem in adult learning does not necessarily have to be viewed as negative.

Second, K. Patricia Cross reports, "Most adult learning begins because of a problem or a responsibility, or at least a question or a puzzle."[4] Adults do not usually learn only for the joy of learning; they are motivated by very practical concerns. They are moved to learn when they sense a problem that needs to be solved or are given a responsibility to fulfill. Sometimes it may simply be a question they want answered; but usually the concerns are quite pragmatic. Adults are motivated more by the outcome of their learning (the results that their learning will achieve) than by the process of learning. They search for answers rather than embarking on a quest.

Third, adults are motivated by a desire to meet needs. Monroe Marlowe and Bobbie Reed observe that "adults are looking for learning situations that allow them to think a little better of themselves, meet their needs, become more proficient in their daily lives and which help them master a subject."[5]

Again, it is evident that adults are motivated by the results of learning. They are not as interested in knowing for knowing's sake as they are in learning so that their needs may be met. The desire to enhance the quality of their daily lives is an important motivational factor for adults.

3. ADULTS ARE PROBLEM-ORIENTATED TOWARDS LEARNING

Growing out of their pragmatic motivation for learning, adult learners tend to be oriented towards the solving of problems. This is quite different from the motivation of younger learners. Knowles observes that as a person matures "his time perspective changes from one of postponed application of knowledge to immediacy of application, and

---

4. K. Patricia Cross, *Adults as Learners* (San Francisco: Jossey-Bass, 1981).
5. Monroe Marlowe and Bobbie Reed, *Creative Bible Learning for Adults* (Glendale, Calif.: Regal, 1977), p. 57.

accordingly his orientation toward learning shifts from one of subject-centeredness to one of problem-centeredness."[6]

Younger learners are interested in acquisition of knowledge regarding a subject, because they want to know about it. Adults on the other hand are much more motivated by immediate concerns and practical solutions. In relation to this, Warren Wilbert notes, "Learning for adults hinges on the connections the learner is able to make between the content, context, and his personal life situation."[7] This view is substantiated by Cross, who observes, "Research generally supports the notion that most adults who voluntarily undertake a learning project do so more in the hope of solving a problem than with the intention of learning a subject."[8]

When adults sense a problem in their own lives or communities, they are motivated to learning so that they may solve the problem. The problem may be major or minor; but adult learning does not take place in a vacuum. Because adults are very interested in the issues of life, and because their life experiences dominate their thinking, they approach learning in response to the life issues which confront them. Therefore, sensitivity to the issues in adult life will provide important insight for teaching adults. Being aware of the problems that adults face will help us to know both how to teach them and what to teach them.

4. ADULTS ARE SELF-DIRECTING

One key insight for treating adults as adults is to recognize that as people mature they become increasingly self-directing. Children need a great deal of direction from the teacher, but the teacher of adults needs to realize that the more mature students will want to be self-directing. Regarding adult educators, Wilbert observes that many "have established beyond doubt that adult learners simply thrive best under conditions which promote, enhance, and develop self-directed learning."[9]

The difficulty is that many adults have been trained so well to depend upon teachers in the classroom that they have difficulty expressing their self-directed desire when it comes to education. Charles Sell, professor of Christian education at Trinity Evangelical Divinity School, offers the following observation:

6. Malcolm Knowles, *The Modern Practice of Adult Education* (New York: Association, 1972), p. 39.
7. Warren N. Wilbert, *Teaching Christian Adults* (Grand Rapids: Baker, 1980), p. 84.
8. Cross, p. 189.
9. Wilbert, p. 84.

Anyone involved in adult seminars or classes is too well aware of how entering a classroom situation transforms even the boldest leaders into helpless followers. On the edge of my memory is a recent Doctor of Ministry course where I asked pastors to be responsible for just four hours of small group experience, a small fraction of the whole course. I have vivid, painful recall of several scenes of complaining and pleading from men who are usually opinionated, bold, independent leaders. To them, entrance into the pupil role was equal to entering a follower's role.[10]

In the church, we tend to create dependency in our learners when we teach them that they must always turn to the minister or the teacher for insight and understanding in Scripture. By maintaining an authoritarian and controlled approach to education we create within Christian adults a feeling that they cannot learn on their own. Because adults are normally self-directed in their learning, and because the Holy Spirit is given equally to all believers, we need to be careful to trust adults to be self-directed learners and to allow for a more nondirective approach to education that allows them to choose and direct their own educational endeavors. If we are to treat our adults as adult learners, there must be much greater freedom to learn and openness in our educational process to allow them to direct their own educational inquiries. One way to begin moving in this direction is to provide an opportunity for choice within the curriculum. The offering of several electives simultaneously within the larger adult departments allows adults to have some say regarding their own educational experiences. If there is only one adult class in a church, the class could be presented with a variety of options as to the content and method of study to be pursued.

IMPLICATIONS FOR TEACHING ADULTS

An analysis of how people learn will provide insight into how we may best teach them. In light of the characteristics of adult learners seen above, the following four implications for teaching adults in the church are set forth.

1. PROVIDE FOR ADULT EDUCATION IN THE CHURCH

Perhaps the most obvious implication is that adult education should not be seen as optional but rather as imperative in the educational programs of our churches. Rather than viewing the ministry of the

10. Charles Sell, "The Emerging Shape of Adult Christian Education," *Christian Education Journal* 4, no. 1 (1983): 69.

Sunday school as primarily children-oriented (although this certainly is an important emphasis of the educational ministry of the church), we should also put a great deal of energy into the education of adults.

It is often wrongly assumed that adults have ceased to learn or are not interested in learning because they are adults. Unfortunately many churches seem to believe this, because they emphasize childhood education without an equal emphasis on adult education. But the nature of the adult is to want to learn; and so it is imperative for us to provide creative educational experiences for our adults.

Because our ultimate objective is to bring our people to maturity in Christ, we must recognize that learning is essential to spiritual growth and development. Whereas it is possible to be knowledgeable of spiritual truth and yet not be mature, it is impossible to be ignorant of biblical and theological truth and be spiritually mature. The receiving of instruction and the acquisition of knowledge is essential to spiritual growth and development. If our people are to grow spiritually, it is important that we provide for them learning activities and events designed to help them learn in ways that respond to their own characteristics. Therefore it is essential that we provide for adult education in the church.

2. MOTIVATE BY OUTCOMES

A second implication for teaching adults is that we should motivate them by means of the potential outcomes of our instructional tasks. That is, if students can see the benefits of learning, they will be much more inclined to participate in our classes. We need to make clear to our adult learners what they will gain by studying with us.

A survey of the offerings of adult continuing education programs at local colleges almost always will reveal skill-oriented classes. It is obvious by the titles and topics being offered that the students will be able to do something as a result of their study. The outcome of the education is always made clear to the adult learner so that he is motivated to be involved in the study.

Applying this principle to the church, we must be careful to offer courses of study that will show tangible results. For example, rather than simply offering a course in the book of James, we should help the learner to see how a study of the book of James will help him in his personal walk with God. Such a theme as "James—Faith at Work: The Integration of Faith and Life" shows that there will be some practical outcomes to the study of the book. Because adults are extremely pragmatic in their orientation towards learning, that kind of motivation helps the student to see the value of a particular study.

We must be careful not to carry this principle to an extreme. Not all of our study should be geared towards specific pragmatic results. For example, it is important to study the character of God simply so that we can know Him better and worship Him more appropriately. Even this kind of a study can be promoted by means of its outcomes, by indicating that a study of theology proper will help the learner in his worship. We can motivate adults to learn by means of emphasizing the potential outcomes of their study in the practical terms of their daily life experience. However, we must guard against the danger of bringing all of our lesson content down to a functional level.

3. PROVIDE PROBLEM SOLVING LEARNING

Because adults have a problem orientation to learning, it makes sense that we provide for problem solving learning in the church. Malcolm Knowles indicates that the learner should diagnose his or her own needs, and that this process of diagnosis involves three distinct steps. First, they should develop an example or model of the skills and insights they wish to develop. Second, they need to check their own abilities against the desired outcome stated in the first step. And third, they need to assess the differences between where they want to be (step one) and where they actually are (step two).[11]

If we are going to treat adult learners as adults, we must allow them to diagnose their own needs and determine the problems they want solved. Rather than dictating the issues to the students, it is much better to allow them to determine the areas and ways they need to learn, and then to allow them to design their own learning experiences in order to solve those problems or meet their needs.

Leon McKenzie states:

> First, adult education programs in parishes and local churches will never be effective as long as adults do not participate in selecting the learning objectives. Second, learning is not simply the receiving of a lecture or sermon; teaching is not merely the telling of theology. Third, adults will never grow or develop along the lines prescribed by religious values until they decide to grow and develop.[12]

It would be very easy for us to make all the decisions for our learners and dictate to them the problems that need to be solved. However, it is

11. Knowles, *The Modern Practice*, p. 273.
12. Leon McKenzie, *The Religious Education of Adults* (Birmingham, Ala.: Religious Education Press, 1982), pp. 181–82.

much better to allow them to discern the objectives of their education themselves and then to help them in the process of their own learning.

Again, Malcolm Knowles has a critical observation in regard to the learners' readiness to solve certain problems. Knowles states:

> Andragogy assumes that learners are ready to learn those things they "need" to because of the developmental phases they are approaching in their roles as workers, spouses, parents, organizational members and leaders, leisure time users, and the like. The critical implication of this assumption is the importance of timing learning experiences to coincide with the learners' developmental tasks. It is my observation that a good deal of professional education is totally out of phase with the students' readiness to learn.[13]

It may be that as we attempt to solve problems through the education of our adults in the church, we are offering to them perfectly good education at the wrong time. The benefit of allowing students to determine for themselves when they need certain information is that we can then teach in response to their readiness to learn. Although Knowles's observation is made in reference to the professional education of adults, the same observation can be made regarding theological education. It seems most appropriate to allow adults to determine for themselves what problems they would like to solve and in what order they would like to approach them.

4. ALLOW FOR SELF-DIRECTED LEARNING

The final implication is that we should allow for self-directed learning in the church. Beyond allowing the students to choose the topics to be studied, it is also best to allow adults to be actively involved in the learning process. Cross notes that "group learning in which the planning is done by a leader or teacher, appears to be the least satisfactory of all. People feel that their gain in knowledge or skill is relatively low, and they are not especially enthusiastic about what they have learned."[14]

Beyond active involvement in planning, the adult learner should also be self-directing in the actual learning activities. The use of teaching techniques that call for active involvement by the learner is critical in aiding self-directed learning. Cross states: "The message should not be lost that the most frequently used methods in self-directed learning are

13. Knowles, *The Adult Learner*, p. 47.
14. Cross, p. 199.

all active, involving the learner directly; the least commonly used techniques are passive—watching or listening to someone else do something."[15] The following two chapters will develop this idea of methodology that is appropriate to teaching adults and that emphasizes self-directed learning.

The purpose of this approach to adult education in the church is to treat adults as adults, and allow them to be responsible for their own learning. This may require some training at first; the adults will need practice in being self-directed learners; but with effort it can be accomplished by posing questions to the group and allowing them to make the decisions for themselves.

We need to remember that many adults will assume a role of dependency when they come to a learning situation especially in the church; we are going against the grain of the adults' experience when we move them in the direction of self-directed learning. Nevertheless, to help them grow in the Lord, it is important that we produce in our people the ability to design and direct their own learning experiences. With that comes not only the responsibility for their own spiritual growth and development, but also the new freedom of being able to study and learn on their own as adult learners should.

GUIDELINES FOR ADULT EDUCATION IN THE CHURCH

As we work toward a more complete understanding of the adult learning process, the following guidelines are especially important to adult education in the church.

1. DESIGN LESSONS FOR A LIFE RESPONSE

We must remember that Scripture is a means to an end and not an end in itself. The simple acquisition of biblical facts and data apart from having our lives changed by that information is of no real value. The proper result of Bible teaching is a changed life, not simply more information about Scripture. Therefore it is important for the Bible teacher to design his lessons for a life response.

In designing our lessons for a life response we must remember that it is the teacher's task to help bridge the gap from Bible knowledge to life.

15. Ibid., p. 197.

Our philosophy of Bible teaching must help the student understand not only what God says in a particular passage, but also what that truth means in their daily lives and how they should respond to that truth.

Two mistakes must be resisted in order to accomplish this objective. The first mistake is simply to encourage the class to "live this passage this week." Without exploring specifically how the passage should be lived on a daily basis, we have not really helped our students to understand the Scripture in relationship to their own lives, and we have not taught Scripture effectively. Therefore it is important to work with the class to determine what the implications of this passage are to their daily experiences.

The other mistake is to simply tell the students how the passage applies to their lives. Moralizing a passage and telling people specifically how they should live will lead to dependency by the adult learner and will not ultimately foster spiritual growth and development. It is much better to help the students think through for themselves the implications of a passage to their own life experiences and to allow them to discover ways in which they may appropriately apply a passage to their lives. This requires greater patience and is more time-consuming for the teacher but ultimately results in more effective learning. Therefore a proper philosophy of Bible teaching recognizes that Scripture is a means to an end and that it is the task of the teacher to design the lessons so that a life response is accomplished.[16]

2. DESIGN PROGRAMS TO SERVE ADULTS

Many times we have the mistaken notion that people are in the church in order to serve our programs. We design a program and then expect people to attend it; we become angry with them if they fail to attend. This betrays the notion that the people are there to serve our programs. We need to remember that our programs should be designed to serve people.

We must ask ourselves why this particular course or class is being offered and how it will help our people to grow in Christ and to serve God more effectively. If we find ourselves conducting programs simply because the traditions of our church dictate that we do so, or because we somehow vaguely feel obligated to offer a program in order to be "spiritual," our programming philosophy is in need of strengthening. Every program should be designed either to fulfill a biblical imperative

16. For a more fully developed statement of this philosophy of Bible teaching, see Lawrence O. Richards's *Creative Bible Teaching* (Chicago: Moody, 1970).

or to meet a specific need. If we are sensitive to the needs and interests of our adults, we will then be willing to design programs to meet those needs and to eliminate programs that have ceased to be necessary.

One of the more difficult tasks of the church is to eliminate the extraneous programs that have ceased to be needed. It is very important that we regularly evaluate all of the programs of the church and be sure that the programs we have designed are there specifically to serve the adults and not to have the adults serve them.

3. CONSIDER A VARIETY OF TEACHING TECHNIQUES

As the next two chapters will show in much greater detail, we must be willing to approach the teaching of adult learners creatively. The expectation in many adult classes is that there will be a lecture and that adult learners will listen. By observing how few learners actively take notes in an adult lecture, we can gain insight into how much they actually value the content being offered to them. It may be that the content or the method of presentation needs to be changed.

We should consider a variety of active learning techniques that cause adults to take responsibility and to be actively involved in the learning process. The teacher of adults in the church must learn to develop a variety of skills in teaching and to use a variety of techniques to draw the adults into the educational process. Even outside class activities such as projects and community involvement should be considered as teaching techniques.

4. WORK ON PERSONAL RELATIONSHIPS

The experience of adult education in the church should be uniquely Christian. That is, the process of feeling loved, of caring for each other and establishing warm relationships, should be an important strategy in adult education. In order to have uniquely Christian education, we should focus not only on Christian content but also on a uniquely Christian experience of learning in the context of loving relationships.

Perhaps the key to this guideline is the attitude of the teacher. The teacher of adults must have a "pastoral heart" that has specific loving concern for each of his students. Our Lord taught His disciples that "all men will know that you are my disciples if you love one another" (John 13:35, NIV). The theme of love is dominant in the New Testament and one that should be applied to the context of adult education. Students should come into the class and feel welcomed, valued, and loved by the teacher and by the class. Good relationships in the context of adult education can do a great deal to make the experiences pleasant for the learners and insure that the adult education experience will be distinctly Christian.

Moreover, class members should be encouraged to establish strong relationships with one another and with new people who may visit the class. A loving relationship can be an important motivational factor for learners and can enhance spiritual lives. We must guard against becoming so oriented toward the process of education that we create a situation that is not uniquely Christian in its caring and love for each individual. Regardless of age, we all have a need to be loved.

This chapter has presented an overview of the process of adult education in the church. The diagram showing the basic differences between andragogy and pedagogy establishes the foundation for the process of adult education.

Adults want to learn in order to solve problems, and they tend to be self-directed in their learning.

In light of those characteristics, we must see that adult education is important to the church, that it is best to motivate adults by means of the practical results of their study, that it is most effective to provide problem-solving learning for adults, and that we should allow for self-directed learning by adults in the Christian education programs of our churches.

Specific guidelines for educating adults include a philosophy of Bible teaching that leads the student to respond to Scripture, a strategy to design programs to serve adults, an invitation to consider a variety of teaching methods for adults, and a reminder of the importance of personal relationships in the process of Christian education.

For Further Study

1. Briefly design two lessons on the same topic, one lesson plan using the principles of pedagogy, the other using the principles of andragogy.

2. Choose a possible topic of study for an adult course, such as a doctrine or a book of the Bible, and suggest how this course could be presented to adults in a way that would appeal to their interests.

3. Suggest several ways you could determine the needs and interests of adults in the church, which could be used to design educational programs for them.

4. Discuss the following proposition: Because adult learning should be self-directed, it is wrong for a Christian education committee to choose the curriculum for the adult department in the church.

5. What practical steps can be taken in the adult departments of our churches to enhance the quality of relationships there?

7

The Use of Impressional Methods

One of the most practical expressions of our love for people is to teach them the Word of God. At one point in the earthly ministry of our Lord, He attempted to call His disciples away to a quiet place for solitude (Mark 6:31). The crowds followed them, and we are told that Jesus had compassion on them because He saw them as sheep not having a shepherd. As an expression of His love for the multitudes, Jesus "began to teach them many things" (Mark 6:34).

In the next two chapters we will focus on teaching methods that are especially effective with adults. Love for our people must be our motivation as in Mark 6, and love must also be our manner, as indicated in 1 Corinthians 12-14. Taking care to develop skills in teaching is the responsibility of a loving teacher.

THE PURPOSE OF METHODS

The teaching process is best understood as a dynamic interrelationship of three components: the teacher, the learner, and the content to be taught. Each component must have relationships with the other two for effective teaching to take place. If any one of the three elements is removed, a true teaching situation ceases to exist.

This interrelationship is called dynamic because it is always changing. As students they grow and develop, the teacher's understanding of the content may deepen, or the students' needs may change. Thus each teaching situation will be unique. The rigid adult Sunday school teacher who never varies his content of approach to teaching will surely miss the mark because the dynamic aspect will be missing.

When teaching is understood in that way, it can be seen that methods become the means of opening the channels of communication between the teacher, the student, and the content.

Methods are the mechanics of teaching; that is, methods are what the teacher does in order to cause this dynamic interrelationship to take place. Therefore, methods must never be understood as ends in themselves. They are the means used by the teacher to establish open communication so that learning may take place. The methods used should cause the student to interact with the content and with the teacher, as well as having the teacher interact with the content and the student. When this happens the triadic interaction pictured below takes place.

Methods are as essential to the teaching-learning process as words are to conversation. Understanding the variety of methods that will be

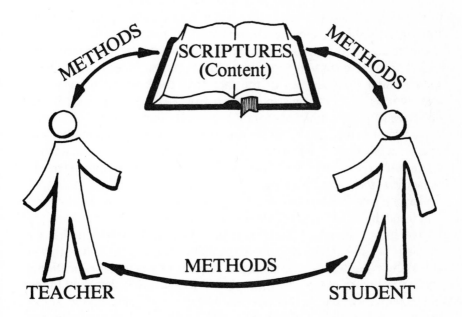

appropriate for adult learners in a church is our next concern. The Christian educator must be aware of the critical role teaching methods have in adult education and then must choose the methods in accordance with the desired objective.

Teaching methods are best categorized according to the kind of involvement they elicit from students. Generally methods may be categorized as either impressional or expressional, depending on the sort of experience you want to provide for your learners. There is no best teaching method. Rather, it is critical to determine which method is the most appropriate for achieving your learning goals in each situation.

In the church a primary concern is the communication of content (propositional truth, normally the Word of God). Impressional methods are especially efficient for this purpose. Impressional methods involve the student through hearing, seeing, teaching, tasting, smelling, or touching. The purpose of these methods is to impress content or information onto the students by means of his five senses. Tasting and smelling were extensively used in ancient Hebrew education; today we focus on hearing, seeing, and, to a lesser degree, touching.

Probably the most common image of adult education in the church is that of a teacher employing an impressional method such as lecture. Lectures are often appropriate in that adults want new information and expect to receive content input from their classes. Indeed, the value of impressional methods lies in the fact that they are an efficient and effective means of transmitting content from teacher to student. If your objective is to communicate content to your students, you should choose an impression method. In addition to lecture, impressional methods include visual aids, demonstrations, and reading assignments. Each of those methods involves the student as a receiver of information by means of hearing, seeing, or touching.

Anyone who has been involved in adult education in the local church has from time to time seen classes in which content has not been presented in a stimulating manner. It is critical to understand that the problem lies not in the content (the Bible is not boring), but rather in the skill of the teacher. Because the content of Christian education is the eternal truth of God, we dare not allow poor methodology to hinder our communication. Rather, we must work to develop highly skilled teachers in the adult department, teachers who can transmit the content of Scripture effectively.

THE LECTURE METHOD

The most common impressional method used with adults is the lecture method. A lecture is an oral discourse on any subject, presented in a systematic, orderly way for the purpose of instruction. Depending on the skill of the teacher, lectures can be one of the most exciting and effective means of teaching—or they can be lifeless and ineffective. When the lecture method is misused it can deaden the learning process. Research indicates that as a teaching method lecturing is especially effective in helping students to acquire factual knowledge.[1]

1. VALUES OF THE LECTURE METHOD

There are several distinct values of the lecture method in relationship to adult ministry in the church. The first is that lecturing is an especially effective way to communicate content in a systematic way. In an adult Bible study or a theological lecture where precision and logic are important, a lecture can be one of the best means of guiding the students in acquiring the information.

The efficient use of time is a second value of the lecture technique. A carefully designed and delivered lecture can communicate a large amount of content in a relatively short amount of time. Especially in the Sunday school hour where time is at a premium, the lecture can be extremely helpful. When the curriculum calls for teaching extensive amounts of material, as in a Bible survey course, the lecture method should be considered.

The teacher has more direct control of the class when the lecture method is used. He is able to control the pace of learning, the terms being used, the direction and emphasis of the study, and the specific points of application. This may be especially significant in an adult class composed of people with a wide variety of backgrounds. By maintaining control of the class, the sensitive teacher is able to emphasize what will meet the needs of the majority of the students, and the danger of a small minority of students with special needs or interests dominating the class can be avoided.

2. POTENTIAL PROBLEMS WITH THE LECTURE METHOD

When considered in relation to adult education, there are two primary dangers in the lecture method, both of which can be avoided. The first

---

1. Frank Costin, "Lecturing Versus Other Methods of Teaching: A Review of Research," *British Journal of Educational Technology* (1972): 3-31.

potential problem is the high degree of skill required to be an effective lecturer. The primary reason lecturing is criticized as a teaching method is that many people have heard many poor lecturers. The problem resides not in the method, but in the person using the method. Therefore, it is important that teachers be skilled as lecturers if they choose to use this method. In a following section, specific guidelines for effective lecturing will be discussed.

The second potential problem with the lecture method is lack of active student participation. An improper assumption held by some adults in the church is that they are not responsible for their own spiritual development. That perspective may come, in part, from the fact that no demands are placed upon them to actively participate in their own maturing process. If the process of adult education is exclusively impressional and if the only expectation placed upon the student is to come and listen to a lecture, an unhealthy dependence on the "expert" for spiritual growth may result. Therefore, the teacher must use a variety of methods, some of which call for active involvement by the students, and must structure the lecture to promote independence rather than dependency in the adult learner.

3. WHEN TO USE THE LECTURE METHOD

As with all other methods, the key to deciding when to use the method is to determine its appropriateness to certain circumstances. First consider the teacher. If he is a skilled lecturer and enjoys lecturing, then it would be appropriate. It is important to consider the personality traits of individual teachers and to help them discover the teaching style that is most compatible with their own capacities and needs. Some people are excellent in small group discussions but are poor as lecturers. They should be made aware of their own strengths and weaknesses.

A second consideration is the pupils. The number of people in a class and their competencies play a role here. Regarding class size, Ronald Hyman makes the following observation:

> The minimum number of students for a lecture class is about fifteen to twenty. With less than this number it is difficult for the teacher to lecture, since the small number of students discourages him from presenting a formal address. Small groups invite, rather, an informal relationship where one person does not talk *to* the others.[2]

2. Ronald T. Hyman, *Ways of Teaching,* 2d ed. (Philadelphia: J. B. Lippincott, 1978), p. 24.

In addition to class size, the background and abilities of the students should be considered. If an adult class is composed of new or uninformed believers, a lecture would probably be most appropriate. If, however, the students are quite familiar with the content, more active participation should be elicited by the instructor.

If the content is highly factual, technical, or simply new to the learners, then the lecture method is appropriate. If the purpose of the class is other than the communication of content (such as the development of skills or the exploration of personal life implications) then a method other than lecture should be used.

A final consideration is the context of the learning situation. Such factors as the time of day, the location, and the situation of the class should be considered. For example, an informal home Bible study would not naturally lend itself to lecture, but a larger Sunday school class meeting in the church building would. It must be remembered that not every educational setting is appropriate to lecture, but many are.

4. EFFECTIVE LECTURING

As mentioned earlier, it is important for the adult educator to develop his skill as a lecturer. There are a number of areas to work on.

Preparation. Because most adults in the church have some background in Bible and theology, the adult teacher must be willing to study his content carefully. Thorough preparation is the key. Effective use of commentaries, dictionaries, encyclopedias, and theological reference books will greatly enhance the quality and depth of the content presented by the lecturer. A good rule of thumb is that the teacher must study until he is excited about what he has learned. Wilbert McKeachie, in an excellent book for beginning college teachers, states:

> Vocal variety, audibility, and movement are overt cues to your own enthusiasm, and if there is any teacher characteristic related to learning, it is enthusiasm. Enthusiasm probably cannot be successfully faked, but it is possible to influence the degree to which your enthusiasm shows. Moreover, my enthusiasm about a lecture topic seems to be a function of the degree to which I've prepared for it. I find it hard to be enthusiastic about most lectures I've given before, but if I've reworked a lecture, learned some new things, and come up with some new ideas, I approach the lecture with much more enthusiasm.[3]

3. Wilbert J. McKeachie, *Teaching Tips*, 7th ed. (Lexington, Mass.: D. C. Heath, 1978), p. 24.

Preparation includes the organization of material. A properly organized lecture should have a clear, logical progression that guides the student's thinking and leads from an attention-gaining introduction, through a clear presentation of the content, and on to an appropriate conclusion. Relevant illustrations will illuminate and enliven the presentation. Preparation includes thinking not only about *what* will be said but also about *how* it will be said.

Effective preparation also includes anticipating questions that may arise in the minds of the students. Sensitivity to the class is necessary so that the teacher may then raise and answer those questions in his lecture. Because adults can and will think deeply regarding issues presented to them, it is important that the lecture does pose the difficult questions that may arise, and then deal with them honestly.

Presentation. Practices such as proper posture, eye contact with students, and voice control are important. It is not necessary to make a formal presentation (indeed, extreme formalism may hinder the lecture), but the lecture must be effective. If, for example, the teacher speaks so quietly that people cannot hear, the most effective preparation will be lost. Several factors can aid in effective presentation.

The teacher's attitude should be one of interest and excitement about the content. This will come as a result of good preparation. In addition, the teacher's attitude should be confident and positive. If the lecture begins with a note of apology ("I really shouldn't be teaching this") or negativism ("I don't know why we are supposed to study this") the mindset of the students will immediately shift against the class.

Concern. At the center of the teacher's attitude must be a sincere commitment of love to the class. Because the ultimate purpose of the class is ministry, the teacher must guard against the desire to impress class members with his expertise, or to demean them for their weaknesses. Rather, like the apostle Paul, his attitude should be: "Having thus a fond affection for you, we were well-pleased to impart to you not only the gospel of God but also our own lives, because you had become very dear to us" (1 Thess. 1:8). It is highly appropriate for the teacher to pray for this love for his students and to see his lecture as his personal gift of love to them.

Not only must the teacher be excited about his lesson, but he must also be excited about his students. He should be concerned for their needs and sensitive to their response to the lecture. If particular points of the lecture elicit significant response (such as nodding of heads or frowns), the teacher should be willing to acknowledge the responses and deal accordingly with them. The purpose of any class is to teach students, not simply cover the content.

Teaching aids. Because the skill of effective lecturing is difficult to develop, the untrained teacher especially should avail himself of teaching aids as a supplement to the lecture. Prudent use of pictures, displays, chalkboards, or overhead projectors can greatly help the visual communication of a teaching situation. In addition, such audio aids as tapes and records can be used. Because a lecture is easily combined with other teaching methods, it is wise to do so.

INSTRUCTIONAL MEDIA

It is clear that today's adult learner is the product of a media-oriented society. Heinich, Molenda, and Russell conclude:

> Learners of all ages are to some extent "different" today from learners of previous generations simply by virtue of their exposure to mass media. There is no question of whether or not modern communications technology should be brought into the learning situation. It is already there, as it is in other aspects of society, in the experiential and environmental background of teacher and student alike. The real question is, How can we best use this pervasive technology for effective education?[4]

Instructional media are any form of communication media that are used to aid in teaching such as films, slides, filmstrips, and overhead projections.

THE VALUES OF INSTRUCTIONAL MEDIA

Beginning in the early 1900s and on up to the present, the effectiveness of educational media has been analyzed and tested. At times, statistics have been inflated; but when the studies are summarized, it is safe to conclude that media is indeed valuable for education.

The use of media in the instructional process makes learning faster. When a large amount of content must be covered in a small amount of time, pictures, charts, graphics, and other resources allow for rapid communication and assimilation of material. Even in hospitals, physicians are finding that computer-generated graphs of patients' vital signs are quicker and easier to read or analyze than the traditional printed list of numbers. Especially in a Sunday school context, when class time is at a premium, the effective use of media can greatly reduce the teacher's frustration over the lack of time for instruction.

4. Robert Heinich, Michael Molenda, and James D. Russell, *Instructional Media* (New York: John Wiley, 1982), pp. 5–7.

The use of instructional media also tends to produce more permanent learning. When a student both sees and hears a concept, he will have greater recall of that concept. Jerome Bruner, a psychologist who has studied how people learn, believes that visually representing concepts by means of pictures, films, diagrams, and so on is essential to the development of proper understanding. Moreover, he believes that this applies to all learners, regardless of age; we must avoid the common misconception that visualization is important only for children.[5]

Learning can also be more enjoyable for the student when media is involved. A variety of sensory input makes the classroom experience more interesting, especially for the media-oriented adult of the 1980s. Communication in church tends to be primarily verbal; legitimate use of media can provide a variety of sensory experiences for the student.

INSTRUCTIONAL MEDIA IN THE ADULT BIBLE CLASS

In order that the media truly aid the learning process, certain steps should be followed as the adult teacher plans to use teaching aids.

First, the teacher should study the lesson to determine where teaching aids are needed. Such indicators as complex ideas, abstract ideas, rather detailed content, or geographical content all should trigger ideas for teaching aids. Diagrams, outlines, or maps will help the student to grasp the content more quickly.

Second, the teacher would be well advised to look for professionally prepared aids to meet his particular teaching needs. The church resource center, public library, Christian media organizations, or local Christian bookstores are possible sources for professionally prepared instructional media. Slides, films, filmstrips, and transparencies for the overhead projector may be rented or purchased.

Third, the teacher should carefully and purposefully develop any aids that he can personally prepare for the class. Perhaps the creative use of personal slides or the creation of a poster or a handout sheet could be considered. Even thinking through the best use of the chalkboard will be appreciated by the adult learner.

Finally, the teacher should practice the skills necessary for using the teaching aids properly. The effectiveness of media may be destroyed by the teacher's lack of skill. The purely mechanical aspects of media should be practiced so that the communication of content will not be hindered. Being comfortable and thoroughly familiar with the tools of

5. See, for example, Jerome S. Bruner, *Toward a Theology of Instruction* (Cambridge, Mass.: Belknap, 1966).

the trade is indispensable. Most instructional media is designed to be used not by a technician, but by a teacher, and is therefore quite easy to use. But still, a few minutes of practice before classtime can give the teacher increased confidence and skill.

THE EXPANDING HORIZONS OF MEDIA IN THE CHURCH

Technological advances in home-oriented media are allowing for its expanded and creative use in the field of Christian education. As of this writing, it appears that two media will have strong educational impact on the church: video cassettes and computer-aided instruction. Although not all churches will adopt these techniques, it is probable that many churches will.

With the ever-widening use of video cassette recorders in homes, a natural extension of that media into educational practices is not only inevitable but warranted. The use of films in Christian education has been widely accepted since the 1950s, so it is appropriate that the advances in technology available through video cassettes should also be used in the local church classroom.

The New Media Bible[6] is an attempt to put all of Scripture into video format for use in educational settings. This kind of project will never replace the written word (and it is not intended to do so), but it does provide a strong visual expression of the biblical narratives to help the stories of Scripture "come alive" more vividly for the learner. A variety of publishers are currently expanding into the production of video cassettes for use with their curriculum materials.

The danger of extensive use of this kind of media in adult education is that the instructor could become depersonalized. To simply watch the television screen without any kind of human interaction would be detrimental to spiritual growth, because a critical aspect of truly Christian education is personal interaction (see chapter 9). But if the video cassette is used as a means of content input and is coupled with appropriate discussion periods, it can be an extremely effective teaching aid. The role of the adult teacher in such cases will be changed from content implanter to content clarifier.

The early uses of video cassettes were basically recorded lectures, so that the picture on the screen featured only a "talking head," that is, only a picture of a lecturer speaking. But as the state of the art is being improved and more creative concepts are being used, dramas, brief story

6. The New Media Bible, The Genesis Project, Inc., Washington, D. C.

vignettes, documentaries, and creative graphics are being combined to provide more exciting and provocative media for Christian education.

The second remarkable technological advance that is beginning to affect Christian education is the use of the computer as a teaching tool. The marked increase in capability of the personal computer, coupled with its rapid decline in cost, is creating a large market for the product.[7] Increasing numbers of home computers are being purchased both by individuals and by churches. The inclusion of computer literacy as a basic skill for elementary and secondary school students will hasten that trend.

The use of the computer as an aid to record keeping is obvious. Financial data, attendance figures, and growth projections can all be easily computerized for greater efficiency. But some of the most promising uses of the computer are in education.

Recent studies have shown that computer-aided instruction can be used in a wide variety of settings with marked success.[8] Although early studies focused on elementary education in the public schools, it is apparent that this technique will be equally effective with adults.

The key to effective use of computers in education will be writing programs that are truly educational. Alfred Bork writes:

> Most of the personal computers that are now being sold as educational devices will perform a very limited educational role. It is only through the development of sophisticated learning material, coming from excellent teachers with great understanding of the learning process, that we can hope to achieve the full potentials of the personal computer as a learning device.[9]

The key to designing programs that are educationally effective will be to take proper advantage of the interactive capabilities of the computer. By designing programs that interact in effective learning modes such as review, correction, and rapid advancement, instructional programs that are personalized for each student can be achieved.[10]

7. "One of the most striking aspects of this has to do with fact memory for storage of data and programs. During the past several years fact memory has decreased in cost each year by approximately a factor of two. Another way of stating this result, even more revealing, is that in each year the computer industry has succeeded in placing twice as much memory on a single chip while the cost of chips has stayed constant. Several factor doublings are projected."
8. Robert J. Seidel and Martin Rubin, *Computers and Communication, Implications for Education* (New York: Academic, 1977), p. 95.
9. Alfred Bork, "Educational Technology and the Future," *Journal of Educational Technology Systems* 10 [1981–82]: 8–9.
10. In the school year 1982–83, a computer club was established among the students of Trinity Evangelical Divinity School in Deerfield, Illinois. Students produced an interactive program to teach the basic content of the book of Romans to high school students.

The potential for linking computer programs to video cassettes and even more versatile video disk players should result in remarkable educational systems. The potential for these systems in Christian education has not yet been fully explored, but the future looks bright. A computer-aided and graphically visualized instructional system would allow for amazing potential for personal learning. That potential should be harnessed for adult education in our churches so that by means of educational technology we can produce men and women who are knowledgeable as Christians and ready to be brought to maturity by the power of the Holy Spirit of God.

The future of adult education will be greatly enriched by the continuing development of diverse and stimulating teaching methods and technology. From the skilled lecturer who can enthusiastically impart content in a personal and creative manner, to flexible and adaptable educational technology that is rapidly gaining acceptance, the opportunities that lie ahead are mind stretching. The only limitation seems to be the hesitancy people have to accept change, even change for the better.

1. What is the critical issue in determining which teaching method to use?

2. What are the potential problems of lecturing, and how can they best be overcome?

3. Describe a situation most appropriate for the lecture method. Compare that with your situation to determine whether lecture is appropriate for you.

4. List some of the factors that make for effective learning. Discern which are your strong points and weak points, and note how to concentrate on your strengths and strengthen your weaknesses.

5. Describe some instructional media and determine how you can avail yourself of them in your teaching situation.

8

The Use
of Expressional Methods

If ever there was a teacher who had the right to be a pure lecturer, it was our Lord. As a result of His divine nature He had sufficient information to do nothing but impart information to His students for the three years of His teaching ministry. But the gospel records clearly show that He chose not to use the lecture method exclusively. Rather, His dominant mode of instruction appears to have been interaction and discussion with His followers. A brief survey of the gospels shows the numerous times that His students spoke as they learned. If Jesus is in any way an example for teachers of adults today, we can safely conclude that active student involvement is an important factor in adult education.

EXPRESSIONAL METHODS

An expressional method involves the student in talking or acting. It allows him to express his feelings, understandings, or reactions pertinent to the class. When communication from the student is desired, an expressional method should be used. Examples are role play, group discussion, reports, debate, student skits, and creative writing. Each calls upon the student to express his ideas or feelings.

Expressional methods are especially appropriate for adult education in the church because the adult has a great deal of information and background life experience that can and should be shared with the rest of the class. Because experience is an important part of Christian life, it is especially important for adults to share experiences with one another. Moreover, an expressional method makes the learner a more responsible participant in the educational experience, because more is expected from him than simply listening. He is called upon to be an active participant in the teaching/learning process. As was noted in chapter 6, that is a critical aspect of the adult educational process.

THE DISCUSSION METHOD

Perhaps the most common expressional method used with adults is group discussion. Due to improper use of the technique, many people have had poor experiences with the discussion method, but when it is used correctly it can be an exciting and productive teaching method. Based on the concept of expression, discussion allows people to discover for themselves scriptural content and its subsequent life implications.

VALUES OF THE DISCUSSION TECHNIQUE

Discussion allows the learners to generate knowledge themselves. Most adult learners will have a vast fund of experiences and data from which to draw in a discussion. Adults have the capacity to put facts and experiences together in new ways to create new information for themselves. As the students are prompted to work with facts through deliberation, argumentation, and judgment, they are able to come to new conclusions regarding their data. Adults have the ability to relate data to new situations by their own intellectual powers, and the discussion method prompts this process in the learner.

The discussion method also encourages students to think issues through for themselves. Because the learners are actively involved in the process, the teacher's role becomes that of an enabler rather than a teller. The teacher using this method is in effect telling his students, "If you want to know, you must exercise your own intellect." Rather than simply receiving answers from the teacher, the student is required to actively consider options himself.

This value is especially important to Christian education. As people grow in the Christian faith, they need to understand *what* is important— but also *why* it is important. By means of discussion, the teacher can help students to think through the reasons behind Christian content, and thus prompt a deeper level of learning. When a person needs to think through meaning for himself, the potential for that answer's being "owned" is even greater. Our goal is to produce mature Christians who are secure in the faith for themselves; discussion can be a very important means of accomplishing that end.

It is important to understand that a good teacher, when he leads a discussion, is teaching on two levels simultaneously. On the first level, he is teaching the principles of the subject matter by means of class presentation and questions. Simultaneously, he is also teaching the way of grasping and generating such principles. Therefore, the student is allowed to see not only the conclusions, but also the logic used to reach those conclusions. In reference to this concept of learning, Ronald Hyman states:

> This notion is connected to the idea that an individual must expand and deepen his knowledge all through his life. He must do so early in formal school situations where teachers are present to guide him. Indeed, the raison d'etre of schools is precisely to facilitate the student's effort in this task. But, since the person spends most of his time away from his teachers even during the years he attends school, he must be able to further his knowledge on his own, and to acquire knowledge when teachers are not around to teach him. Discussion in this way serves both the purpose of schooling and the purpose of preparing for a life after schooling is completed.[1]

Further, the discussion method helps the student develop independent thinking, and this can then lead to personal independence. Through discussion the focus shifts from *what* to think to *how* to think. Because ultimately we want our adult learners to learn to think Christianly regarding any life situation, it is essential that we teach them how to think. The process of discussion can show how to think Christianly regarding the issues of life. The result is that students can gain a proper degree of independence from the teachers. While the Scriptures teach that all members of the Body of Christ are related to one another and need each other, there is also strong emphasis on the importance of a growing independence in a mature believer. For example, John reminded his readers in 1 John 2:27, "As for you, the anointing which you received from Him abides in you, and you have no need for anyone to teach you; but as His anointing teaches you about all things, and is true and is not a lie, and just as it has taught you, you abide in Him." Continued dependence on a teacher will not result in spiritual maturity in our

1. Ronald T. Hyman, *Ways of Teaching,* 2d ed. (Philadelphia: J. B. Lippincott, 1974), p. 75.

believers. We need to help students to think independently so they can have a growing faith that is also personalized. The ability of discussion to cause the student to think is an important means to that end.

The discussion method, with its emphasis on personal discovery, is highly motivating for the student. When a student begins to gain knowledge on his own and his confidence in his own capacity to discover increases, it can be very stimulating to his learning. As our students begin to discover that they can make valid observations regarding a scriptural passage or develop good theological insights in regard to life issues, they become more motivated to think and to become more effective students of the Word. The reward of achieving personal insights is an enhancement of individual study.

The discussion method also provides for a variety of insights in class experience. Especially when we have competent adult learners, we should respect and value the input they can have. By allowing them opportunity to voice their concerns and ideas, the whole class can benefit from the value of their insights. Discussion is a very practical way of allowing the truth of 1 Corinthians 12, that we all have something to contribute to the Body, to be included in our teaching philosophy.

Finally, by means of discussion students can accomplish a more personalized application of the truth to their lives than we can effect through an impressional method. Discussion allows students to explore the meaning of a biblical truth in a much more intimate and personal way than by one-directional input by the teacher. The fact of the matter is that the class may be more sensitive to its needs than the teacher is, and the class may also probe more deeply into life implications than the teacher could ever do. Therefore, allowing the class to explore implications and to apply the Scripture itself may result in a more personalized application of the truth.

LIMITATIONS OF THE DISCUSSION METHOD

Although most limitations can be avoided by proper use of the method, it is important that we realize the potential problems that lurk within the discussion method.

Discussion requires that the group have prior knowledge of the subject matter. Prior Bible knowledge is almost always necessary. Without it, the discussion is only a pooling of ignorance rather than a growing and learning experience. Without sufficient information the class simply cannot engage in intelligent discussion. For example, the hypostatic union of Christ's humanity and deity cannot be discussed if the group does not know that Jesus is both God and man simultaneously. Therefore, we need to realize that not every group is capable of effectively discussing every subject.

Also, discussion can easily degenerate into aimless talk, if the leader is not careful or skillful. Unless it has been carefully thought through by the leader, a discussion can fail to reach a proper conclusion so that people know what to do or to think as a result of the discussion. Aimless comments and unrelated information may be included in the discussion until it becomes an exercise in futility rather than a dynamic learning experience. We have all had experiences in a discussion when at the end we wondered what we actually had accomplished. As will be shown later, a careful guiding of the discussion by the leader can avoid or avert this limitation.

It is also possible that even though the entire discussion group is in agreement, its conclusions will be wrong. A teacher may give up a large part of control of the group and not guide it to his conclusion. He may let it reach its own conclusion, regardless of what that may be. Normally, in an adult class that will not be a problem, but the potential is definitely there for the group to come to an incorrect conclusion.

The final limitation of the discussion technique is that it can be very time consuming. What the teacher can lecture on in ten minutes may take the group thirty or more minutes to discover for itself. Discussion is a slow process and cannot be used when there is a great deal of content to be dealt with in a short amount of time. Discussion is not effective for a fifteen-minute Bible study. At some points the teacher may conclude that there simply is not enough time for an effective discussion. The teacher is best advised not to attempt a discussion in a short amount of time and thus frustrate himself and the class but rather to wait and have discussion when there is sufficient time to use the process properly.

EFFECTIVE DISCUSSIONS

There are four interrelated factors that can contribute to an effective discussion. Each factor must be considered when a discussion is being planned to insure the potential for success. These factors are the topic, the group, the physical setting, and the teacher.

The topic. An effective discussion topic must be something that the group is able to discuss and something that the members want to discuss. When the students find a topic challenging, interesting, and relevant, they will enthusiastically participate in discussion. If, however, they find that the topic is too ethereal to have immediate practical significance to them or if they think it is basically a closed issue, they will not participate in the discussion. The key here is to choose a topic that has immediate significance to the group and to pose the discussion question in such a way that the students might quickly see the issue's relevance. For example, if the class has been studying a doctrinal subject such as the holiness of God, a good discussion topic might be the question, How does the holiness of God affect our lives? No doubt the class will need some help in thinking through these issues, but if they have sufficient information regarding the holiness of God they will be able to begin to draw some specific conclusions as to how the doctrine affects their daily experience.

The group. If the group is not willing to discuss, the discussion technique will not work. A group needs to be willing to disagree, willing to be open-minded, willing to be objective, and willing to be honest. Willingness to disagree is not the same as being disagreeable. Rather, it implies that group members are not so concerned with the avoidance of conflict that they cannot or will not express an honest point of disagreement among themselves. Not all Christians agree on everything, and proper discussion of disagreements can be an important factor in the development of our understanding of the Christian faith. But if people are not willing to be open minded and objective and to state honestly their feelings, attitudes, and ideas, they will not be able to work together for deeper understanding. Therefore, the group must be willing to participate in the process and to speak honestly.

That kind of attitude needs to be fostered by the teacher. A warm, open, and trusting environment will create an atmosphere where it can be developed. But if the students do not trust one another or the teacher, they will not risk the involvement of open, honest discussion. We need to remember that discussions can be threatening until people feel comfortable in the process.

The physical setting. The actual "feeling" of a room will change according to the room arrangement. A formal arrangement of students in rows creates an attitude and atmosphere of observation by the learner. But a more informal circular arrangement will create an attitude of participation. If, for example, an adult class meets in the sanctuary where the pews are bolted to the floor, it may be difficult to develop an effective discussion. If it meets in a more informal setting where the chairs can be arranged in a circle, the atmosphere will be more conducive to effective group discussion.

The teacher. If a teacher is not willing to be open and honest, the group members will not have that willingness either. The teacher must be open and interested in the topic. The teacher must see the topic as of vital concern and important to discuss. His attitude and approach to the discussion will set the tone. Some teachers tend to monopolize and dominate a class, and this will greatly hinder discussion. But if the teacher's attitude is one of openness and warmth, this will help to set the class much more at ease, and effective discussion may result. For that reason, it is important for the teacher to know himself and to understand how his own personality traits will affect the dynamics and functioning of his class.

LEADING THE DISCUSSION

The key to leading a discussion effectively is preparation on the part of the teacher. Leading a discussion properly requires at least as much, if not more, preparation than does the lecture method. A well-prepared teacher appears to be natural and almost spontaneous as he skillfully guides the discussion to the main issues by means of probing questions. In actually leading the discussion, the leader performs four functions: he orients the group, presents the problem, guides the discussion, and draws the discussion to a close with a summary.

The discussion leader *orients the group* by first creating a comfortable and relaxed mood. If the leader himself is relaxed and at ease, it will help to create an atmosphere that will promote free discussion by the group. In addition, the leader should also orient the group to any procedural instructions that might be necessary. These would include the basic ground rules of how the discussion will be run so that people will know what is going to happen and what their role in this discussion will be.

As the leader *presents the problem,* or the issue to be discussed, he needs to establish the topic's relevance to the group. A clear aim for the discussion should be presented, so that the group has a sense of progress and a goal towards which it is aiming. A clear presentation of the topic will do a great deal in setting the direction for the discussion so that the predetermined objectives will be met.

The leader *guides the discussion,* but does not dominate it. Careful guiding of the discussion includes keeping it on track. The leader needs to listen carefully to the content being discussed and must graciously keep the discussion from going down blind alleys and off on issues that are not really relevant to the topic at hand.

The leader must also provide logical transitions, so that the group can clearly move from point to point in the development of the topic. Transitions are provided by first offering a brief summarization of what has been said to that point, and then providing the next logical question in the line of the discussion. As a result of providing careful transitions during the discussion period, the group will have a sense of progress, and the learners will be satisfied that something is being accomplished.

Also included in guiding is the task of maintaining the process of the discussion. Because the goal of discussion is to draw people into the process, the leader must be aware of who is talking too much and who is not talking enough. The effective discussion leader must find ways to naturally and easily draw out the more quiet people and at the same time subdue the more talkative ones. As the discussion leader builds rapport with the group that task will be less difficult than it might be initially.

Finally, the discussion leader *draws the discussion to a close* with a summary. An important factor for satisfactory learning is to have some sense of closure and conclusion at the end of a class period. By careful summarization of the discussion and insightful analysis of what was said, the discussion leader can provide that sense of closure for the students so that they know what the discussion accomplished. That does not mean that hard and fast conclusions must be reached but rather that the learners have at least a sense that something was accomplished. If the learners have a sense of direction and accomplishment they will feel that the discussion was a satisfying experience. Because adults desire to see results from their efforts, this final step is critical.

ASKING QUESTIONS

Another important strategy in the art of expressional teaching methods is the effective use of questions. Hyman observes:

> Teaching involves questioning. It is virtually impossible to think of teaching (over a period of time) that does not involve questioning. Indeed, questioning is the teacher's chief means of directing or channeling discourse. No doubt the teacher will ask fewer questions in a discussion than in a recitation. However, precisely for this reason he must be aware of the various types of questions. He must deliberately frame the questions appropriate to the context of the discourse of the students involved. By varying his questions the teacher can elicit a wide range of responses, thereby developing in the students a broad set of cognitive skills.[2]

WHY USE QUESTIONS WITH ADULTS?

As the above quote indicates, there are a number of advantages to using questions in teaching, some of which are critical for the adult

2. Ibid., p. 324.

learner. The cognitive values of questions are obvious. The use of questions will cause students to think through the issues at hand. When a student is asked to think and respond to a specific issue, his involvement in the learning process will become much more active than it would be in simply listening to a lecture. Perhaps this is why our Lord used questions on a regular basis in His teaching ministry.

Kenneth Gangel suggests that questions are effective because they tend to promote student "ownership" of the class.[3] As students become more actively involved in the process of the classroom, they feel a deeper sense of responsibility and association with it. By helping them become more active participants they will feel more that this is their class rather than the teacher's class.

Questions can also be important in adult education, for they tend to "stimulate students to think to seek out additional data on their own."[4] In adult education, it is extremely important to build independence in our learners. The posing of stimulating questions that are not always answered in class can aid growth toward independence by creating within the students the desire to study on their own. That will help adult learners become more responsible for their own spiritual development.

A critical problem with some adult learners is that they feel insecure regarding themselves and lack confidence in their own ability to understand and feed themselves as believers. Therefore, it is important when working with adults to ask questions that allow the students to build up positive self images. When the learners can successfully answer the teacher's questions, they quickly discover that they need not worry about their own abilities in regard to personal Bible study for spiritual growth.

A final reason for asking questions with adults is to "assess the degree of success in achieving the goals and objectives of the lesson."[5] One of the most effective ways to determine whether learning has in fact resulted from a lesson is to question the students. By means of properly phrased questions the teacher may discover how much his students understand and whether or not his objectives have been met. Questioning can be an evaluative tool for the teacher as well as the student.

3. Kenneth O. Gangel, *24 Ways to Improve Your Teaching* (Wheaton, Ill.: Victor, 1971), p. 39.
4. Arthur A. Carin and R. B. Dund, *Developing Questioning Techniques: A Self-concept Approach* (Columbus, Ohio: C. E. Merrill, 1971).
5. Ibid, p. 24.

BASIC KINDS OF QUESTIONS

Although there are many complex classification schemes for identifying the types of questions that may be used in education, it is helpful to think in terms of broad categories in which questions may be asked. These categories are based upon the kind of student reaction the question is designed to elicit.

The *identification question* asks of the student, "What do you know?" It may be very simple, such as "Where did God send Jonah to pronounce His judgment?" or it may be rather difficult, such as "What was the place of Nineveh in the political structure of Jonah's time?" Both of those questions ask for a knowledge response; if the student has sufficient background information, he is capable of answering. The identification question is helpful in discovering what the students know and in providing opportunities for the students to affirm for themselves and for others that they are knowledgeable regarding the subject. (Of course, it may also be used to demonstrate to the student that he is not quite so knowledgeable regarding the subject as he thinks he is!)

The *analytical question* asks, "What do you think?" It seeks to gain a judgment or an analysis by the student. Rather than asking students to repeat information they have acquired, the analytical question asks them to deal with information in a creative way, so that higher levels of thinking result. Again, the question may be simple, such as "How would you paraphrase Jonah's experience in chapter two?" Or it may be complex, such as "If Isaiah had been sent to Nineveh instead of Jonah, what would have been different?" It demands more of students because it requires them to use their own minds in creative ways. Especially because of the mental capacities of the adult learner, analytical questions need to be asked with greater and greater frequency in the educational program of the church. That will help the student to become more adept at thinking in deeper ways regarding biblical and theological issues, and in analyzing his own life issues as well.

The *value question* asks, "How do you feel?" It probes not only the cognitive but also the affective realm of the students. Value questions are the most difficult for students to answer because they require delving into the more personal aspects of their own lives. An example would be "Have you ever been despondent over the actions of God in the way that Jonah was in chapter four?" Value questions ask students to divulge the more personal aspects of their own life experience, and therefore require a great deal of trust in the class. But the value of this kind of question is that it causes students to think through the deepest issues of their

Christian lives, namely those that touch values and attitudes regarding the Lord. If the student senses that a value question is being asked from a basis of love and concern, he will feel free to respond openly. That can be extremely helpful in causing students to grow in their depth of understanding and commitment.

GUIDELINES FOR QUESTIONING

Just as with any other teaching method, the effective teacher needs to develop skills in the art of questioning. To enhance the effectiveness of questioning, first vary the kind and difficulty of your questions. Adults become bored with predictable teaching techniques. If the teacher always asks the same kind of questions of the same level of difficulty, students lose interest. Therefore, a helpful procedure is to pre-plan several pivotal questions in a lesson, questions that ask the students to respond on either a knowledge, thinking, or feeling level. Also, the teacher must be careful to design both simple and complex questions for the different levels of students in the class.

A critical skill in the art of questioning is that of giving students time to respond. The more mature teacher is not threatened by silence in the classroom, but is willing to allow students time to think. Especially when a more difficult thought question or a feeling question has been posed, students will need time to think. If the teacher is willing to wait, a more insightful answer may result.

Also, when asking questions, be sure to affirm all student responses. This does not mean that the teacher must treat an incorrect answer as though it were correct, but rather that the student must be praised for an attempt to respond. If the student is not personally secure, attempting to answer a question can be a rather frightening experience. If the teacher will affirm the student for his involvement and his attempt to answer, even the offering of an incorrect response can be a positive experience for him. Especially for adults who may have had years of experience at being silent in the church, this is especially important. It is the task of the teacher to be sure that responding to questions is a positive experience for the student.

One final suggestion: the teacher must ask many questions for which he does not have the answers. Again, Hyman offers insight when he states:

> The reason for asking questions for which the teacher has yet no correct answers is to eliminate the pointless game wherein the student tries to guess what is in the teacher's mind. Moreover, these questions put the

teacher and the student in the role of co-inquirers. For the student, this means stimulation. For the teacher, this means that he is taking on the role of acting as guide to the student and as a model of an adult inquirer exploring new ground.[6]

Because we are dealing with adult learners, we desire to foster both critical and creative thinking in our students. One of the best ways to do this is to pose questions for which there is no "right" or clear answer. Questions of this kind lead teacher and student together in attempting to discover answers, and put them on the mutual ground of learners. Although not all questions need to be of this type, it is important that the teacher pose questions that allow the learners to function as adults.

Given the nature of the adult learner, and the ultimate objectives of the educational program of the church, a high level of concentration on expressional teaching methods seems appropriate. Some students will resist, but for those who desire and need to be more actively involved in their own spiritual growth, teaching methods that cause them to contribute and respond are essential. Teachers in the adult department can foster more independent learning in their students by means of effective use of expressional methods.

The two most practical and productive expressional techniques for teachers of adults are discussions and questions. As with other methods, these must be carefully planned and skillfully executed. God's first recorded question, "Adam, where are you?" (Genesis 3) was designed to get Adam to evaluate his situation and get new information from that evaluation. God knew where Adam was geographically, psychologically, physiologically, sociologically, and spiritually. Adam, on the other hand, needed that information so that God could begin to do a new work in his heart.

6. Hyman, pp. 325-26.

1. Compare and contrast the impressional and the expressional methods. Tell why both are needed for effective instruction.

2. Design a lesson plan for a young adult class using the discussion method as the primary approach. Clearly outline how you will orient the group, present the problem, guide the discussion, and summarize.

3. Prepare fifteen questions to ask a middle-aged adult class, covering the material presented in John 14 (or some similar narrative passage). Five knowledge questions, five analytic questions, and five affective, or feeling, questions.

4. Write a letter to an imaginary teacher of adults who has been lecturing all his life, trying to persuade him to use either the discussion or the question-and-answer method.

9

The Curriculum of Adult Education

How can we lead a person to maturity in Jesus Christ? What ideas and experiences are essential to promote the development of faith in adults? What does a person need to know and to do in order to become mature? These are questions that must be answered if a proper curriculum of adult Christian education is to be developed.

The question of curriculum is a very complex educational issue, because it touches on such foundational areas as the content and total educational plan of the church. Therefore, this chapter will provide a brief introduction to some of the foundational issues in curriculum theory and will show how those issues can be understood in relation to the educational program of the church. Of necessity, each of the issues raised can only be examined briefly, but they will provide some important guidelines for understanding the curriculum of adult education.

DEFINITIONS OF CURRICULUM

Curriculum is defined by the lay person in one way and by the professional in another. When curriculum is defined on the popular level, it normally refers to a course of study or the content of an educational experience. Thus, curriculum is normally assumed to refer specifically to the subject matter that is covered by an educational program.

However, to the professional, curriculum has a broader meaning. Although the content of study is part of the curriculum, in educational theory, curriculum normally refers to the total educational program.[1] This definition embraces the program of study, but also includes other educational experiences.

For the purpose of this chapter, curriculum will be understood as *the plan the instructor follows to direct the experiences of his students so that predetermined objectives are met.* This definition views curriculum as larger than simply content. However, it is limited to the plan the instructor follows in attempting to have his objectives of education met. The experiences of the students may include, but are not necessarily limited to, involvement with content. For example, a period of informal fellowship and refreshments as a means of helping the students get to know one another is part of the curriculum plan, because it is an experience designed by the teacher with certain objectives in mind.

FOUNDATIONAL QUESTIONS

In his classic book on curriculum theory, Ralph W. Tyler of the University of Chicago presents four basic questions that are extremely helpful in considering the curriculum of adult education in the church.[2] Although first published in 1949, this book continues to be a foundational study in curriculum theory. The four issues raised by Tyler deal with objectives, experiences, organization of those experiences, and evaluation of outcomes.

OBJECTIVES

The first foundational question of curriculum theory is, *What purposes should the educational program seek to attain?* In general, we know that the goal of Christian education is to lead people to Christ and then to bring them to maturity in their faith. But for effective education to take place, we need to define in more specific terms what we mean by maturity. Therefore, more specific goals such as "The student shall exhibit a consistent prayer life" or "The student shall diagram the logic of the book of Romans" need to be developed.

In order to have a properly developed curriculum, objectives need to be clearly defined. We need to consider carefully what changes we want

1. James E. Gress and David E. Purpel, eds., *Curriculum: An Introduction to the Field* (Berkeley: McCotchen, 1978), pp. 8-9.
2. Ralph W. Tyler, *Basic Principles of Curriculum and Instruction* (Chicago: U. of Chicago, 1949).

to see in the lives of our students so that we can help them to mature. In thinking through those objectives we must consider both the age characteristics of the adult learner and the imperatives of Scripture. The objectives must be both distinctly Christian and related to the adult learner.

In determining the objectives for the adult department of our Sunday schools, two helpful sources of information can be used. First are the professionally produced curriculum materials. Most curriculum writers are well aware of the needs of adults and suggest objectives that are in keeping with adult needs. However, some curriculum writers set their objectives a bit below the true interest and needs of adults. For example, some basic Bible courses for adults tend to survey content without probing the deeper questions of implications for life, which would challenge the minds of adults more than survey alone can do. (Wayne R. Rood, in his book *On Nurturing Christians,* suggests that a proper approach for adult education is to work towards "philosophical interpretation of biblical stories."[3]) The point is that we should consider the objectives for adult education presented in curriculum materials in relationship to the higher cognitive needs and interests of adults. The second source for determining objectives is the group which we are teaching. Consideration of the needs and interests of a particular congregation or denomination will be important in determining the specific objectives of our instructional program. Sensitivity to the needs and interests of the group will be a critical factor in choosing curriculum materials that will be both interesting and helpful to the spiritual development of our people.

EXPERIENCES

Curriculum theory also asks, *How can we select learning experiences that are useful in attaining those objectives?* Specifically for adult education in the church, this question asks, What experiences can we design to promote Christian maturity? Although observation of our adult departments might lead us to think that sitting and listening to lectures is the single most important means of spiritual growth, we know that is not true. Even a cursory observation of our Lord as a teacher shows us that He brought His disciples through a variety of experiences in order to help them to grow spiritually. He had them involved in many kinds of educational and life experiences. All were designed to aid in their training for spiritual maturity. Therefore, as we consider the various educa-

3. Wayne R. Rood, *On Nurturing Christians* (New York: Abingdon, 1972), p. 94.

tional experiences for adult education, our thoughts must be broader than just the designing of appropriate lectures for adults to hear.

It is important that educational experiences be geared toward what the *student* does, not what the teacher does. The teacher must consider what the student should do in order to be aided in his spiritual growth. Our curriculum should be designed in such a way that the student is led through experiences that will be beneficial to his maturing in Christ.

Generally speaking, there are four kinds of educational experiences through which a student can be brought. They are experiences to develop skill in thinking, information, social attitudes, and interests.[4] Each of these general educational experiences is important in adult education and should be considered in the designing of curriculum.

Classically, adult education in the church has emphasized the second kind of experiences, namely, those helpful in acquiring information. Above all else we have wanted our people to know the Word of God. Although that is extremely important to spiritual growth and development, we must remember that it is possible to know Scripture and still not be spiritually mature. Our Lord condemned the Pharisees on this point when He said, "You diligently study the Scriptures because you think that by them you possess eternal life. These are the Scriptures that testify about me, yet you refuse to come to me to have life" (John 5:39-40, NIV). We must not confuse the acquiring of information with spiritual growth and maturity.

ORGANIZATION

What is the best way to group the educational experiences so that the desired outcomes are achieved? The concern of this question is that the cumulative affect of our educational effort be achieved. All aspects of the adult educational program should be coordinated so that the final desired outcomes of spiritual growth and maturity can be attained.

The organizational factors of time and content need to be interwoven. Sequence, duration, frequency, and when educational experiences will be conducted all need to be considered. In addition, the content areas of Bible, theology, church history, and social concerns need to be coordinated into those timing factors to have a unified organizational structure. The meshing of those two foundational issues form the basis of proper organization of adult curriculum.

There is no single best way to accomplish this organization, but the two factors of when (time) and what (content) need to be considered.

4. Tyler, pp. 72-75.

The chart below diagrams the way those organizational factors integrate. As the curriculum is being designed the planners should consider each content area in relation to each time factor so that a balanced curriculum results.

To demonstrate how it works, consider the content area of the doctrine of the Holy Spirit (a theological issue). As the overall curriculum is planned, you must consider how long (duration) the study should take, how often (frequency) you want to include a study on the Holy Spirit, and in what part of your total educational program (when) the study should be held.

That kind of careful planning can help each church design a course of study that is best suited to its interests and to the needs of its people. When the planning is accomplished, the curriculum will then be organized according to a design rather than by a haphazard approach based only on convenience.

In order to have a well-developed curriculum in adult education, these questions of organization must be considered. They are difficult to think

CONTENT

	Bible	Theology	Church History	Social Concerns
Sequence				
Duration				
Frequency				
When				

The Organization of Adult Curriculum

through because it is obvious that the issues become quite complex, and there are no hard and fast rules to be followed. But we must not simply ignore these questions of organization. Through careful planning in the adult department they should be considered and resolved.

EVALUATION

The last foundational question of curriculum theory is, *How should the effectiveness of the curriculum be evaluated?* The concern of this question is the attainment of objectives. Are our people actually growing in maturity, and in what ways are they growing? These questions are very threatening to some people but are essential to curriculum development. The goal is not to condemn our people but rather to gather important information to assist in determining the effectiveness of our educational experiences. If the things we are doing to help our people grow in Christ are not bringing about the desired changes, then we need to change them to cause them to be more effective.

Tim Couch of the Ligonier Valley Study Center has written a penetrating article entitled "Anyone Learning Anything?" In it he describes a test conducted by a friend on participants in a very popular Christian seminar (which he does not identify). His friend developed a validated test procedure to determine what kind of learning actually took place at the seminar. The ability to remember specific ideas was tested. Couch reports:

> The results of this experiment, done under the best up-to-date practices and procedures of modern, scientific learning measurement, were surprising and alarming. Every person in the seminar was pleased and very animated in his or her praise of the program. However, what they actually learned from the experience was abysmal. They had been entertained but not educated![5]

Clearly, it is very possible for us to entertain our students but not meet our objectives.

The process of evaluation may appear to be somewhat competitive and inappropriate for the church, but if we are attempting to accomplish anything through our educational programs, it is essential that we take this final step of evaluation. The form of evaluation may vary, but the fact of evaluation is imperative.

It is obvious that evaluation in adult education must start with clearly stated goals. If we have clear-cut objectives for our curriculum,

5. Tim Couch, *Table Talk* 3, no. 3 (July 1982), p. 10.

it is then possible to attempt to measure those objectives to determine if they were met.

The measurement of foundational Christian knowledge is achieved rather easily. By means of such standardized examinations as the "Eternity Basic Bible Exam,"[6] we can measure the knowledge level of our people. But when we try to evaluate such things as attitudes or decisions, evaluation becomes more difficult. However, by means of careful observations by the teacher, and through creative use of teaching procedures such as role plays or creative writing, it is still possible to determine to some extent at least how our people are thinking and feeling in regard to their Christian faith. Those procedures are essential to effect evaluation of adults.

The matter of curriculum is a very large and important issue in adult education. Careful thought must be given to the foundational questions, so that we can provide an educational plan that, when coupled with the power of the Holy Spirit, can lead people to a growing faith. Such a plan cannot guarantee spiritual growth and development, but it can take the best ideas of educational science and apply them to the church so that the possibility of growth from the human perspective is increased.

ADULT EXPERIENCES FOR SPIRITUAL GROWTH

Both Scripture and theories of religious education help us to see the kinds of experiences we can design for our adult learners so that they can grow spiritually. We must, of course, understand that designing those experiences will not guarantee spiritual growth. People can go through the same educational experiences and have completely different results. That is because each individual learner is different and will, therefore, interpret educational experiences differently. The Holy Spirit also works in each individual's life in different ways. But still there are certain foundational experiences that are critical to spiritual growth.

INTERACTION WITH CONTENT

Because to a certain extent Christianity is a propositional faith, that is, a faith that has content to be known, interaction with content is essential to spiritual development.

Much of the New Testament epistles is highly theological in that they contain information to be known. Over and over again Paul instructs his readers in the knowledge of God and Christian faith so that they can

6. "Eternity Basic Bible Exam," *Eternity* (September 1982). Copies are available by writing to *Eternity* Magazine, 1716 Spruce St., Philadelphia, PA 19103.

be mature. Knowledge and maturity are not the same, but it is impossible for a person to be spiritually mature and yet be ignorant of spiritual truth. Harold Mason states:

> The aim of Christian education involves transmissive teaching so much frowned upon by those whose views of democracy extend to freeing the person of any doctrinaire or imposed values as absolute. The principle of authority is involved here, and the relativity of truth. Jesus said: "I am the Way, the Truth and the Life." This is an authoritative statement to be taught a person as final truth. There is more to Christian education than self-expression and activity from the evangelical point of view. In Christian education there is a body of knowledge to be transmitted, an ancient book to be perpetuated.[7]

Therefore, impressional teaching methods that cause students to interact with Christian content are essential to the design of the adult curriculum. A discussion of the specific kinds of content that are helpful to spiritual growth and development will follow later in this chapter.

INVOLVEMENT IN THE BODY OF CHRIST

It is clear from Scripture that the primary context for spiritual growth is within the Body of Christ. Romans 12 and Ephesians 4 teach us that we are not alone but are inextricably linked together with other believers to form the Body of Christ. Involvement with other believers is essential to our spiritual development. Lawrence Richards, in a book on youth ministry, states:

> The supportive, loving concern of Christians gathered in the body relationship is, together with the Word of God, the primary means God uses to remold us from within—a dynamic, divine power that growth in Christ demands we experience in life together as a new community; a community created and marked by love.[8]

As we design learning experiences for our adults, we must design experiences that allow them to interact with each other. If our educational experiences cause the students to be isolated receptors of our teaching and do not allow for the free exercise of their own abilities while relating in love with each other, we will hinder one of the primary aspects of spiritual growth.

7. Harold Carlton Mason, *The Teaching Task of the Church* (Winona Lake, Ind.: Light and Life, 1960), p. 25.
8. Lawrence O. Richards, *Youth Ministry* (Grand Rapids: Zondervan, 1972), p. 231.

Many churches provide for this need by fellowship groups, socials, or home Bible studies. We should design experiences that allow our students to interact with each other so that spiritual growth may be enhanced.

EXPOSURE TO MODELS

Our Lord taught, "A pupil is not above his teacher; but everyone, after he has been fully trained, will be like his teacher" (Luke 6:40). If the outcome of teaching is that students will become like their teachers, teachers must model what they want their students to become. We tend to think of modeling in relationship to children and youth, but Richards argues that it is appropriate to all age groups:

> It is relatively easy to see that a socialization process takes place in the case of children, and that they grow as linked beliefs, attitudes, values, and behaviors are communicated through shared experience with adults with whom they identify. It is also, perhaps, relatively easy to see that the church body may learn the same way from the local leadership teams. But we often lose sight of the fact that adults that come into the Christian community through conversion—and even adults who have been Christians for years— are also discipled in the same kind of process. For all ages the model is essential; relationship with the model in which identification is encouraged and significant sharing of the inner life of the teacher and learner takes place is critical; a "real life" rather than formal setting for shared experience is vital.[9]

We are encouraged in Scripture to be examples to each other. When we encounter a living, breathing example of what a mature Christian is to be, that can be very important in our own spiritual development. Therefore, it is crucial to design learning experiences that provide our students with exposure to maturity.

The models can be either literary or flesh and blood. A literary model could be the apostle Paul, a secular historical figure, or a current Christian who is presented through books, films, or other media. A flesh and blood model could be a Sunday school teacher or another person who is there to interact with students. In any case, it is extremely important to allow our adults to see examples of what we are talking about. Many times such theological concepts as "faith" are hard to understand in theoretical terms; but they come alive as we see them lived out in others.

9. Lawrence O. Richards, *A Theology of Christian Education* (Grand Rapids: Zondervan, 1975), pp. 250–51.

Therefore, we should incorporate in our teaching exposure to people who exemplify the qualities that we see as essential for spiritual maturity.

DIALOGUE WITH OTHER BELIEVERS

A final critical factor for spiritual growth in adults is the opportunity for dialogue and interaction with other believers. The gospel narratives indicate that our Lord spent a great deal of time in dialogue with His disciples. Many extensive conversations are recorded; that kind of interaction seems to be extremely important for spiritual development. The pattern is continued in the book of Acts, where Luke often records that the apostles spent time discussing spiritual truth with those they had won to the Lord. Because adults are reasoning and thinking people, this kind of interaction is essential.

Our curriculum designs must allow our students to interact with teachers and with other adults. Expressional teaching methods, which allow and encourage interaction, are necessary for adult learning. As was seen in chapter 3, this kind of learning is especially important for adult maturation.

Learning strategies that encourage interaction by adults are readily available. Discussion groups, study groups, and "teacherless curricula," which allow a group to function without a designated expert teacher, are possible options for the adult department. The specific ideas for this kind of interactive education will be developed further in following chapters.

Careful curriculum design calls for integrating all four kinds of experiences into the adult educational program. We must not emphasize one above the other or eliminate any from the procedure. Because of both the theological and learning issues that were raised, we must be careful to have an integrated curriculum that allows for each kind of experience.

THE CONTENT OF ADULT CHRISTIAN EDUCATION

A critical question in developing adult curriculum is: What should we teach? In general, our content choices should come from the areas of the Bible, theology, church history, and life issues. Within those large categories specific choices can be made by individual teachers. It is important that the *depth* of the studies be commensurate with the abilities of the adults. Because much of the material may be familiar ground for them, especially those who have been raised in the church, we must be sure to take them to deeper levels of meaning and understanding.[10]

THE BIBLE

Obviously, the study of Scripture is essential to spiritual growth. It would be a foundational error to assume that because people have studied Scripture in the past they therefore have no further need of Bible study. Knowledge of the Word of God is essential to spiritual growth and to Christian living (2 Tim. 3:16-17). Adults never outgrow their need for knowledge of the Word of God.

In order to help adults understand more fully the content of Scripture, it is very helpful to teach them not only the meaning of individual verses but also the logic of an entire book of Scripture. Although it is appropriate to expect children to grasp only small segments of Scripture, it is appropriate to help adults think through the logic of an epistle such as Philippians or Galatians, or to see the differences between the gospels of Mark and John. That kind of training in Scripture will not only help adults to think in more biblical ways as they see the logical development of entire books, but also will challenge them to think more deeply regarding the issues of Scripture. It will be challenging for teacher and for students, but the ultimate outcome will be worth the effort. The careful use of Bible handbooks, commentaries, and other study tools, by both the teachers and the students, will enhance biblical understanding. Helping adults to grasp the larger concerns in Scripture will ultimately help them mature.

THEOLOGY

Theology is simply the systematic organization of biblical teachings into logical categories. The purpose of theology is to help us think systematically regarding the teaching of Scripture. Because we desire to produce adults who can think Christianly regarding God, themselves, and life, it is imperative that we teach them good theology.

Studies that focus on the character and nature of God, or the Person and work of the Lord Jesus Christ, or man and his relationship to God, can only enhance spiritual growth. Although some may want to argue that this kind of study is not practical in daily living, nothing could be further from the truth. If the studies are left only in the theoretical vein

10. For a basic overview of deeper levels of cognitive learning see Benjamin Bloom, ed., *Taxonomy of Educational Objectives; Handbook I: Cognitive Domain* (New York: Longman Green, 1956).

and are never related to life, then the study of theology could be perceived as irrelevant. However, the purpose of theology is to help us to understand more fully the important issues of life so that we know how to live to bring glory to God. Therefore, the careful study of theology is not only helpful but imperative if adults are to grow.

The value of theological studies for adults is that they are based upon logic. Because adults have well-developed thinking abilities, helping them to think about God and His relationship to mankind makes good use of an age characteristic. Well-developed theology helps them to think in systematic ways. The study of theology is not only in keeping with the purposes of God, but also with an age characteristic of the learner.

CHURCH HISTORY

Church history may not be a major thrust of the adult curriculum, but it is a very helpful way to show people that God has continued to work in the world beyond the close of the book of Acts. Understanding of how the church was formed, how Scripture came into unified form, and how basic theological doctrines were established can help people to appreciate more fully their Christian heritage.

Of particular significance to any local church would be a study of the history of its own denomination. For a non-denominational church, an understanding of the history of independent churches in general, and its own church in particular, can be equally helpful. Each church can specialize in terms of its own distinctives to help its people understand the heritage of their beliefs and practices. Historical analysis can be especially helpful in understanding current issues within the local church. For example, the study of different ideas and practices regarding Communion can help adults to more intelligently and more reverently partake of the Lord's Supper. Most people realize that the small symbolic meal in the church is not the same as the Passover Feast. A study to help them understand how Communion came into its present-day form would lead to more meaningful worship in the Communion service.

LIFE ISSUES

As was seen in chapter 6, adults are extremely need oriented. They tend to study in those areas where they feel the greatest need. Therefore, sensitivity to the needs of adults will provide direction for the kind of life issues that should be studied. Developmental issues of adulthood, such as career changes and aging, should be studied; also, the particular pressures of twentieth-century life can provide impetus for the selection of content areas.

The complex pressures on today's adults cause a variety of needs that can and should be studied in the church. Such issues as communication, marriage, parenting, unemployment, and entertainment all provide opportunities for studies from a Christian perspective. Each of those areas can be examined from both a biblical and experiential perspective to help our people understand how to live godly lives in this present age.

The study of life issues is a very good way to get adults actively involved in the process of learning. They will have many experiences, successes and failures, and insights to share with a group. A good strategy is to draw from the experience of the group in developing the content of the study.

Perhaps not everyone in the church will have the same life needs, but if there is a significant group with a shared concern, it will provide the opportunity for an elective. The offering of studies related to life issues should be based on the specific needs of any individual local church.

ELEMENTS OF EFFECTIVE ADULT CURRICULUM

Regardless of what content area is studied, certain elements should be included in any adult curriculum. These elements are geared to the specific needs and interests of adults and are designed to make the adult an active participator in the development of his curriculum.

CHOICE

The first element of effective adult curriculum is the element of choice. Because adults are adults, they should be allowed to choose what they want to study. Certainly we can provide some guidance, but the element of choice immediately makes the adult learner an active participant in the educational process. Even if there is only one adult class, as in the case in many of our churches, the students should have an active role in deciding what their class will study.

ACCOUNTABILITY

Although many people resist accountability in the church, it is important for adults to have some responsibility for their own education. They should be expected to study and participate. They need to feel responsible for their own spiritual development and need to choose in some way to be involved in the process. If all we expect of them is to show up

Sunday morning, the potential for achieving our objectives will be diminished. If, however, there is an element of accountability that requires them to give to the educational process, the potential for spiritual growth will be enhanced.

DISCOVERY

An effective adult teacher must help his students discover meanings, implications, and imperatives for themselves. Certainly there is a time for telling the students what they need to know, but in the long run it is usually best to have as part of our strategy a plan to involve adults in the process of discovery, so that learning becomes their own. The effective use of expressional teaching methods (see chapter 8) can help.

REFLECTION

Adults should be encouraged to reflect upon what they have learned so that meaning can be determined. Reflection asks adults to think about what they have learned so that they might more fully understand the importance of that learning. Rather than simply storing away factual data, they should be encouraged to consider carefully the implications of their studies.

RESPONSE

The curriculum should allow students to respond to the truth that they have learned in some practical ways. Class projects, individual activities, or family activities will allow people to put learned truth into practice. Rather than simply telling them what they should do in response to biblical truth, we should let them think through implications of the truth to their own lives and help them decide on an appropriate life response to the truth. Perhaps the most important concern for spiritual growth is the response of obedience by the believer to the truths of Scripture. Our curriculum must be designed in such a way that it helps students to respond in obedience.

When we think of curriculum we must think of all the experiences adult learners need if they are to mature. The content of our teaching is essential, but the objectives we have, the experiences we design, the organizational patterns we follow, and the results we get all need careful analysis.

The education of the adult believers, according to the Scriptures, also involves person-to-person sharing and helping. The biblical model is the human body, where every part performs a different function but all are interrelated and interdependent. The past, the present, and future also play a vital role as a total experience is developed. Today's adult Christians have centuries of past truth and godly heritage to build upon. May we take advantage of all God has provided for us and continue to produce until Jesus comes.

1. List the four foundation questions to ask when considering the curriculum of adult education in the church. Seek to answer each question relative to your situation.

2. Define the three criteria suggested under foundational question 3, and then apply them to your teaching style and content.

3. Write down the objective of your next lesson, and determine how you will evaluate that lesson, that is, how you will know the objective has been achieved.

4. Four adult experiences for spiritual growth were suggested in this chapter. What are they and how can you best organize your class so that your students are exposed to those experiences?

5. Five elements of effective adult curriculum were named. Determine how you can utilize those elements in the planning of the adult curriculum of your church.

PART THREE

ADULTS
IN THE CHURCH

Gilbert A. Peterson

10

Enlisting and Preparing
Adult Leadership

Launching into a consideration of leadership can be an exhilarating or exhausting venture. There are more people who are actually engaged in the enterprise of leadership than ever before in the history of man. In spite of this, more and better leaders are needed in all types of organizations and situations.

We are warned on the one hand that "in no country have as many volumes on the subject of leadership appeared as in the United States. The reading of them is a dismal, when it is not a ludicrous experience"; and again, "There are at least three subjects . . . on which no wise man should ever attempt to write: love, genius, and leadership."[1]

On the other hand, the abundance of leadership literature contains the recurring theme that the study of leadership and the development of leaders are crucial needs for our time, even though they tend to be baffling. Philip Selznick writes, "leadership is not a familiar, everyday idea, as readily available to common sense as to social science. It is a slippery phenomenon that eludes them both. What leaders do is hardly self-evident. And it is likely that much failure of leadership results from an inadequate understanding of its true nature and tasks."[2]

1. Stephen R. Graubard and Gerald Holton, eds., *Excellence and Leadership in a Democracy* (New York: Columbia U., 1962), pp. 1–2.
2. Philip Selznick, *Leadership and Administration* (New York: Harper & Row, 1957), p. 222.

It is obvious that there is a great need today, especially in Christian leadership, for a more adequate understanding of the Christian leader's role, function, and task. A challenge to commonly held concepts of church leadership has been introduced by Lawrence Richards and Clyde Hoeldtke in their book *A Theology of Church Leadership*. Leaders, they say, are called to minister, not administer. Leadership in the church is to create community and to care for members; management of the body is the prerogative of Jesus Christ. In a persuasive and almost propagandistic manner, using many carefully selected case studies (with leading questions), Richards and Hoeldtke sharply divide leaders into two categories: the institutional leaders, who are leaders *over* people; and body leaders, who are leaders *among* people. This issue will be discussed when the role, function, and tasks of leaders are presented.[3]

THE HISTORY OF LEADERSHIP

When attempting to understand leadership, one naturally turns to the person who leads. That is done by almost all writers, whether they are writing descriptively or evaluatively. Here the investigator finds prime raw data on the subject of leadership. A better understanding of leadership comes from a study of leaders, followers, situations of leadership, methods of dealing with people in various settings, and various viewpoints on methods and objectives. For the Christian leader, the filter through which all of this is passed is indeed the Scriptures.

Different authors see different ways of dividing up the history of leadership. Dalton MacFarland sees everything before 1900 as assumed leadership, and everything after 1900 as studied leadership.[4] Murray Ross and Charles Hendry, on the other hand, find three divisions in the history of leadership. The period prior to 1920 they call the speculative period, when not much thought was given to the meaning and development of leadership. From 1920 to approximately the end of World War II came the period of scientific leadership; gathering and analyzing data through modern techniques was held to be most vital. The present period is characterized by a scholarly approach, with hypotheses being developed and tested.[5]

3. Lawrence O. Richards and Clyde Hoeldtke, *A Theology of Church Leadership* (Grand Rapids: Zondervan, 1981).
4. Dalton E. McFarland, *Management Principles and Practices* (New York: MacMillan, 1958), p. 7.
5. Murray Ross and Charles E. Hendry, *New Understandings of Leadership* (New York: Association, 1957), p. 66.

A fourfold approach, looking at leadership from inherited, individual-istic, interactional, and investigative perspectives may prove most help-ful. The concept of leadership by inheritance primarily based upon birth, rank, and position, held sway with some notable exceptions until the time of the Renaissance.

The next attempt to define and explain leaders and leadership was centered in the idea that there are certain types of personality and particular traits that combine to enable a person to be a leader. A high premium was placed on the rugged individualist. That viewpoint of individualist leadership was commonly held from the Renaissance until approximately 1920, when studies indicated that leadership was more a combination of circumstances: it simply occurred in different situations depending upon the needs and factors that arose. That could well be called the interaction concept of leadership, since it identified leadership in terms of the interaction of individuals within a given situation.

The present leadership scene is marked by leadership literature at-tempting to retain the best of the past concepts while presenting a factual and practical approach to the discovery, understanding, and development of today's leaders. It could well be termed the period of intensive investigation and instruction.

THE NATURE OF LEADERSHIP

Leaders are often faced with the problem of adequately describing the nature of leadership. A clear perception of the essence of leadership will immeasurably aid men in more fully performing whatever leadership role they assume. More often than not, the question "What is a leader?" is answered with the response "One who leads." That is a long way from the helpful insight we need.

Definitions of leadership offered by much of the current literature tend to describe what a leader does, rather than what a leader is. It is fascinating to note that when the New Testament describes leadership, it does not talk in terms of gifts or skills, but rather in terms of qualities of character. Three ideas surface in the New Testament, formed around three roles that individuals had in ancient society, namely, shepherding, servanting, and administering. The first and most often used role model is that of the shepherd. In John 21:16, Peter is told to tend or shepherd (*poimainō*) the sheep. Jesus had earlier taught extensively about His role as the Shepherd of the sheep (John 10). When the Good Shepherd was going away, Peter was told that a new role needed to be assumed by leaders in the body of Christ, namely, shepherding the sheep. The shep-herd had to prepare a feeding area for the sheep so that the sheep could eat. The shepherd had to tend to the wounds and general well-being of the sheep. The shepherd had to discipline the sheep to keep them from harm's way. In other words, the role of the shepherd was that of all-inclusive involvement with the lives of those he was shepherding.

The second term, found in Luke 22:27, has to do with servanting. Jesus told His disciples that the "greater" person is not the one who lords it over others (*kurieuō*) but "the one who serves" (*diakanos*). Leadership from a Christian perspective is not to be a boss or to exercise autocratic control over people. The servant was one who did the bidding of his master and stood ready at all times to serve. He had to be skilled, available, and under the authority of his master—three good guidelines for Christian leadership today.

The third term used in the New Testament is *kubernesis,* "administration" or, more literally, "steering a ship." In 1 Corinthians 12:28, the term bears the connotation of administering or caring for details in an orderly manner. For an excellent discussion of *diakanos* and *kubernesis* in terms of Christian leadership, chapters 1 to 3 of Kenneth Gangel's book *Competent to Lead* are recommended.[6]

Four major concepts of leadership appear in various definitions. Leadership is seen as a process, a relationship, a set of qualifications, or a method of directing people and things. The tendency is to center too much attention on one aspect, as in the case of those of the past who stressed the traits of leaders, and therefore leadership gets defined in very narrow terms. Lawrence Richards[7] stresses the relationship aspect of leadership. Ted Engstrom and others with whom he writes describe the process aspect of leadership.[8] Then there are those who stress the qualities of leaders, such as David L. Hocking in his book *Be a Leader People Follow.*[9] And leadership as a method of directing is illustrated in books like Robert Bower's *Administrating Christian Education.*[10] Each of those approaches, seeking to simplify the concept of leadership, make it understandable to the public, and identify single causes, tends to overlook certain factors that are essential to a complete understanding of a complex process.

I believe that leadership is a dynamic and complex process in which a minimum of at least five elements needs to be carefully analyzed. *Leadership is a process of dynamic communication whereby one person is in the position of influencing others toward a particular objective.* This definition

6. Kenneth O. Gangel, *Competent to Lead* (Chicago: Moody, 1974), pp. 9–39.
7. Richards.
8. Ted W. Engstrom, *The Making of a Christian Leader* (Grand Rapids: Zondervan, 1976).
9. David L. Hocking, *Be a Leader People Follow* (Glendale: Regal, 1979).
10. Robert K. Bower, *Administrating Christian Education* (Grand Rapids: Eerdmans, 1964).

involves the leader, or influencer; an ever-changing communication process, which is the method of influence; the recipient of the influence, or the follower or followers; the goal toward which the influence is directed; and the setting in which the entire process takes place.

THE LEADER

A Christian leader must study both the forces and variables at work within himself (personal value system, personal spiritual life, characteristics of personality, degree of confidence in self and others, etc.) and the forces and variables at work in his relations with individuals and groups (interests, needs, degree of independence, commonness of goals, etc.).

A trained leader attempting to properly influence others will draw upon his knowledge of himself, others, the immediate situation, the resources available to him at the time, and the nature of the objective. The key concern of a leader is to influence others to the satisfactory attainment of established goals. He is an educator, a communicator, and modeler of that which needs to be accomplished.

THE METHOD OF INFLUENCE

To influence action toward a specific goal, a leader can choose from many methods. These range all the way from physical coercion to non-threatening suggestions. Most methods of influence used by normal leaders employ verbal and non-verbal communication.

The non-verbal facial expressions and the hand gestures that may go along with the verbalizations are a part of a leader's characteristics and personality. A person is seldom conscious of the effect of his non-verbal messages. A leader must develop awareness of the influence each non-verbal message has on followers. The influence on people can many times be stronger when it is non-verbal.

Verbal messages, whether written or spoken, make up the largest segment of the method or process of influence. To be successful in his task, a leader must be more than just a communicator; he must influence by his communication. A leader could send a clear message that is both received and understood, and yet not acted upon. However, if a leader lacks the ability to convey values and ideas effectively and without distortion, he will be severely limited in his resources.

For leadership to be successful, a message must be thoughtfully, accurately, and purposefully sent, received without distortion, and acted upon in accordance with the intent of the leader.

THE FOLLOWER

An obvious ingredient of leadership is an understanding of the follower. Until recently, however, not much attention has been given to the role followers play in the leadership process. As long as leadership was considered to be a gift of inheritance or a unique combination of traits, little thought was directed toward followers. As the concept of leadership as an outcome of interaction between people began to take hold, more attention was focused on the follower.

It was not until the 1960s, however, that leadership literature began to attach importance to the follower as an active agent in the leadership process. One management writer pointed out that "every organization is a human enterprise whose success depends upon the coordinated efforts of its members."[11] In earlier considerations of the role of the follower, the main concern had been to discern the changes brought about in the follower as a result of the behavior of the leader. The follower had been viewed as a target at which the leader could aim his skills and through which he could accomplish his goals. The most recent discussions of leadership, when referring to the role of the follower, stress his contributions as an *interactive agent* who exerts independent influence in a dynamic process.

Group size, purpose, experience, and a host of other factors increase the variety of ways the follower may exert his own influence in the leadership situation. In studying his role as a leader, each person must develop a sensitivity to, and an understanding of, those individuals with whom he works. This is true regardless of the group's purpose, type, or structure.

THE SITUATION

Leadership takes place when people are joined together in the pursuit of specific goals. A group, whether it be a church, committee, or a board, can be defined as two or more people who bear an explicit spiritual and psychological relationship to one another. One of the common confusions in the study of leadership is the failure to distinguish between the different types of groupings within the Body. There are learning groups, for example, whose purpose is to learn, share, and understand each other, and whose goal is individual growth. Then there are action groups, where the purpose and need is to cooperate, decide, and plan.

11. Rensis Likert, *New Patterns of Management* (New York: McGraw-Hill, 1961), p. 178.

The group goal here is group productivity. The motivations of the two types of groups are very different, but both are present within the Body.

The type of leadership required also is different for each and God has provided within the Body a diversity of leadership personality and style. Learning groups are such things as classroom groups, League of Women Voters, and other groups that have common concerns of an informational nature. Action groups are church building committees or missionary committees that are attempting to plan and carry out projects. Leadership may be discussed in abstract terms but actually takes place in the concrete realities of life.

The leadership situation may be relatively simple, with only two people involved and the objectives simply obtained, or highly complex, with large numbers of people performing numerous tasks in a long-range project. In either case, there are forces that have a direct bearing on any consideration of leadership that come from neither the leader, the follower, nor the method of leadership. These are forces of the situation. They include the type of organization, the effectiveness of the group, time, and the problem being addressed. The spiritual condition of group members is the most critical situational force.

The "situation" is the entire complex of interactions, influences, relationships, and forces that are woven together in the formation of the fabric of leadership. As in the making of cloth, where choice of thread, color, texture, pattern, and method of weaving are of vital importance if the desired end result is to be achieved, so it is in the construction of the fabric of leadership.

THE GOAL

Of prime importance to every leader is the goal toward which the process is directed. Goals can be short or long-range, physical, personal, group, or a number of other alternatives. They are normally related to the overall purpose and objectives of the organization within which the groups function. Further, they will often be measured in terms of their ethics and value.

Goals form the guidelines by which the entire leadership process is judged effective, ethical, and efficient. Leadership is judged effective if the goal is successfully achieved; it is judged ethical if the goal fits harmoniously with the accepted standards of the group. For the believer, of course, the standards must be biblical. Leadership is further judged efficient if there has been a minimal expenditure of resources in the attainment of the objective. The leadership process by nature is goal-directed, and thus well-defined goals are of primary importance.

RECRUITING AND TRAINING LEADERS

Let us view a typical scene. A group of boys are in need of help. The church senses the need and chooses to establish a Christian Service Brigade group to meet those needs. It may be that just one man cares enough to spur the church to initiate the group. The benefits seem to be very apparent. The boys will have a group with which to identify, and will be able to learn and enjoy a variety of activities. The men, in turn, will have numerous opportunities to serve the Lord and help boys.

Assume that there are a few men who have some zeal and enthusiasm for working with boys in a leadership capacity. What comes next? The next step *should* be enrolling those men in a program of leadership development. But normally what we find is a needy group, a willing helper, an initiated program, and ultimately frustration for all involved. Lloyd Perry in *Getting the Church on Target,* discussing the motivation for leadership, says,

> First is a sense that one grows as he does something important. Men motivated to leadership recognize that the value of a life is computed by its donation, not by its duration. Next is what is termed as developing of a trust level. The leader has the feeling that others have confidence in him and are trusting him. A third factor is the development of a support system. When leaders feel that they have adequate backing from others, they are stirred to advance.[12]

Leadership development, recruitment, and training must be a conscious and concerted effort on the part of the church.

Lowell Brown, discussing the "teacher and leadership training," says

> Several different kinds of training are needed. New teachers and leaders need orientation to your organization, educational philosophy, and training methods. Your current staff members must constantly upgrade their teaching skills and their knowledge. All Sunday School leaders and teachers need training in basic educational philosophy, organizational principles, objectives of the Sunday School, and the basics of how to personalize learning. They also need specific training relating to the age group with which they work.[13]

Although the recruiting and training of leaders is often named as one of the greatest needs in the church, it is also one of the most neglected

12. Lloyd Perry, *Getting the Church on Target* (Chicago: Moody, 1977), pp. 81–82.
13. Lowell N. Brown, "Teacher and Leadership Training," in *Introduction to Biblical Christian Education,* ed. Werner C. Graendorf (Chicago: Moody, 1981), p. 276.

functions. It takes prayer; it takes detailed work; it takes a personal approach; and it takes the enthusiastic follow-up of one or more individuals committed to leadership development. Whether you are seeking teachers for adult groups, administrators who can help organizational groups in their proper functioning, special task-oriented people such as secretaries, treasurers, and ushers, or whether you are looking for people who can help to coordinate groups and maintain effective communication within the Body, training is necessary.

First, recruiting and training leaders requires prayer. Since in the Scriptures we see only a small portion of the life of our Lord (of His 30-plus years on earth, only a little over thirty days is recorded), it is difficult to determine the actual leadership development process that He used. A. B. Bruce in his marvelous volume *The Training of the Twelve* gives us some practical help.[14] One thing that does stand out in the gospels is that our Lord prayed for leaders and with leaders. Our Lord was prone to pray, but His disciples were prone to sleep. Prayer for the discovering and developing of leaders needs to be a regular part of local church and parachurch ministry.

A second great need is for detailed work to be done regarding those whom God has brought together as a group or a local church. God has promised to equip the church for the work of the ministry, and He does that not only in a supernatural way through the Holy Spirit, but also by bringing together individuals of differing skills, abilities, and talents so that they can minister to one another. A small group of leaders in the church needs to be formed into a praying, planning, and leadership recruitment and development team. A talent sheet needs to be developed on each individual in the group or church, containing all of their interests, experience, and expertise. The Evangelical Teacher Training Association and other organizations have developed forms for this purpose; they can be distributed to the entire congregation and then gathered and analyzed by the small leadership recruitment and development team. Discerning the talents and abilities of the individuals in the congregation does take detailed work, but it is rewarding and essential. Steps one and two must then be put together, with careful prayer going into each individual and each potential leadership position that is needed.

The third phase in the process is the personal approach. Too often individuals are approached on a Sunday morning, handed a teaching quarterly, and asked if they would fill in because the teacher could not come or something prevented their having a teacher that Sunday. In too many cases, this then becomes a life-long position—without training or

14. A. B. Bruce, *The Training of the Twelve* (Grand Rapids: Kregel, 1971).

proper orientation. Far better would be to analyze the gifts and talents and abilities of the individuals in the congregation. Analyze the needs. Pray through the list and come to a consensus of who should be approached for a particular task. The Holy Spirit will direct and even prepare the heart of the individual in such a process.

Careful attention needs to be given to the approach, so that the individual is given a complete picture of what the particular ministry entails and what the responsibilities are. Also, the individual should be informed as to what the church or group is prepared to provide for him in terms of support and helps. Time should then be given for the individual to prayerfully consider this responsibility before accepting it.

The fourth and final step is to give enthusiastic follow-up and support-type evaluation to all leaders. Again, the sad story is often that an individual recruited for a particular task is then left alone in that task to carry it on without support or even fellowship. People need to be appreciated and recognized for the work they are doing. The recruitment and development committee, the overall leadership of the church, and the group where the individual is working all need to maintain contact. Leaders are people who are growing and as such need encouragement to grow, as well as direction for growth. This can come in a very supportive and Christlike manner.

One of the things that we have assumed in this overview is that the individual recruited has experience, expertise, and/or training in the task to which he has been called. In the vast majority of situations, this is not the case. What is first needed is a time of training and orientation to the responsibility and to the people who are involved in the particular ministry. Several approaches are possible.

Self-development, of course, is basic to any type of leadership development program. This requires motivation or desire on the part of the individual for growth and change. The leader, or potential leader, must want to change, restructure, modify, or adapt his knowledge, skills, and attitudes in the direction of increased effectiveness. Willard Claasen adds an important dimension for the Christian leader when he says, "When we think about leadership from a Christian perspective, we must reckon with the fact that there are many motivations to leadership which are less than Christian. Why does the leader want to lead?"[15] The Christian leader needs to consider his philosophy of life, his theological convictions, his concept of leadership, his own personality, and, of course, the task that is set before him. A potential leader should consider questions such as:

15. Willard Classen, *Learning to Lead* (Scottsdale, Pa: Herald Press, 1963), p. 15.

Do I like people in general?
Do I consider people to be of great importance?
Is my present relationship with God a growing one?
What do I believe about leadership?
What is my style of leadership?
What are my gifts and abilities?
Why do I want to lead?
Where do I need to improve?
What is the job that needs to be done?
What do I feel is the best way to achieve in this particular ministry?

Desire, then, must be united with discipline, whether the self-development program involves reading, tapes, video tapes, program learning materials, or classroom learning. Positive attitudes have to be energized by productive action. This was emphasized by the apostle Paul when, in his letter to the church at Philippi, he exhorted them to follow a pattern of joy, peace, prayer, positive thought, and powerful action (Phil. 4:4-9). He had set before them, as a leader, an example to be followed. The pattern was valid, the example or test case was demonstrated, and the enthusiasm of the leader was evident. What remained was action on their part. "Those things, which you have both learned and received, and heard, and seen in me, do" (Phil. 4:9, KJV). Discipline to see a job that needs to be done and to move toward accomplishing it, is vital.

Another form of leadership development is the leadership training conference or workshop concept that has grown in the past ten years. The individualized self-study method is extremely valuable but does demand a great deal of personal discipline and motivation. A formal course is often helpful because it provides a disciplined framework: study is in the company of others and is held over a long enough period of time that concepts can be integrated into experience.

The short-term conference or workshop also has value in our time-conscious age and can more readily attack skill development and attitude building—the keys to effective leadership. Many have great knowledge but do not have the skill to put the knowledge into practice. Others have both the knowledge and the skill, but lack the desire or the proper attitude with which to move forward. All three elements must be part of an effective leadership development program. Individuals in evaluating themselves, and recruitment and development committees in evaluating individuals, need to determine which area needs the strengthening: knowledge, skills, or attitude.

It is important that leaders actually lead. Leaders must be involved in doing the type of work and ministry they expect others to do. Leroy Eims discusses this in an practical way:

> I once agreed to teach a Sunday School class for the summer. One of my goals was to increase the attendance of the class, which had been running at about twenty college-age kids who came fairly regularly. For the first two or three Sundays, I encouraged them to bring someone to class the following week. No one did, so I began to make it a matter of prayer. During one of my prayer times, the Lord revealed to me why no one was bringing anyone else to class: I wasn't.

Eims goes on to describe how he and his family noticed some young servicemen hanging around the park near his church on Sundays. They invited them to church for a number of Sundays and by the end of the summer, scores of young men had met Christ and the class had gone from an average of 20 college-age young people to around 180 per week. As Eims summarizes it, "My job was to teach the class and to provide leadership for them. It's summarized in Proverbs 4:11, 'I have *taught* thee in the way of wisdom; I have *led* in the right paths.'[16] The road to success and leadership and leadership development is putting into practice what we know personally.

Many people do not serve because they are not asked. Many do not serve because they are not asked in the right way. Having every member of the congregation responsible for some aspect of ministry should be the goal of every church leader.

Although potential leaders need certain qualities as raw material, leaders are made, and leadership is a process of communication influence. The process of learning as it relates to a leadership development program stresses the ideas that "learning is an internal process . . . learning is most efficient when goals are clear . . . learning involves change and behavior—and change tends to be resisted . . . learning can be facilitated and strengthened through *group experience* . . . learning is enchanced by evidence of progress."[17] It follows then, that a leadership development program must be (1) accepted and understood, (2) applied, and (3) evaluated by the trainee if it is to accomplish its purpose. Those

16. Leroy Eims, *Be the Leader You Were Meant to Be* (Wheaton: Victor, 1975), pp. 78–79.
17. Malcolm S. Knowles, *The Leader Looks at Self-Development* (Washington, D.C.: Leadership Resources, 1961), pp. 1–3.

three factors are basic principles or guidelines in the construction of any leadership development program.

One final analysis may be helpful in recruiting and developing adult leaders for adult ministries. Ross and Hendry present a helpful framework for constructing a leadership development program.[18] They suggest six phases in planning a leadership development program:

1. An inventory of possible leaders based on intimate contact
2. An audit of all tasks within the organization for which leadership is required
3. A plan or strategy for placing and developing leaders
4. The development of a framework of appraising groups, tasks, and leaders
5. The development of a program of supervision
6. The development of leadership courses

Leadership is a dynamic process of communication and influence. The educating and training of people for leadership roles must be life-centered and individual-involving. Many helpful materials are available today from various publishers. Some stress content; some stress skill development; and a few are attitudinal in their orientation. Also, the use of video tape and other media forms can increase interest. In other portions of this text suggestions are given for specific development of teachers and leaders of family life groups. Commitment to a training program that is designed to develop people, not simply fill jobs, should be the desire and design of every Christian organization.

18. Murray G. Ross and Charles E. Hendrey, *New Understanding of Leadership* (New York: Association, 1957), pp. 138-49.

FOR FURTHER STUDY

1. Write out your own definition of leadership. Identify what you consider to be the key elements and biblically support your presentation.

2. Compare and contrast the presentation of Richards with the presentations of other authors like Engstrom, Hocking, LeBar, and Bauer as cited in the text.

3. Draw up a leadership recruitment and training program for adult Sunday school teachers.

4. It has been said that "it is easier to work with paid employees than volunteers. When you're paying them, you can tell them what to do and they will do it." Evaluate this viewpoint. Is it true or false? Why or why not?

5. Why can one leader be effective with one group but not with another group?

6. Evaluate your own church's (or group's) program of leadership recruitment and development. What are the strengths? What are the weaknesses?

11

Adults in the Sunday School

More adults are involved in planned learning experiences today than at any other time in history. They are studying everything from auto repair and tennis to Transcendental Meditation. Adults are studying in small groups, in large classes, and independently via audio and video cassettes and home study courses. The field of learning today for all ages is exceedingly ripe.

Adults are learners. They must be if they are going to cope adequately with this ever-changing world. An adult never stops learning unless hampered by some physical or mental handicap. As we have seen in chapter 4, the rate of learning is not always the same, but the potential and the ability to learn are present in normal, healthy human beings of all ages.

Many tests have been devised to measure learning ability. These tests show that people learn at an almost constant rate between the ages of eighteen and forty. Between forty and sixty, there is a decline in both the rate and the ability to learn, but this decline is slight. After sixty, adults still learn, but the decline of ability and rate is somewhat sharper normally due to a decline in their visual and audio capacities.

ADULTS NEED TO STUDY THE BIBLE

The Word of God—a book penned by adult human writers to mostly adult readers—was written to be learned. The apostle John wrote, "But these have been written that you may believe that Jesus is the Christ, the Son of God, and that believing you may have life in His name" (John 20:31). Obviously, John expected adults of the first century to be well aware of what was written in order that they might fashion their lives according to God's truth.

Luke praised the Jews in Berea because they not only listened to the gospel message but searched the Scriptures daily to confirm that what was said agreed with what had been written (Acts 17:10-11). Peter criticized scoffers who were willfully ignorant of what the Word of God plainly stated (2 Pet. 3:3-7). It is a sad fact today, however, that even in so-called Christian nations there are many people who have never studied the Bible with an adult mind. They may remember bits and pieces of Bible stories they learned as children, but they have never taken the time as adults to consider the claims of Christ or the message of the Scriptures.

ADULTS NEED TO STUDY THE BIBLE
FOR THEIR OWN PERSONAL GROWTH AND GUIDANCE

In his second letter, Peter warned his readers to be diligent in their study of the Scriptures and in adhering to what God specifically stated. He warned that some who were unlearned in the Scriptures would twist them to their own destruction. He then challenged believers to know the things God had said and therefore to "grow in grace and knowledge of our Lord and Savior Jesus Christ" (2 Pet. 3:16-18).

Adults need to experience the Word of God, both as a belief system and as a life experience. Growth is a slow process, but a steady one. It comes by being properly nurtured. Proper development involves both healthy nourishment and healthy exercise. The Word of God is food for the soul, to be absorbed and used in life.

Adults also need personal guidance. The Psalmist wrote, "Thy Word is a lamp to my feet, and a light to my path" (Ps. 119:105). One benefit of Bible study mentioned by a number of adult teachers recently surveyed was the guidance they had received. God's truth is applicable to daily living.

ADULTS NEED TO BE ABLE TO TEACH THEIR CHILDREN

When adults have the responsibility of raising children, special attention needs to be paid to what the adults learn. Parents are the key to family life and learning.

When God told Israel to reverence Him and keep His commandments, He said their obedience should come from a heart relationship. Jesus in summing up the Ten Commandments quoted Moses: "You shall love the Lord your God with all your heart, and with all your soul, and with all your mind" (Matthew 22:37).

In Israel, parents were obviously to be key teachers of their children— and in order to be good teachers, they first had to be good learners. They needed to learn the truths of the Word of God so that they could teach them to their children. The relationship moved from a personal and individual relationship with the Lord to that of a family.

Moses explained that out of family relationship there would come public testimony: "You shall bind them [these words] as a sign on your hand and they shall be as frontals on your forehead. And you shall write them on the doorposts of your house and on your gates" (Deut. 6:8-9). The home was to be a visible witness of God's truth.

Parents also need to know *how* to teach and train their children. If there is one area lacking in Christian education, it is the training of parents to be teachers of their own children. God challenges us as teachers and leaders of adults to handle His Word accurately and to teach parents to be teachers of their children. This responsibility is one of the most important tasks in Christian education today.

Only a few years ago, sociologists and psychologists were predicting the decline of the family and the demise of marriage. More recent articles in major news magazines predict the resurgence of family life and marriage. The church of Jesus Christ must lead the way, not just in the preservation of marriage and family living, but in their vital development for the glory of God. Sunday school can be a significant base for this type of development.

ADULTS NEED TO STUDY THE BIBLE
TO DEVELOP LEADERSHIP IN THE LOCAL CHURCH

One of the primary needs across the country and around the world is for well-trained, prepared leaders. Churches have a great need for mature believers who know the Word of God and are able to apply it to daily conduct and living.

Those who qualify for leadership in the church of Jesus Christ are the men and women of good reputation who are able to instruct others in the truths of God's Word (1 Tim. 3:2). Our job as teachers is to develop spiritually mature students "who will be able to teach others also" (2 Tim. 2:2). Although not everyone can have the opportunity for formal study in Bible colleges or seminaries, it is important that all believers be involved in the Christian education process that takes place in churches and Sunday schools. What takes place in the classroom must be the best possible learning experience that can be provided. We must not settle for less than the best.

Adults need to be instructed in the absolutes and the basic principles of Scripture. They need to understand the great truths God's Word clearly sets forth. They also need to see the relationship of those truths to their lives as they relate to one another even in a classroom experience.

The writer of Hebrews chides his readers for being dull of hearing and not receptive to the Truth. He says, "Though by this time you ought to be teachers, you need someone to teach you the elementary truths of God's Word all over again. You need milk, not solid food!" (Heb. 5:12, NIV). Does that description fit any of the adults in your Sunday school class? Unfortunately, it is an accurate description of adults in many Sunday school classes.

Adults need to know more than what the Bible says. They need to discover how they can make it a living reality in their daily experience. They need to see it in terms of personal living, family living, and leadership in the church.

ADULTS NEED TO STUDY THE BIBLE
TO BE ABLE TO COMMUNICATE THE GOSPEL TO OTHERS

Philip was moved by the Holy Spirit to make a forty-mile journey in order to talk with a single individual. The man, an Ethiopian eunuch, was reading Isaiah when Philip met him. He asked if he understood what he was reading. "'How can I,' he said, 'unless someone explains it to me?' So he invited Philip to come up to sit with him" (Acts 8:30–31, NIV).

Philip explained what the passage meant, and as the man came to understand the Scripture, he desired to obey it. The account in Acts 8 indicates the remarkable follow-through of this learning experience from mind to life.

Adults need the Word of God because faith is born in the heart by hearing and receiving God's Word (Rom. 10:17). It is the Word of God that bears fruit in the life, and not the wisdom of man. Adults need to grow so that they will be a challenge and a testimony to those round about them. As a result of their lives, questions will be asked and answers can be given to lead people from spiritual darkness to light.

The challenge is great for every adult Sunday school teacher and class. Every class member has great potential for personal growth and for a vital ministry. This ministry can take place in the family, in the church, and in the community. Only as the truth of the Word of God is planted in hearts and minds and nurtured through practical Christian living will the potential of teaching adults the Word of God be realized. Our challenge is to teach the Word clearly and to help adults to live the Word thoroughly.

THE ORGANIZATION OF THE ADULT SUNDAY SCHOOL PROGRAM

Adults are people, and people are important. Many churches, however, have taken a haphazard approach to the development of their adult programs. We need to recognize that adults have vital needs just as children and youth do. Further, adults enjoy continuing opportunities for learning and growth. Many adults have a keener awareness of what their needs are than do members of the younger age-groups but are no better prepared to fulfill them.

Churches usually pay considerable attention to ministries for children and youth. Their programs are well-structured, and all types of programs are provided. The same careful planning and attention to detail needs to be given to adult programs. Continuing education for adults, or as it is more popularly called today, life-long learning, has become big business in the United States. This should encourage us to make use of adult education programs to advance the cause of Christ and the church.

Concepts of design, purpose, and organization come directly from God. They are expressions of His nature and are evident in the universe He has created. If we are going to be serious about Christian education for adults, then effective planning and organization is necessary. For this reason, it is important to look at the divisions and grouping of adults, the organization of classes, and the program of activities.

GROUPING BY AGE

The most common way of organizing adult Sunday school classes is by age. The age span of groups in the adult department of the Sunday school is normally, and ought to be, larger than the other departments. A minimum of ten years is usually recommended. With the exception of young adults, whose usual age span is seven years (from 18-24) a ten-year span within the adult department would be as follows: 25-34; 35-44; 45-54; 55-64; 65 and over.

Another way of dividing the age groups is to use a fifteen-year span, again beginning with a seven-year 18-24 age group breakdown, then running from 25–39 and continuing on in fifteen-year age group divisions. Another way would be according to the four major age groupings: young adults (18–33), younger middle adults (35–49), older middle adults (50–64), and senior adults (65 and older).

Any attempt to define the age limits of these groups is arbitrary because, first, there is no consensus among educators about these limits, and second, individuals vary widely in levels of maturity, personality development, experiences, and interests. There are twenty-five-year-olds who are more mature than others who are more than fifty in chronological age. Individual differences among people make it very difficult to set limits.

Though organization by age divisions in Sunday school is traditional, it does impose certain limitations, especially in a married couples' group where there is an age difference between husband and wife. Also, it tends to cause people to limit social interaction to their own age group.

Some churches allow for a ten- or fifteen-year age span in a class but then permit the class to remain together over the years, moving from young adults through young and older middle adults to senior adults. A new class of young adults is then started and the process repeats itself. Where this occurs in churches, classes usually select names that do not reflect the age of their members.

In churches where classes are divided by age, there is usually some overlapping of ages and the categories are used for general division rather than rigid classification. Flexibility, tact, and concern for individual needs should be taken into account in any age-graded adult department.

ALTERNATIVE GROUPINGS

Two major alternatives to using age as a criterion for grouping adults are social criteria and interest. They may also involve some age differentiation.

The social criteria for adult grouping can lead to a men's class, a women's class, a class for singles, a class for businessmen and/or businesswomen, a class for young marrieds, a class for parents of young children, another for parents of teens, and so on. In churches that have separate men's and women's classes, age divisions are often added as well. For example, a Sunday school might have a young men's class, a senior men's class, a young women's class, and a senior women's class. In some cases, a professional couples' group is added.

A second major alternative is to group adults according to their interests and/or needs. Elective programs, which establish classes on the basis of subjects to be studied, generally fall into this category. But even where electives are offered, most churches also maintain a basic core of age level classes for stability within the adult department.

New converts' classes are another example of grouping according to special need. Whether the grouping arrangement in an adult division is made on the basis of age, social criteria, or interest/need, most Christian educators believe it is important to have a new converts' class because of the differences in Bible knowledge and spiritual maturity.

Many adult classes are organized in accordance with a published curriculum, and thus the age breakdowns, interest needs, and other considerations are already taken care of. This can be a very helpful approach, because most Sunday school teachers do not have the knowledge, skill, or time to construct their own curriculum. They need the help a published curriculum gives in providing structure for a series, lesson content, and teaching methods. Even many experienced teachers could increase their effectiveness by following a published curriculum and giving the time saved in the development of original materials to improving their lesson plans and teaching techniques—and to visiting class members and prospective members.

Published lesson plans for adults, with some variation, follow either a uniform, graded, or elective approach. The uniform lesson pattern means that the entire Sunday school studies the same portion of Scripture, usually about fifteen verses in length, with each department using different methods and having somewhat different applications.

The graded curriculum approach means that each department or age level in the Sunday school studies a different portion of the Scriptures, especially selected as appropriate for that age group. In the graded curriculum there is often, however, one course of study for all ages of adults. This usually covers the entire Bible, using a variety of teaching approaches, such as verse-by-verse, chapter study, book study, doctrinal, biographical, and topical.

The elective approach means that individuals or groups are allowed to choose their courses of study from selections available. This approach is usually reserved for young people and adults. Each course generally lasts for a quarter (three months), after which a student can select another elective or return to a regular core class depending upon his adult department's structure.

The size of a church also affects the organization of its adult Sunday school. A department is normally created when there are not less than two nor more than six classes for a major age group. After there are six classes within a department, it is often suggested that another department be created as soon as possible. This also is affected by the size of the classes, and the trend toward smaller classes certainly affects the number of departments created. Experience has dictated that adult sections or departments where the enrollment is between 100 and 125 normally function at maximum efficiency. John T. Sisemore suggests that the minimum number of departments be arranged to total church membership as follows:[1]

Total Church Membership	Adult Departments Needed
Below 250	1
250–500	2
500–750	3
750–1000	4
1000–2000	5–7
2000 and up	8 or more

There is a certain level of commitment, feeling of belonging, sense of responsibility, and contribution that comes from belonging to a smaller group. When that smaller group is related to a number of smaller groups, you also have the benefit of feeling a part of a larger corporate enterprise. Adult departments need to consider this in their structuring and organization.

CLASS STRUCTURES

One distinctive of the adult Sunday school department is class officers. In addition to teachers, adult departments may have officers, committees, and other sub-groups. Children's and youth programs usually have related activities, but many adults are limited to their Sunday school class and congregational meeting. For this reason, class structures have been developed for adults.

The teacher is, of course, the primary person in any class structure. In most Sunday schools he is appointed either by the board of Christian education, the Sunday school board, or the Sunday school superintendent. In some cases, the teacher is elected by the class or the church. That approach, however, is not recommended. The teacher's work and responsibility should be confined to teaching, counseling, and ministering to the spiritual needs of the members. He should not be responsible for the social and business aspects of the class.

In order to care for those necessary social and business matters, adult classes often elect officers. The role of the president in an adult class is to open the class session, take care of announcements, and coordinate

1. John T. Sisemore, *The Sunday School Ministry to Adults* (Nashville: Convention, 1959).

class functions. The secretary/treasurer cares for correspondence, notification pertaining to the class, special financial projects, and coordination of funds.

Adult classes, as a general rule, should not support separate missionaries, have separate budgets, or take on separate projects that are not coordinated with the rest of the Sunday school and the church. The purpose of the president and the secretary/treasurer is simply to coordinate the activities and the functions of the class and meet needs that are not part of the teacher's responsibility. That frees the teacher from details and enables him to do his work more effectively. Both teacher and class benefit from such an arrangement.

Adult classes often find it profitable to have committees, made up of members, to care for such matters as the spiritual needs of individual members, outreach ministries, and social activities. The *Spiritual Life Committee* is concerned with the spiritual needs of various class members and also makes contact with those who may be hospitalized or are suffering grief, loneliness, or bereavement.

The *Outreach Committee* is normally charged with the responsibility of making sure the class does not become ingrown but rather reaches out to others in the community who need Bible teaching and a personal relationship with Jesus Christ. This committee is generally responsible for witnessing and service ministries.

The *Social Committee* is responsible for scheduling and overseeing regular social events for the class—providing for meaningful contacts outside of class as well as in. The social activities can be varied: anything from having coffee and doughnuts prior to Sunday school to special class dinners from time to time, with or without outside speakers or music.

A more recent development in adult Sunday school classes has been the institution of "Care and Share" groups. Normally the entire class is divided into groups of six to ten people, usually along geographic lines, keeping husbands and wives together. One person is in charge of each group and is responsible for coordinating its activities. The purpose of the Care and Share group is for Christians to maintain close contact with a few other Christians and to meet whatever needs—physical, spiritual, and social—arise within the group. Many such groups meet once a month in the home of one of the group members for a time of fellowship and prayer. Some churches have found that restructuring the caring groups every six to twelve months is helpful in allowing Christians to get to know other believers in the church in a deeper way. This may be too brief a time, however, for meaningful caring and sharing to develop. Each group must find its own timing.

THE TEACHING SESSION

A popular idea has descended upon the American scene in recent years: the do-it-yourself approach to building, repairing, and even creating artistic things. Some people buy do-it-yourself kits; others buy raw materials and create things using their own imaginations.

People who undertake such projects meet with varying degrees of success, depending upon the complexity of the project, the skill of the individual, and the amount of prior knowledge. Most do-it-yourself kits, however, include a step-by-step instruction for the inexperienced to follow. Many Sunday school teachers follow the do-it-yourself approach when it comes to teaching the Word of God. Unfortunately, some have laid aside or lost the step-by-step instructions that came with the "kit." In building a bookcase by the do-it-yourself method, ruining a piece of wood simply means that you have to replace that piece and start again. When it comes to spiritual matters and the lives of people, serious mistakes in our teaching cannot so easily be undone.

THE LESSON PLAN

The adult educational process and teaching methods are discussed in chapters 6, 7, and 8. It is important here, however, to focus on the Sunday school teacher and the work that teacher has in weekly ministry. A lesson plan is a teacher's blueprint for teaching. The teacher has established what lesson or material is to be taught (the content) and what he anticipates the final result will be (the aim). From the lesson aim comes a lesson plan. The lesson plan is not a word-by-word script of the lesson but rather a detailed outline with the helps, questions, and ideas for conducting the class session clearly set forth. A good lesson plan enables a teacher to move through the teaching process step by step.

A lesson plan is designed to remind the teacher where he intends to go with the class God has entrusted to his care, and how he intends to get there. It tells him how he plans to guide the class members through each step to achieve his anticipated objective. Without such a plan, or blueprint for learning, a teacher is sidetracked and prone to overlook areas that need attention. Experienced and successful teachers know that a good lesson plan is their most effective tool in guiding learners and targeting the instructional process. It is the teacher's "game plan," subject to some adjustments as the class progresses. It serves as a constant reminder to the teacher of where he is and where he ought to be during the process of teaching.

TEACHING AIMS

Aims are important, first, in focusing on life-related teaching. Without clearly defined learning objectives, a teacher will convey content without seeing its necessary relationship to the people being taught. One of the most common failures in many areas of education is the lack of defined aims. Though we do not want to fall into the trap of saying that all learning must have immediate application to life, we still must be concerned that our students see the value and meaning of what is being taught in terms of its usefulness for their thinking and living processes.

Aims are also important. In fact, selecting the aim is one of the first things a teacher should do when developing a lesson plan. If a lesson plan is like a blueprint for building a house, the aim is the decision that is made prior to drawing up the blueprint; it determines the type of house that will be built.

Aims are also important in measuring achievements in the teaching process. Only if a teacher knows what he intends to have happen as a result of his teaching can he determine whether or not he has been successful.

The three most common types of teaching aims are intellectual, emotional, and volitional. Intellectual aims are the simplest and probably the most common in Sunday schools. They normally have to do with the development of systematic knowledge of the Word of God or of Bible doctrines. The teacher desires the student to master a certain biblical passage or book and might state: "My aim for this week is for my class to be able to recall the Ten Commandments in correct order." Or, "To have my class be able to summarize the content of each chapter in the book of First Peter." Intellectual aims are necessary because of the appalling lack of information people have about what the Bible teaches.

The second kind seeks to elicit a certain emotional or attitudinal response. An example would be "To have my class feel the love of God for each one of them through praying and sharing with one another." Or, "To have my class sense the anticipation of the Lord's return as the apostle Paul experienced it."

A third type of teaching aim seeks to lead a Christian to act on a biblical truth. An example of this type of aim would be "To have each member of the class engage in regular devotions every day for the next week." Or, "To have each member of the class speak to one person this week concerning his need of the Savior."

Although the knowledge aim is common, the attitude and conduct response aims are seldom considered. There is need in evangelical churches for teachers to give careful thought to life response and emotion aims. They should not attempt to accomplish too much in any one teaching session. To try to accomplish knowledge, feeling, and conduct response aims in one class session is not advisable. It would be better to plan the teaching approach week by week to build from one to another, but to give proper balance and weight to each of these important aims.

LESSON PLAN FORMULAS

A lesson plan helps the teacher remember what he is to do, when he should be doing it, and even why the activity is being engaged in. It also enables the teacher to see the lesson as a whole and to quickly identify where he is in the progress of the lesson.

Different formulas have been developed by educators to accomplish this. In his excellent book *Creative Bible Teaching,* Lawrence Richards set forth a fourfold pattern that he popularizes with the words: "hook," "book," "look," and "took." Except for when teaching the very young, Richards says, "Make sure that your Hook gets the attention, sets a goal, and leads into the Bible. Plan the Book to communicate both information and meaning. Check the Look to be sure you guide your students to implications. Finally, construct a Took that will aid and encourage response."[2]

Sharpen the Focus. It is important, obviously, to begin where the learners are. A good lesson plan, therefore, begins where the students are at the moment the learning session gets underway. Most people come to a Sunday school class with a vague idea of what the lesson is going to be about—and perhaps with some notion as to how it might relate to their lives. The teacher begins the lesson by helping the students focus on what is to be studied and then sharpens their perception of the subject matter under consideration. Though it is the teacher who constructs this opening portion of the class experience, it is the student who must be reached. The experience is similar to taking a picture with a 35-mm camera. When the camera is put to your eye, you have a general view of your subject, but you must adjust the lens, or focus the camera, if you are to get a sharp view of the subject. Introducing a lesson is like focusing a camera. It helps teacher and student sharpen their understanding of what needs to be done.

To focus the lesson, the teacher can use a variety of methods, but it is suggested that they vary from week to week. One week an article that touches on the subject under consideration could be brought to class. Bringing material from the contemporary scene into the classroom helps

2. Lawrence O. Richards, *Creative Bible Teaching* (Chicago: Moody, 1970), pp. 12, 108–12.

students see the relevance of the subject under consideration and the particulars involved in their learning experience. A teacher can help the class focus on an issue by having several members relate experiences pertinent to what is going to be studied. Or the teacher can notify some class members in advance to bring illustrations out of their experiences that relate to the subject under consideration. Stories also provide an excellent transition from the everyday world to the classroom.

An alternative to the above mentioned four-step lesson plan is the three-step learning cycle, which begins with the sharpening of the focus of the students on the lesson to be taught.

Discover the Truth. The second phase of the lesson plan is that of discovery. Learning is never passive. Students must interact with the material under consideration for it to change their behavior and become a part of their lives.

The transition from the first step to the second must be carefully thought through. Whether one uses illustrations, articles, or stories to focus the attention of the student on the lesson, the introduction of new material should be a natural extension of that first phase.

In the discovery phase of the learning cycle, the teacher attempts to lead the class or group from the area of common experience and common knowledge into areas of experience or information that are new to them. The teacher is again providing the setting and material, and pointing the way to the content to be learned.

This phase is called the discovery phase because it concentrates on what the student is to do. The student is to discover for himself, by personal interaction with the material, the truths and principles that are applicable to his needs, desires, and interests. This is especially true in adult learning, where self-initiative is the strongest.

Guided discovery learning takes many forms for adults. Some adults are verbal participants; others are reflective participants. The verbal participant is willing to speak up and often talks a great deal. He asks and answers questions and participates in small group discussions. The reflective participant is often non-verbal but nonetheless participates in class by thinking through the implication the lesson has for his own personal experience. It is a mistake to assume that the non-verbal person is not really involved or that he is not really learning. The verbal person needs to be challenged to be more reflective, and the reflective person needs to be encouraged to express verbally what he is learning.

A common mistake made by many adult teachers in the discovery phase is to pre-digest and then deliver to the class the content of the lesson. Rather than simply preaching each week, involving the students in a joint discovery learning experience can be most valuable. Study carefully and use the variety of methods suggested in chapters 7 and 8 of this text. It is important for adults to use their Bibles and for the teacher to lead the way. The teacher needs to have the outline of the lesson and various notes necessary for teaching, but some depend solely upon the quarterly—and some have been known to even read from it.

Adults need to see the implications of the Word of God in their own lives. In each class session adults, as new truth is uncovered, should consider the effect of that truth upon their lives. Time must be given for this.

Respond to the Truth. The third and crucial stage of the learning cycle is the response. It is designed to give students an opportunity to do something with the truth they have discovered. Applying truth to life is probably one of the most difficult parts of teaching. For one thing, it comes at the end of the lesson, at a point where time is running short and teachers normally have not planned their lessons carefully. The tendency for most teachers is to end the class with the bell rather than ending it by giving students an opportunity to respond to God's truth. Once a student has grappled, during the discovery portion, with what the Bible says and with what the truth should mean in terms of his life, the vitally important third phase begins.

The role of the teacher in the third stage of the lesson plan is to provide an opportunity for each student to make a decision based on the biblical material studied. Adults differ in terms of maturity and needs. A simple question such as, "This week, how can we practice what God has spoken to us about?" can set the stage for them to respond.

Students can respond verbally or by writing things down on a card or piece of paper, or by praying silently. They can even use the method called "neighbor nudging," which is expressing their ideas with the person or persons seated next to them in class. A specific response or commitment of this kind allows the teacher at the beginning of the next lesson to ask how God enabled the individuals in this class during the week to respond to the truths He revealed to them. Some adult teachers encourage their students to respond by dropping them notes or cards during the week to remind them to put into practice what they have learned.

The focus-discover-respond learning cycle provides the teacher with a meaningful outline of the teaching-learning process. The total learning experience must be viewed as a unit, and the instructor's strategy for conveying biblical content through meaningful, participative, adult learning experiences, while at the same time providing for diversity of participation, is the objective in teaching adults in the Sunday school.

THE LEARNING ENVIRONMENT

A word must be added concerning the actual teaching environment. In scores of churches across America, adult classes meet in the main auditorium, which is normally outfitted with pews. That suggests to all who are there, teacher and pupil alike, that a sermon is about to begin. Little provision is made for students to take notes or for the teacher to use visuals. Wherever possible adults should have a classroom location that is conducive to the teaching-learning process. Where this is impossible, every effort must be made by the teacher to provide visuals and handout materials that the students can use to take notes and be totally involved with the learning experience.

The adult learning environment should also be a friendly place, where openness and sharing are expected. Many adult departments have a refreshment time at the beginning of the class hour that allows adults to fellowship with one another and begin to talk to one another even before the classroom experience begins. That is a most helpful procedure.

The setting of the room can be enhanced if there are pictures, posters, maps, and other materials relating to or highlighting the material being studied. A key verse, a poignant expression, a visual reminder of lesson highlights helps to reinforce what is being taught. Adults, like youth and children, learn through all their senses, not simply through the hearing gate. Effort must be made in adult teaching to use all the senses whenever and wherever possible. In the Passover feast, God saw to it that the family, and particularly the adults, were reminded of truth through various articles of food that were present. The verbal message was reinforced by both what they saw and what they tasted. Those lessons left an indelible impression upon them. Every lesson is not designed for us to taste, feel, smell, as well as hear and see. However, whenever we can appeal to multiple senses, it is important that it be done.

THE APPRAISAL PROCESS

It is probably heresy to suggest that adults in Sunday school be tested on what they are learning. People shy away from tests, and with 90 percent of American adults not involved in Sunday school experiences of any kind, we are most likely fearful of driving even more away if we expect them to really learn something. It is also true, however, that you "cannot expect what you do not inspect." People will normally rise to the level of expectation, and one of the great failures of the entire Sunday school movement from childhood through adulthood has been the lack of true expectation. We have seen the Sunday school as a great evangelistic outreach and an arm of the church, and it has also been viewed as the agency that "teaches the Bible." However, when tests are given, to incoming freshmen in colleges and universities across America and questions are included with regard to Bible content (even such simple things as the number of disciples, the name of the first man and woman, and the names of the writers of the gospels), the results are rather dismal. We must begin to include an appraisal process in our adult Sunday school program.

Appraisal can take a variety of forms. It could be in the more traditional true-false, multiple choice, and fill-in-the-blanks questions. That probably would create two problems, the first being the fear on the part of many adults in taking any type of exam, and second, the impression that simply learning Bible content is what is needed for Christian maturity. We must be careful, as we have seen earlier, not to go to the opposite extreme of saying that one can be spiritually mature without knowing Bible content.

Another approach has been advanced that is experience-oriented. Here people are encouraged with open-ended questions and essay responses to give their opinions as to the meaning of various passages or truths. This approach, by itself, also has a flaw in that it often assumes that wisdom is arrived at by the sharing of pooled ignorance. Opinions may be right, but there must be some standard and coherent pattern of truth by which opinions are evaluated.

Having a variety of appraisal techniques is probably the safest and best solution. It is probably best to start non-threatening, open-ended questions, to get adults into the habit of making choices and thinking sincerely about what they are studying. Periodic content-oriented evaluation is also necessary. Modern advertisers know that repetition and drill are important learning techniques. In our effort to try to teach "something new each week," we often end up at the end of fifty-two weeks having taught nothing very well. Perhaps it would be better to highlight some major truths and Christian life experiences and have them repeated so that the truth will truly be learned.

It is also worthwhile to consider evaluating the total operation of a department, including its biblical study program, its fellowship experiences, and its outreach ministries. The famous last words of the church, "We've always done it this way," need to be reviewed and revised. Just because something has been repeated for a number of years does not make it wrong or right. The leadership of the local church today must take a serious look at what is happening in the adult department. We may say that the children's department is "the church of tomorrow," but the adult department is "the church of today."

The adult class in Sunday school can be one of the most remarkable places for the effective, systematic teaching of God's Word to Christian adults. For this to happen, however, effort must be expended and time given to plan and organize experiences.

Different adults have different abilities, and the use of those diverse abilities is necessary in our adult departments. Seeing each adult become a spiritually growing, learning, helping person is our goal, as is making each lesson meaningful to adults and applicable to the learner's life.

1. Prepare a tract or a pamphlet that can be used to motivate adults to get into a regular habit of Bible reading and Bible study.

2. "Lifelong learning" has become a major enterprise in the United States. Does this phenomenon have any relevance to adult Christian education? If so, what is it? If not, why not?

3. Dividing adults into groups (by sex, age, marital status, etc.,) has been going on in adult Christian education for years. Is this proper? Why? Why not? What should be considered if this approach is taken?

4. To what degree should the local church attempt to provide for the physical, social, and emotional needs of adults? Support your response with biblical documentation.

5. Prepare a lesson plan for an adult class using the focus-discover-respond pattern; teach it; and prepare a written appraisal of the results.

12

Single Adults and the Church

The most diverse and growing group in the second half of the twentieth century is single adults. Since 1960 hundreds of magazine articles, books, and even magazines have been written analyzing the complex subject of singleness. There are certain threads that run through the literature, and the development of a healthy sensitivity and a meaningful ministry to this age-old problem is the focus of this chapter. There are different perspectives on singleness that need to be understood: the married, the never married, the divorced, and the widowed. And there are special problems that the different categories and age groups within singleness present: single parenting, divorce and its biblical and social implications, and the variety of needs and prospects that the widowed face, and male and female viewpoints.

THE SINGLE SCENE

Statistics differ, yet there is a growing number of individuals alive today who are adults and who are not presently married. One writer puts the number at one out of every three adult women and one out of every four adult men in our society.[1] Another writer in the same year

---

1. William J. Peterson. *Evangelical Newsletter* (Philadelphia: Evangelical Missions Incorporation, 1978).

indicated that for every married couple in America, there was a single adult. In 1981 the estimate was 56 million single adults living in the United States over the age of 21.[2] No matter how you view the statistics, a significant portion of our population fits the category of single adult, whether they are individuals who have never been married, are divorced, or are now widowed. They are not just statistics either; they are individuals who have names, personalities, dreams, and problems. Gail is recently widowed after just four years of marriage. She has a young son, and the suddenness of her husband's death in a car accident has left her bewildered, lonely, and facing complex financial problems. John is also single, but it is because his wife of nine years became involved with one of the men where she worked, and a divorce followed. He tried every way possible to preserve his marriage, but nothing worked, and he is bewildered and hurt. Susan is 28 years of age and has never been married. After graduation from college, she entered into her profession as a teacher, and the investment of her time and energies in the lives of students and her professional pursuits have been rewarding and fulfilling. Others are concerned about finding her a husband, but that is not a priority with her. Different people; different needs; different walks of life: a complex group of individuals.

There are also differences between the needs and outlooks of younger, middle, and older singles. The life prospects and problems for a 25-year-old, a 45-year-old, or a 65-year-old widow are indeed different. Likewise, whether divorce occurs after 2 years, 15 years, or 25 years of marriage makes a difference in terms of responsibilities, resilience, and remedies. A survey of your local church may well reveal some tremendous and startling facts regarding the complexity of the ministry to singles. Too often when singles are mentioned, only young singles are considered.

NEEDS SHARED BY ALL SINGLES

Terry Hershey's *Single Adult Ministries Kit* identifies some of the needs all singles have, regardless of their special categories: relational, social, spiritual, intellectual, and emotional.[3]

After God had created a single, "Adam," He observed that Adam needed someone with whom he could be intimate, and so God created Eve. The entrance of sin into the world had a disrupting influence on

2. Nicholas J. Cristoff. *Saturday Night, Sunday Morning* (San Francisco: Harper & Row, 1978), p. ix; Richard Kraus, "Leisure Today," *Journal of Physical Education, Recreation, and Dance,* October 1981, p. 52.
3. Terry Hershey. *Single Adults Ministries Kit* (Garden Grove, Calif.: Positive Christian Singles, 1980), p. 2.

relationships. Both the Old and New Testaments have much to say about establishing and maintaining proper human relationships by means of a vital living relationship with God. Meaningful life implies human relationships. Sharing joys and sorrows, sharing discoveries, and sharing victories and defeats are all part of the human experience. Intimacy is one great area of need in all single lives, and in everyone's life.

Human beings are social beings. Closely tied to personal relationship needs are social relationships. Singles' groups have often been formed so that the individuals can have a comfortable place in which they can share common interests, concerns, and dreams with others who share their common experience. It has been encouraging in recent years to see the singles' retreats and conferences shifting their emphasis from the "problems of singles" to a more positive emphasis on personal growth and fulfillment. People need people—and that means people of the same sex, as well as a different sex, to interact with and thereby grow.

In a superb article entitled, *"Don't Single Yourself Out,"* Nancy DeMoss writes:

> To avoid the potential pitfalls of singleness, it is important to make some non-negotiable spiritual commitments, based on the principles of God's Word. I would like to share seven commitments I have made as a Christian single. . . .
>
> (1) *I am committed to serve Christ with all my time, abilities, and energy* . . .
> (2) *I am committed to relinquish all my expectations of material and physical security* . . .
> (3) *I am committed to develop personal discipline* . . .
> (4) *I am committed to relate to family* . . .
> (5) *I am committed to honor and care for my widowed mother* . . .
> (6) *I am committed to give extravagantly rather than live extravagantly* . . .
> (7) *Finally, I am committed to pursue God's will above all else.*[4]

The basis of her commitments are biblical. The positive nature of her argument dispels the twin myths that singles are either footloose and fancy free on the one hand, or trapped, doomed, and inferior on the other.

Singles also have intellectual needs. As indicated in other portions of this text, life-long learning is a privilege of all adults. All adults explore new channels of learning, experience changes in life-style and relationships, and cope with diverse problems.

One need that is all-pervasive is the emotional need. Melanie Margaron deals with this issue in a very helpful and positive way. She says:

4. Nancy DeMoss. "Don't Single Yourself Out," in *Worldwide Challenge* (Colorado Springs, Colo. 1981).

Some people choose to be single, but for most it is a circumstance in which they find themselves. Of first importance, then, is to make that commitment to follow Christ wholly. This is the only way to have peace in circumstances we do not choose. There must be trust in the sovereignty and goodness of God. There must come a point at which, by faith, we are willing to *lay aside* the questions without having received the answers. This isn't easy to do, and it doesn't necessarily make everything less difficult, but it is a necessary step.[5]

Margaron goes on to indicate that in order to have solid emotional stability, the single must come to a peaceful acceptance of the fact that apart from marriage, they must forego the sexual relationship and unique companionship that comes in marriage. They must also be willing to resist self-pity, live in the present, be careful about being overly sensitive about the single issue, be active in ministry, and be willing to do some things that are difficult. Conquering in any, or all, of these areas produces positive healthy growth.

STEREOTYPES

One of the greatest difficulties married individuals or organizations such as churches have in thinking about the single life is the stereotypes that exist. In our family-oriented society, it is easy to discriminate unconsciously, even if it is against 40 percent of the U. S. adult population. David McCasland, in a penetrating article, identifies these stereotypes as:

(1) Never marrieds. Nice people, but obviously there is something wrong with them under the surface or someone would have latched on to them long before now. They are basically unhappy, only marginally dependable, and the thing they most need in life is an introduction to the "right" person.
(2) Divorced woman. Attractive . . . very attractive. Married men wonder why any man wouldn't be happy with her. The women think they know. She has no children, works for a TV station or an advertising agency. She is financially independent, intellectually stimulating, and sexually available.
(3) Divorced man. The whole thing was probably his fault. He has no sense of responsibility to his wife or children and is probably keeping more money for himself than he sends to his family. He is not to be trusted and spends most of his spare time with divorced women.

5. Melanie Margaron. "Aren't You Married Yet?" *Conservative Baptist* (Fall 1983), p. 11.

(4) Widow. She needs our sympathy and support for about six weeks; then it is time for her to get her act together and get on with life. If she is young, someone nice will turn up for her. In the meantime, she needs to really ride herd on those unruly kids of hers. Never invite her to dinner unless you invite a top-of-the-line, never-married man, too.

(5) Widower. His dear wife's death was untimely; but his kids are grown, he has his job, his house is paid for, and there are a million things he can do. About six weeks of support should get him on his feet, too. But he had better not even look at another woman until his wife has been dead for at least a year.[6]

Unfortunately, too many people really do hold these thoughts in their minds, and the result is harmful for all concerned.

MANY PERSPECTIVES

While we can talk about singles as a group, the only thing that actually brings them together is that they are not presently married. The diversity among them is considerable, and the perspectives vary greatly. One church in Texas, grappling with the need to form a Sunday school class to meet the needs of unattached adults, struggled with the problem of naming the class. "Young Adults" did not fit, for age was not the issue. "Singles" was not popular either, because some might get married and want to remain with their friends in the class. They finally solved the problem and called it the "Come As You Are" class. Many churches, and many singles, have found that the healthy mix of marrieds and singles is the real answer. Let us look at some of these diverse perspectives.

MARRIED

Adults who are married have made a conscious decision to spend their lives in an intimate relationship with another adult of the opposite sex. There can be many reasons for this decision. As mentioned earlier, companionship can be one of a complex set of reasons, and is part of the overall plan of God. In Genesis 2:18, God pronounced that the relationship of aloneness that Adam was experiencing was not good, and rather than creating for him another man to have companionship with, he created a woman so that the companionship could be deep, lasting, and intimate. This is not to say that close friendships with those of either sex are not significant. It does mean, however, that from Genesis to

6. David McCasland. "What Are You Doing About Singles in Your Church?" *Leadership* (Summer 1981), pp. 109-10.

Revelation, God used the marriage model as a constant reminder of His relationship with His people. In the New Testament, it becomes specific when the church is called the Bride and Christ is called the Bridegroom.

In 1 Corinthians 7, Paul shows concern that he had that married people could be too encumbered to minister effectively. Yet he clearly recognizes the problem of passion and encourages those who cannot resist physical temptation to marry. Jesus addressed the same problem in Matthew 19, when He indicated that there were a select number of individuals who, because of their desire to give themselves totally to ministry, had consciously decided not to enter into marriage.

A third reason to marry is in order that children might result. Children are a gift from God to those who are married. When these three elements—companionship, desire, and children—are bonded together, an individual has good reasons for marriage.

Margaron suggests a fourth reason which is worthy of consideration. The purpose of serving Christ in an effective way as a team can be a very important reason for entering into matrimony.[7] There are some ministries that can be best accomplished by a person who is single and free to devote his time to it. Other ministries, however, can better be carried on by couples or families.

Some people see marriage as a way of solving their present problems or getting out of a family situation that they find too confining. Escape is never a good reason for marriage, and is never condoned in the Word of God. Some people also feel that if they marry they will be complete as a person, because singleness, in their thinking, means to be incomplete. Biblical teaching, however, reminds us that security, significance, and completion are only found ultimately in Jesus Christ. The marriage relationship is a way of demonstrating visibly on earth the vital relationship you have with Jesus Christ, but can never become a substitute for it.

Probably the most difficult and dangerous notion that a married person can have is that marriage is life's goal. As Linda Strain points out: "It is no longer, 'How can I best serve God?,' but 'where can I find a mate?'" Many a young person desperately rushes into a marriage prematurely, only to wind up on the crushing rocks of divorce. As Strain so aptly puts it, "The Westminster Confession reads, 'The chief end of man is to glorify God and enjoy Him forever.' It isn't 'to get married and enjoy marriage forever.'"[8]

7. Margaron. "Aren't You Married Yet?" p. 10.
8. Linda Strain. "The Single Saint in a Couple's Culture," *Interest* (February 1984), pp. 8-9.

Having been married for over thirty years, and having observed many marriages begin and develop, as well as observing some marriages end, I can safely say that in marriage, as in singleness, you will only get out of the relationship what you put into it. Attention must be given constantly to all aspects of your life and your relationships, and the biblical guidelines must be carefully followed. The missing ingredient in today's society appears to be commitment; and that is something everyone must have, be they married or single.

SINGLE

"People are single because . . . " You fill in the blanks. Each individual has a certain viewpoint on why others did not marry or are not married at the present time. Of course, in the case of the death of a spouse, it is very obvious; but in the case of divorce, it is not. As society has been changing, there have been also changing viewpoints toward singleness. Consider the following comparison:

	Older Viewpoint		**Newer Viewpoint**
Being single is —	Unusual	—	Accepted
Being single is —	Unfortunate	—	Advantageous
Being single is —	Unnatural	—	Appropriate
Being single is —	Undesirable	—	Attractive

The older viewpoint was that it was unusual and somewhat strange not to be married. Marriage was economically feasible and often necessary. It was the expected role and goal for daughters to be wives and mothers. Today singleness is accepted as not only a statistical fact of life (with more adult women living single in the world than adult men in the same situation), but it might even be preferred.

The older viewpoint said that it was unfortunate for people not to get married; they obviously were missing the "best part of their life." But in today's world singleness is often considered advantageous, for the single individual can pursue both vocational and avocational interests in an unhindered way. The financial resources they produce do not have to be shared with another, but can be used at their own discretion.

The past viewpoint suggested that singleness was unnatural, and certainly not intended by God. But the newer viewpoint suggests that it is not only natural, but is appropriate and desirable for a vast number of people. In the past if persons chose singleness, questions were raised with regard to their sexuality, but in most cases today, that is not the issue. That is not to say that homosexuality has not increased; but just because a person is single, it is not necessarily for unnatural reasons.

The older viewpoint also suggested that singleness was undesirable, whereas today it is often looked upon as attractive. One thing that can be said for sure is that singleness is a stage of life for every adult, and for some it is a lifetime.

A biblical approach to singleness must include the fact that singleness is a gift from God. When Paul said, "I have learned to be content in whatever circumstances I am" (Phil. 4:11), he was expressing a conviction that God had given him the internal resources to deal with whatever his situation might be; in his case, that involved singleness. Also singleness is a gift that is not chosen, but given.

Since it is a gift that is given by God, we can rest assured that it was not given carelessly, but rather suited to the individual and appropriate for his circumstance. This does not mean that we do not have to draw upon the resources God gives us for the development of the gift, but it does mean that we need to be appreciative of who we are and the state that God has planned for us.

Further, singleness is purposeful, and the more current viewpoints provide opportunity for the use of this gift in a very positive manner. Elizabeth Elliot has gone through various states of singleness and marriage, and writes with clarity and sensitivity. Must reading for both men and women is her volume entitled *Let Me Be a Woman*.[9] Although written in a tender way to her daughter on the threshold of her own marriage, the lessons she has learned are valuable to both men and women. She sets forth the values and benefits of both the single and the married phases of life. Her discussions of topics like yieldedness, independence, and interdependence of men and women, single and married, are insightful and provide the basis of fruitful thought. There is a serious need for dialogue between different types of groups within the church: single men with single men; single women with single women; single men with single women; and marrieds with singles.

DIVORCED

Although society, and even the church, may be becoming more tolerant regarding the divorce problem, the word *divorce* still evokes an emotional response from all who hear it. The now all too familiar, "Did you hear that so-and-so is getting a divorce?" elicits a negative emotion and a feeling of emptiness in the pit of one's stomach.

9. Elizabeth Elliot. *Let Me Be a Woman* (Wheaton, Ill.: Tyndale House, 1976).

The stigma of the divorce label is widespread. Titles of books suggest the trauma of divorce: *But I Didn't Want a Divorce, Our Family Got a Divorce, Who Am I Now That I'm Alone?, After Divorce Survival Guide.*[10] A person who has gone through the process of divorce is experiencing special tensions. There are feelings of failure on the part of the partners, the parents, and the children involved. Each does soul-searching to try to discover what they could have done differently that would have prevented the problem. Scars are often deep and permanent.

The subject of divorce also raises significant theological questions, particularly with regard to the church's responsibility, the divorced persons' responsibilities toward each other, and of course, the inevitable question of remarriage. Divorced persons normally have a deep layer of guilt, and whenever the subject of marriage or divorce is mentioned from the pulpit, in a classroom, or in general conversation, there is always anguish and sometimes anger—even though it may not be expressed. Also, divorced people have been the object of statistical and behavioral studies, and can come to feel as though they are statistical objects rather than people with needs.

There appears to be a plethora of reasons for divorce. Psychologists and counselors in seminars and in articles often point to communication, money, and sex as primary factors consistently involved in triggering divorces. In addition to these specifics, there are general pressures and forces in society that have a significant negative impact on marriages.

The first could be called "microwavism." We live in an instant, microwave, disposable society where instant gratification and quick and easy answers have become the rule. One television show portraying a marriage ceremony had changed the words "til death us do part," to the words "until love doth depart." If there is not excitement, constant newness, and persistent emotional highs, people want out. The Scriptures exhort us to commitment. Past patterns and social customs stressed commitment as an essential and worthy issue. In today's society, however, commitment is viewed as foolishness, and we have replaced the patient development of significance, trust, security, and satisfaction with pills, contracts (even for marriages!), and quick and easy escapes.

A second pressure is materialism. We are living in a two-career society that has reduced the amount of time couples spend with each other.

10. André Bustanoby. *But I Didn't Want a Divorce* (Grand Rapids: Zondervan, 1978). Carolyn E. Phillips. *Our Family Got a Divorce* (Glendale, Calif: Regal, 1979). James Ramsey. *Who Am I Now That I'm Alone?* (Discussion Series, 13222 E. Baily Street, Whittier, Calif. 90601). Harper's Bazaar, "After Divorce Survival Guide," *Harper's Bazaar* 109 (July 1976).

Economics, coupled with the hedonistic philosophy that permeates our age, is creating insurmountable barriers for many families. Things are more important than people. Parents give children gifts rather than time because it is easier. Success, even in church ministry, is determined by numbers, budget and staff size, buildings, and even buses. "Big means blessing" and "Success means money."

The mobility of our society, coupled with movements designed to promote rights over responsibilities, puts more pressures on our families and marriages today. The demise of the extended family with its reunions and traditions is being hastened by job transfers and the relative ease of moving from one area of the country to another. Yes, there is the telephone, but a grandmother or grandfather cannot hug the grandchildren over the telephone. Also, the women's movement, the Human Potential Movement, and others have glorified and magnified old nature characteristics such as pride, selfishness, and greed. The magnification of these negative qualities of life has changed life-styles and has led to a dissatisfaction that is unhealthy.

While the pressure has been on, the relief valves have often been shut off. People going through divorce need help in a variety of ways. They often need physical and financial help during times of transition. Too often Christians have believed that helping those who are going through divorce means condoning the divorce. Sometimes, too, pride or fear of what people will say keeps Christians from helping. The Scriptures are very clear: "let us do good to all men, and especially to those who are of the household of faith" (Gal. 6:10). Physical help in moving and setting up an apartment and financial help during this transition seem to me to be Christian responsibilities.

Emotional help is also called for. Most of these people need someone to weep with them and listen to them, rather than to outline for them the biblical teaching on marriage. There also is a need for social help, especially as they attempt to re-enter the circle of their friends and the ministry of the church. Of course, it is a time when they need to be ministered to, rather than to minister to others; giving them leadership roles at this point is dangerous. Where there are children involved, there is tremendous need for help in the caring and development of the family. The daughter needs to have a proper relationship with her mother and father, and with female and male images. The same is true for the son. Youth workers, Sunday school teachers, pastors, and church elders can be of significant help during those times of critical need.

WIDOWED

The greater number of singles are in the widowed category. Statistics indicate that widows outnumber divorced wives by four to one. Their problems are different from other singles; sometimes that means their transition to singleness is easier, and sometimes it is more difficult.

The widowed tend to be older, and are single due to circumstances beyond their control. The older ones have more memories, and the loneliness that sets in can be intense. A special insight into this loneliness through the eyes of a dying person is presented in the poignant volume entitled *Free Fall,* by JoAnn Kelley Smith. This true story of a person who for six years battled cancer and death, describes loneliness as separation, a sense of emptiness, a sense of being abandoned, and a sense of being without company.[11]

Those who have become single again through the death of a spouse need care beyond the first six weeks of grief. As David McCasland writes,

> My stepmother was a widow when she married my father, a widower. Their life together was a short and love-filled three and a half years. After his death, she said, "I appreciate so much all the things that people at church will do for me, but I know that it will last for about six weeks, and then I will be alone again. They don't mean to drop you, but they get back into the routine of doing things with other couples, and it never seems to occur to them to include half of a former couple in those get-togethers. It happened before and it will happen again, but it will still hurt when it does."[12]

Preparation for future singleness through widowhood is a seldom addressed subject. There is sparse information on how to prepare oneself emotionally, socially, and spiritually for this event. Some materials, of course, are available for estate planning and financial and fiscal futures, but the more intense and non-physical areas are often neglected. It is threatening to think about future singleness, for in so doing one must realistically face the future. It may appear to be selfish; and thus the subject is often avoided.

The church has little biblical data to guide it in its care for widows and widowers—except for the command to do it. Because of the society in New Testament times, the emphasis was on the physical needs rather than on the total emotional and social needs. In the Old Testament, however, there were more specifics given with regard to how families should relate to each other. In our mobile and nuclear family-oriented society, however, the tendency is to avoid the issue. Also, in North America at least, the strong spirit of independency has influenced elderly adults and their sense of need, self-sufficiency, and usefulness.

11. JoAnn Kelly Smith, *Free Fall* (Valley Forge, Pa.: Judson, 1975), p. 88.
12. McCasland, "What Are You Doing About Singles in Your Church?"

SINGLE PARENT

The single parent issue needs to be addressed by itself. In Psalm 146:9 we read, "The Lord protects the strangers; He supports the fatherless and the widow." We have a responsibility to be instruments in the hand of God to help in this area. Jay Adams writes,

> The church of Jesus Christ has failed miserably in helping the single parent. When a woman must raise her children alone without male influence, it is difficult for the child, particularly if he is a boy. The church ought to move in and provide fathering for such children. He needs families to invite him over frequently so that he can see a family at work. He needs men of the church to take him places—to go fishing with him, to go hunting with him, to take him camping.[13]

This problem is not insignificant: according to the U. S. Census Bureau, fifty percent of the children born in 1982 will live in a single parent household sometime during their first eighteen years of life.

Single parents also have to make many adjustments following the separation, divorce, or death of a spouse. Three stages are often identified by psychologists: disruption, adjustment, and integration. In the disruption stage, there is tremendous emotional, legal, financial, physical, and social stress. Although the same problems exist in the next stages, the disruption stage is the most critical. During the adjustment stage, a person is trying to find himself in terms of effective communication, self-image, and security and significance. In the integration stage he has moved toward a new life, the ego is intact, and relationships are more secure and long lasting. There is no exact timing of the length of each phase, because the multiple factors of emotional stability, physical and financial situation, and support of friends make a big difference. The single parent, however, has special needs and needs special ministry.

Church Ministry

Local churches need to have special sensitivity to the needs of their singles. Larger churches seem to have been sensitized to this, and often have well-developed programs and even staff people whose primary responsibility it is to minister to this very needy portion of the Body of Christ. The average church in America, however, is under two hundred

13. Jay Adams. *Christian Living in the Home* (Grand Rapids: Baker, 1979), pp. 129–30.

in attendance. It does not have the resources, financially or physically, to develop a fully-orbed program; and because it is small and people know each other intimately, getting involved in this kind of a ministry often seems threatening.

Years ago, the emphasis in local church ministry was on children. A shift then placed the concentration on youth. Today, it appears the emphasis is on adult ministries. With that has come a concentration on singles ministry. Singles, however, are not rushing to involve themselves in the traditional ministries of the local church, nor is the local church necessarily open to their involvement in these ministries. Sometimes a "singles" group is created for them, but for the variety of reasons suggested in this chapter regarding the diversity of their needs, one group does not seem to be the answer.

PRINCIPLES

There are some principles, however, that make sense when thinking through a ministry *with* single adults—and not a ministry necessarily just *for* single adults. First, we need to recognize that singles are people with their own interests, concerns, personal needs, and expectations. One writer suggests that we involve ourselves as a church one with another, married with singles and singles with married, and do it on the basis of equality and special gifts and abilities rather than considering whether the person is married or single. Too often, married folks who have concerns for singles feel that they must perform total ministry for them, and not let them set their own goals or carry out their own programs. Also, being careful to examine our attitudes by looking at speech can be extremely beneficial. Jokes, innuendos, and lack of sensitivity on the part of some believers have indeed hurt others in the Body of Christ. Humor is important to a healthy perspective on life, but can be used as a weapon. Jokes about "unclaimed blessings," "Miss-ed wonders," and other insulting expressions often betray an underlying hostility and/or fear, and need to be examined and corrected.

A second important principle is the involvement of singles in all phases of church ministry. Some have taken the instructions that church leaders be "the husband of one wife" (1 Tim. 3:2) to mean that an elder in a local church must be married. Other churches have excluded single women from ministry in the nursery or children's departments on the basis that they would not have sensitivity and understanding in handling children. Single men have at times been excluded from the same ministry with the innuendo that their motives weren't pure. Each local church must rethink the mixture of people that

God has brought together in that one assembly and involve each of them in a meaningful ministry suited to his skills, calling, and biblical qualifications, rather than simply using marital status as a qualifying factor.

Third, the church should consider the developing of biblical hospitality. This would include families and singles fellowshiping together outside as well as inside the church program. Linda Strain says,

> Will you ask your spouse what you and your family could do to show hospitality to a single in your church? Could a single be an "aunt," "uncle," or even a "grandmother" to your children? Could you offer to go shopping or out to eat with a single? How about just inviting a single to sit with you and your family in church or in Sunday School, or at the next church fellowship time? How about inviting a single or two over to your home the next time you have a couple in for fellowship? When your children go to the circus or a camp-out, or a hike, is there a child of a single parent you could invite along?[14]

That provocative series of questions opens a whole new vista of consideration as families think about ministry with, to, and among singles.

PROGRAMS

In a practical way, the church can also take some positive steps toward the development of a workable singles ministry. Phase one would be an audit of the entire congregation to determine where all the single adults are and what their present skills, abilities, calling, and future plans are.

Phase two would involve getting the singles together to discuss their needs and to gather ideas as to how the church could minister more effectively to them—and how they could minister more effectively to the church. Pre-cut, pre-planned, packaged programs that move from one church to another or from publisher to church are not necessarily the answer for this very diverse group. Resource materials are needed, but programs must be developed by the people involved. It is not a question of imposing a program on them, but having them identify their needs and state how they best feel those needs can be met in and through the ministry of the local church. It should not be a meeting just for singles, but also for married couples who are involved and concerned about singles because they are people.

14. Strain, "The Single Saint in a Couple's Culture," pp. 10, 19.

Research does need to be conducted with regard to what is being done in other churches and what resource materials are available from other organizations. The SALT I (Single Adult Leadership Training) Conference, conducted in 1980, produced some creative thinking and clear direction for church ministries. *Single,* the magazine published by the National Association of Christian Singles,[15] also provides timely articles and profitable suggestions. Positive Christian Singles in Garden Grove, California, also has excellent resources for the organization and administration of a singles ministry.

This leads us into Phase three. A small group of leaders—three or four at the most—should analyze the needs as expressed by the singles either when they meet together in a group or through their private sharing. The leadership should then develop the kind of ministry that would be best suited to that local assembly. Establishing separate singles departments, creating singles churches, or isolating singles should not be the objective. Rather singles should be integrated into the total ministry of the church while at the same time specialized needs are met through specialized programs. The final stage of the development of a church ministry program ought to be the alerting, informing, and committing of the entire local assembly to a ministry of meeting needs of individuals of which a large portion are singles. People need people. If the singles in our churches are not going to find their worship, instruction, and fellowship, or have their emotional, physical, and spiritual needs met in the congregation of God's people, they will go elsewhere, and we all will be losers.

The potential of singles ministry today is providing the church with a fantastic challenge. Christian singles have special needs, but also are a unique resource. They are diverse as a group, yet can be united as a force for God in this world. The spirit of the age is putting unusual pressures upon both singles and families, and therefore the wonderful grace of Jesus is needed by all. The local church must assess its opportunities for ministry to singles and take positive steps to capitalize on the force available in this phase of adult education. Now is a time for aggressive and creative action.

15. P. O. Box 11394, Kansas City, Mo. 64112.

FOR FURTHER STUDY

1. Interview three types of single people (never married, formerly married, widowed) and identify the needs they have in common, the needs that are different; the attitudes that are common, the attitudes that are different; and their views of how their local church perceives their situation and helps meet their needs.

2. As indicated in the chapter, there is an older and a newer viewpoint on singleness. Is there another alternative? If so, what is it? What is your viewpoint, and why do you feel that way?

3. Using only your Bible, concordance, and a Bible dictionary, do an in-depth study of what the Bible says regarding singleness. Present the results of your study in the form of a series of theses or statements of conviction.

4. What is the attitude of your local church toward singles? Is any "special" ministry provided? On one page, summarize your church's philosophy and ministry for singles.

5. Take a position on the subject: "Singles should be integrated into the total life of the church rather than have separate groups." Write a brief, fact-filled argument for your position.

13

Senior Adults and Church Ministry

The Golden Age of life has become the Gray Age of life in the thinking of much of Western culture. Rather than seeing old age as the culmination of learning, experience, and wisdom, it is dreaded. Youth is glorified and old age is shunned. In fact, hundreds of thousands of dollars are spent every year by those in the 55-to 75-year-old bracket on lotions, dyes, and various preparations in order that they might appear younger, because youth is worshiped in our culture.

Adults, and in particular senior adults, are becoming a major segment of our community. Man has been on the earth for centuries, but in the short hundred-year period between 1840 and 1940, the world population doubled. It has been estimated that between 1940 and 1990 (a fifty-year period), it will double again. In 1840, about 2½ percent of the population of the United States was age 65 and older; by 1970 that number had climbed to 10 percent! As indicated in chapter one, it is projected that by 2000, those 60 and older will be 17 percent of the U. S. population.[1] Whatever the statistics might be, it is clear that two things are happening. First, longevity has been extended through medical and nutritional improvements. Second, there simply have been more adults born in

1. United States Bureau of the Census (Washington, D.C.: Government Printing Office, 1977) p. 33.

years gone by who are now reaching older adulthood. They are a force to be reckoned with, a group to be ministered to, and a fantastic resource to be drawn upon.

The Scripture speaks of the tremendous value that senior adults have, and advancing age is presented as filled with glory, deserving respect, and full of productivity. When speaking of the *glory* of old age and tying it to the last days, Luke quotes the prophet Joel: "And it shall be in the last days, God says, that I will pour forth of My Spirit on all mankind; and your sons and your daughters shall prophesy, and your young men shall see visions, and your old men shall dream dreams" (Acts 2:17). Here we find the glory of anticipation. The Lord told Israel, "You shall rise up before the gray headed, and honor the aged, and you shall revere your God; I am the LORD" (Lev. 19:32). Here glory and honor is bestowed upon the aged and tied to a relationship with God. Again, in Proverbs we read, "A gray head is a crown of glory; it is found in the way of righteousness" (Proverbs 16:31). There is a glory and honor that comes with age to those who walk uprightly.

The Scriptures also speak of *respect* for the elderly. In the classic passage in Ecclesiastes 3 where God sets forth the principle of appropriateness of time for varieties of activities, He raises the question,

> What profit is there to the worker from that in which he toils? I have seen the task which God has given the sons of men with which to occupy themselves. He has made everything appropriate in its time. He has also set eternity in their heart, yet so that man will not find out the work which God has done from the beginning even to the end. I know that there is nothing better for them than to rejoice and to do good in one's lifetime; moreover, that every man who eats and drinks see good in all his labor—it is the gift of God. (Ecclesiastes 3:9–13).

God uses the glory of a lifetime of work that has been committed to Him to honor the aged. Again we read in Proverbs 22:6, "Train up a child in the way that he should go, even when he is old he will not depart from it." While this passage is often looked at from the standpoint of the child, it speaks also of the elderly one who has had a patterned life of belief, trust, and faithfulness; the end result is a godly testimony.

It is not just glory and respect that is due the elderly, but also an expectation of *productivity*. Job, responding to his accusers and underscoring the power and might of God, says, "Wisdom is with aged men, with long life is understanding" (Job 12:12). The lengthening of the days of godly men and women endows younger believers with a great resource of knowledge. Amplifying this, Psalm 92:12-15 says, "The righteous man will flourish like a palm tree, he will grow like a cedar in Lebanon. Planted in the house of the Lord, they will flourish in the courts of our God. They will still yield fruit in old age; they shall be full of sap and very green, to declare that the Lord is upright; He is my rock, and there is no unrighteousness in Him." The tried and tested life of the godly believer continually renews the strength of the younger believer, and fruitfulness and productivity is the end result.

When life on planet earth is over, the believer passes through the gateway of death into eternal life with God. That eternal, endless life speaks of the blessing of God. The prophet Isaiah, when moved by the Spirit of God to write concerning a new heaven and a new earth, said,

> I will also rejoice in Jerusalem, and be glad in My people; and there will no longer be heard in her the voice of weeping and the sound of crying. No longer will there be in it an infant who lives but a few days, or an old man who does not live out his days; for the youth will die at the age of one hundred and the one who does not reach the age of one hundred shall be thought accursed . . . . For as the lifetime of a tree, so shall be the days of My people, and My chosen ones shall wear out the work of their hands. (Isaiah 65:19-20, 22).

Longevity from God's perspective is for the purpose of fruitfulness, productivity, and blessedness. Old age is a time to look forward to with great anticipation—quite a different view from that held by an unbelieving world.

In 1970 it was estimated that as many as one-third of many local church congregations were 65 years of age or older. In the years that have followed, that percentage has increased and yet the ministry to this vital part of the Body of Christ has not grown proportionately. In the remaining portion of this chapter, we shall examine various aspects of the life of a senior adult.

LENGTH OF LIFE

Two words have surfaced in recent years that have to do with the study of senior adults. *Gerontology* is the study of the aging and what it means to be elderly. It is fascinating to note that very little has been written on the elderly by the elderly. Perhaps the next time a study is undertaken regarding the needs, desires, and programs for senior adults, senior adults ought to do it!

In attempting a definition of age, Vern Bengston concludes that "Age can best be defined as the culmination of developmental events, a particular point in time in the life of an individual."[2] Betty Groff, a friend who is a culinary expert and in demand as a speaker, was once asked to make a presentation on "cooking for older people." As she considered carefully what the meaning of "older people" might be, she came up with what I believe is a classic definition. She concluded, "An older person is an eighteen-year-old in the eyes of a seven-year-old." The matter does tend to be somewhat relative. The newspaper in Lancaster, Pennsylvania, recently reported that two children, ages 70 and 75, put on a big birthday party for their 95-year-old mother! The developmental events Bengston talks of include longevity, retirement, death of friends and/or spouse, physical changes, and economic and housing adjustments.

The other term that has come into being is *geriatrics,* which has to do with the treatment of elderly people. Starting in the 1960s, the rapid growth of this field continues today, continually broadening its scope of concern with the needs, concerns, and potentials of the elderly.

It is statistically verifiable that people are living longer than they did in earlier years, and because of the birth rate in earlier years, there are more and more people reaching the elderly stage of life. Of course, the predicting of longevity is not precise, and statistical tables are of little comfort or help to the elderly. As one writer put it, "What, after all is read and done, does the [statistically devoted] gerontologist tell the newly widowed at the graveside of a devoted spouse? 'Your loved one passed away, you see, because his value was significant at the .001 level and his null hypothesis was not confirmed.'"[3] Obviously, more is needed in terms of both comfort and actual help.

Duke University has been actively involved in studying the aged for many years, and Erdman Palmore and his group have discovered that although heredity, and some physical differences, are indeed factors that aid in the prediction of longevity, more significant factors are nonphysical. They include the occupation, education, and intellectual and social activities of the elderly. The four most important ways they discovered to increase longevity were: (1) Maintenance of a satisfying and productive role in society, (2) a positive mental outlook on life, (3) continued good physical functioning, and (4) the avoidance of smoking.[4] Note carefully that the first two and the last one can be controlled by the individual and are influenced greatly by a person's attitude.

2. Vern Bengston. *The Social Psychology of Aging* (Indianapolis: Bobbs-Merril, 1976) p. 16.
3. E. Palmore and F. C. Jeffers, eds., *Predictions of Life Span: Recent Findings* (Lexington, Mass.: Heath, 1971).
4. Ibid.

No one knows precisely why or how some people live longer than others. Certain areas of the country seem to produce greater longevity than others. Studies by insurance companies, the business industry, and government have shown that some professions seem to have a greater longevity than others.[5] And although length of days is of concern, it is generally conceded that the quality of life is more important than its duration.

Adaptation and Adjustment

Studies by various gerontologists indicate that the old adage, "success breeds success and failure breeds failure" holds true for people who are becoming seniors.[6] Individuals who have handled their lives well by having a clear-cut purpose for living, meaningful objectives that they strove for—for the cause of Christ worldwide, for their family, or for mankind in general—normally adapt and adjust in later life like they did in early life. Adaptation involves flexible living that is attuned to changing circumstances; adjustment means a more permanent or fixed choice, based on an unchanging circumstance. The senior adult has to do both. Changing economic conditions call for constant adaptation; the loss of a spouse normally requires a more permanent adjustment. It may be true that in earlier life we make more adaptations, whereas in later life we make more adjustments.

There are some significant myths about senior adults that need to be exploded. Some of them are that senior adults want to disengage from life and activities, are unable to learn, will soon die after retirement, are set in their ways, and are basically all the same.[7] In reality, the opposite is true. Adults are not all the same. They adjust and adapt at different rates and with different abilities. Individual older adults may be set in their ways, but so may younger adults. As we will see a little later in this chapter, the learning ability of older adults does not decline significantly with advancing age, and their need and desire to be involved and productive remains constant.

The factors that seem to be most important in helping adults to adjust to old age are: an early life that was healthy, successful, and productive; a well-thought-out plan for the future; an ability to remain

5. J. V. Quint and B. R. Cody, "Prominence and Mortality: Longevity of Prominent Men," *Industrial Gerontology* 7 (1970), pp. 43–44.
6. M. P. Lawton, "Clinical Psychology?" in C. Einsdorfer and M. P. Lawton, eds., *The Psychology of Adult Development and Aging* (Washington, D.C.: American Psychological Association, 1973).
7. Laurella Bartholomew. *Ministering to the Aging: Every Christian's Call* (New York: Paulus, 1979) p. 10.

active and flexible; an inner security that allows them to be free from the unhealthy restrictions upon them regarding their behavior and activities by the other age groups; and a continued sense of being wanted and useful.[8]

Senior adults tend to be present-past oriented rather than present-future oriented. This is true frankly of all adults. One of the great gaps between youth and adults is that youth tend to be present-future oriented and adults are present-past oriented. As adults get older, there is more past to view, and so they become more retrospective than prospective. So if they have lived productive, healthy lives and have been successful in accomplishing a number of life's objectives, a feeling of success pervades. Some who have studied older adults find four different attitudes toward life's acomplishments. One group feels that life's work is completed, and it is their task now to relax, rest, and enjoy. The second group feels that life's work is never done, and it is their desire to "die with their boots on." The third group resigns itself to what lies ahead, but wishes that things could be different, for example that they could have more strength or resources to keep going. The last, and saddest group of all, are those whose lives were characterized by purposelessness and meaninglessness, and who now are filled with remorse and regret.[9]

If seniors have been active and productive during their early and middle years, then personal contacts, interests, and insights have been developed and expanded. Those now become a fantastic resource to draw upon during the senior days. Activity in church and civic groups can provide a meaningful contact and context for stimulation and growth.

Successful adaptation and adjustment is made by individuals who have planned and made commitments for the future. The anticipation of living and the anticipation of accomplishment allows them to adjust successfully to changing circumstances. Plans made by the elderly need to have the same characteristics as plans made by people of all age groups. The plans must be flexible: a rigid plan will lead to frustration as circumstances diminish financially, physically, and socially.

It is also important that seniors be able to continue to contribute to others and be useful. Retirement years can be years of accomplishing many of the dreams and tasks bypassed earlier. Arranging slides and pictures that have been taken over a 45-to 50-year period is rewarding in memories and in the satisfaction of getting a long-awaited task com-

8. V. Wood. "Age—Appropriate Behavior for Old People." *The Gerontologist,* 1971. M. P. Lawton. "Clinical Psychology?" *The Psychology of Adult Development and Aging* (Washington, D.C.: American Psychological Association, 1973). D. Schonfield. "Future Commitments and Sucessful Aging." *Journal of Gerontology.* 1973.
9. See Ledford J. Bischof, *Adult Psychology* (New York: Harper and Row, 1976), pp. 314–16.

pleted. Engaging in a hobby or sports activity that one never had time for can have both social and physical benefits. Sewing, cooking, travel, woodworking, golf, and a host of other activities now can be pursued with vigor.

Finally, older people need freedom. Younger people have tended to restrict the freedom of the elderly in their activities, dress, and personal relationships. Senior adults have begun to band together in greater numbers in retirement communities and other social and housing arrangements. This is not viewed by them as restriction or confinement (except for those who are physically limited), but rather it is "being with our peers who accept and understand us." It almost has the ring of adolescent challenge!

PHYSICAL, MENTAL, AND EMOTIONAL HEALTH

We turn our attention now to some of the more obvious aspects of aging. In doing so, we need to recognize that aging is a continuum. People do not jump from age ten to age twenty, and age twenty to age thirty; rather, there are a series of slow steps and gradual processes. There seem to be, however, certain critical points in the aging process marked by birthdays that are seen as benchmarks of growth and maturity. They appear to be ages 16, 20, 40, and 65. The first two birthdays are looked forward to with great anticipation. The last two birthdays we would rather not face. Adulthood and senior adulthood do bring with them certain physical and mental limitations. Those limitations are magnified in a youth-oriented culture, and thus the events that signal them are dreaded.

Factors leading to aging include the gradual decline in the reserves that the physical body has both in cellular reproduction and in organ functioning. While in childhood there are more acute illnesses, in the aging there are more chronic sicknesses. It has been estimated that in 1980 more than 85 percent of the adult population over 65 had had one or more chronic illnesses. The most persistent chronic problems are loss of hearing and loss of eyesight. Learning to adjust to hearing aids and being left out of conversations, or being restricted because of poor eyesight or slowing reflexes present special pressures for the aging.

The aging process also normally causes a general decline in physical activity. Physical health and stamina decrease, muscles are weakened, there is less energy, and changes in the respiratory and circulatory systems become evident on a daily basis. Those physical changes are the most noticeable in our society. As one individual put it, "The pains of age and the losses of freedom to do physically what the mind wants to do mentally, gives one the feeling of being a prisoner within one's own body."

Hereditary factors enter into the aging process as well. It is statistically verified that women live longer than men. Also, it has been noted that long-lived parents normally have long-lived offspring. The moral of that story is that if you want to have a long life, choose parents who had a long life.

Many facets of physical deterioration and disease are unknown, but it appears that those who care for themselves well and have a positive mental outlook will generally live out their lives to a reasonable length with a sense of accomplishment and satisfaction.

Tied in closely with the physical are the mental processes. It has been assumed over the years that there is a general intellectual decline during old age. Studies that have been done, especially cross-sectional studies, have generally declared that a person's mental ability peaks at age 24, remains relatively constant through age 30, and then begins a slow gradual straight-line descent from age 30 to old age. But it is not that simple to define. The more straight-line declines appear to be in motor skills, not in mental capacity or creative ability.[10] Remember that Michelangelo completed the dome of St. Peter's Cathedral at age 70, and Handel, Haydn, and Verdi created their most lasting works after age 70. Goethe completed *Faust* after age 80, Charles Hobbs wrote productively until age 91, Tennyson continued to write poetry until after age 80, Winston Churchill became Prime Minister at age 77, and Benjamin Franklin and Thomas Jefferson did some of their most influential work after age 80.

Life-long learning is the order of the day. Senior adults have not only the capacity to learn, but also the desire. Allen Tough, in his work with the Ontario Institute for Studies in Education, discovered that high on the list of reasons for starting and continuing learning projects for adults were the following: (1) usefulness, (2) puzzlement, curiosity, or a question, (3) pleasure from the activity of learning, (4) enjoyment from receiving the content, (5) satisfaction from possession, and (6) in order to impart to others.[11] It is clear from this study and others that adults of all ages have a desire to learn for the love of learning and for the love of sharing.

10. For further study, Matilda W. Riley et al., eds., *Aging and Society* (New York: Russell Sage, 1968), vols. 1, 2, and 3.
11. A. Tough. *Why Adults Learn: A Study of the Major Reasons for Beginning and Continuing a Learning Project.* Adult Education no. 3. Monograph. (Toronto: Ontario Institute for Studies in Education, 1968), p. 10.

When Raymond B. Catell did his research on the learning patterns of senior adults, he concluded that there were two kinds of intelligence: crystallized and fluid. The first kind was constant and did not decline with age, whereas the second was biologically affected by age, and related to things such as dexterity and levels in performance. When one takes an overview perspective on intelligence and the aging and feeds in factors such as motivation, physical skills, and other experiential factors, the stability of intellectual abilities emerges.

Comparative studies between youths and aging adults show something interesting. The average layman has a strong stereotype of the abilities and behaviors of the elders, and this comes through even in television commercials. They are pictured as dottering, forgetful, and totally unaware of new things. But research indicates that there are greater differences in abilities and behaviors among a group of older people than among a group of younger people. In technical terminology, the researcher would indicate that the standard deviations tend to increase with age rather than decrease.

Tied to physical health are mental health and emotional health. Mental health is a great concern in aging, because the declines in motor skills, health, and financial and physical resources often can lead to depression for those who have not made proper adjustments. The suicide rate in older adults is climbing, and the need for mental health services for this age group also is growing.[12]

One factor that affects the mental health of senior citizens is the kind of living accommodations they have. Some live with family and relatives. The usual pattern is for a mother or a father to move in with a daughter, rather than with a son or with grandchildren. Others have lived for many years in their own home; they resist moving. It is the place that they are most familiar with and that holds a storehouse of memories. Several factors obviously affect this decision, however, such as physical health, the security of the neighborhood, and financial ability. Another living situation is the retirement community; those are dramatically increasing in number throughout the United States. Some are trailer and mobile home parks; whereas others are regular retirement buildings and houses. In some situations, there are combination nursing homes and retirement housing in a single complex. Here there is supervision and physical, social, and even spiritual care. Separate from those are nursing homes of different types. Another option is hotels or rooming

12. D. Schonfield, "Translations in Gerontology—from Lab to Life: Utilizing Information," *Journal of Gerontology,* 1973, pp. 28, 189–96.

houses where older adults live. They tend to be in deteriorating areas with very limited facilities.

The effect of the residence on aging is significant. Studies on housing and the aged do not indicate that a person's life is shortened by the stress of relocation, but there are many factors that do need to be considered. They include the community into which the individual is being relocated; the competency of the individual physically, mentally, and socially; the ability to adapt and adjust; and the active involvement of the individual with others in either organized or informal activities.

In terms of mental health, statistics seem to confirm that emotional problems of the aged are fundamentally the same as those in younger persons, but that there is a continuing rise in susceptibility as age progresses. In 1977 it was noted that in people 65 years of age and older, 13 to 15 percent were in need of professional mental health treatment, with another 30 percent living in conditions that were not conducive to good mental health.[13]

The body, mind, and emotions are all intertwined. The body is our machine for living and, like all machines after long use, it wears out. The wearing process continues, and so does adaptation.

LEGAL STATUS

We live in a time when individual freedoms and liberties are at least under scrutiny, if not under attack. For the senior adult it becomes acute. It is even more so if the individual has been hospitalized or institutionalized. Christians and Bible-believing churches must take seriously the injunctions of Scripture to care for the widows, the orphans, and the elderly. One study that was done on the subject of the rights of the aged indicated that once the courts have ruled that an older adult is incompetent, the older adult is then prevented from doing anything further legally to protect himself.[14] The normal pattern is total divestiture of self-management. It appears that too often rather than the estate with its financial resources being used for the senior's own welfare, the courts protect the assets of the estate for the survivors. There is a significant need to abolish the concept of incompetency as the statutes now define it, and to put in its place a law that more equitably cares for the rights of the senior citizen.

13. Charles Harris, ed., *The Fact Book on Aging* (Washington, D.C.: Council on the Aging, 1979), p. 120.
14. G. J. Alexander et al., eds., *The Aged and the Need for Surrogate Management* (Syracuse: Syracuse U., 1972).

Many families, even Christian families that have had good relationships over many years, will come to severe disagreements and even hostility over the subject of estates and inheritances. Good biblical concepts of stewardship need to be taught in our families, in our churches, and practiced by individual believers as a testimony before a confused and oppressed world.

RETIREMENT

Wendall is looking forward to retirement with great anticipation. All during his working life he eagerly anticipated vacations and planned for them with great delight. He has applied the same kind of interest and planning to his retirement, and is looking forward to it with eagerness. Farley does not have the same idea. He sees it as a time when he will no longer be needed, wanted, or useful. His wife is not looking forward to having him "under foot," and he does not know what he will do hanging around the house day after day. Two men—facing the same event with very different perceptions and expectations.

In our age and culture, retirement is a fact of life. In 1900, life expectancy was 47 years and retirement was not an issue. By 1975, however, life expectancy had reached 70 years, and the average number of retirement years stood at 14. It is anticipated that by 2000, life expectancy will be approximately 81 years, and the average person will face 25 years of retirement.[15] The concept of retirement looms large as an issue to be faced and an opportunity to be developed.

Retirement is both an event and a process. It is an event in that it takes place at a certain time in life, but it is a process that goes on from the time of the event until the time of death. As people get older, the age at which they would like to retire and expect to retire goes up. Younger people are thinking more and more about early retirement and older people are attempting to delay it. Most want to stay where they are in terms of residence or community, but all persons face it with certain key questions. What the average older person resents is what they feel is a loss of significance and independence. Another factor that appears to have some significance is the size of company that the individual worked for prior to retirement. The larger the company, the earlier the retirement; the smaller the company or organization, the later the retirement.

Factors that affect the decision include money, health, status, family support, future concerns, and job morale. The matter of adequate fi-

15. For a fuller discussion, see Harold Geist, *The Psychological Aspects of Retirement* (Springfield: Charles C. Thomas, 1968), pp. 3–8. Also, Harris, *Fact Book on Aging.*

nances is a real issue. Inflation makes for an uncertain future and requires careful planning. Health can cause early retirement if the individual is unable to continue work. The status of the early retiree has risen lately; he is more and more viewed as one who has planned well and has something significant to do. And if the family, friends, and fellow-workers are supportive of early retirement, the retiree will view it more positively.

A key question is whether retirement should be at a fixed time or made flexible within a range of time. The most common practice of our recent past is to have a fixed age, usually 65, at which all employees are required to retire. Facing the "event" can be made easier if a fixed time is established. The following factors are worth considering: (1) A fixed retirement age requires planning and forces the individual to do what he would normally like to put off doing with advancing age. (2) A fixed retirement age forces the individual to plan his future financially, and he therefore becomes more future-minded than present-oriented in spending. (3) A fixed age for retirement is democratic and fair because employees of the organization are treated equally, at least as far as the age of retirement is concerned. (4) A fixed retirement age is in keeping with other fixed age concepts such as voting, eligibility for holding office, and even driving cars. (5) A fixed retirement age can make it easier for management to plan staffing and organization for the future. (6) A fixed retirement age prevents the individuals who refuse to quit until they have made "enough" money for retirement from working until just before they are about to die. The story is all too familiar: people who secured what they thought was enough money, and then died just a few weeks or months after retirement. (Perhaps that is a middle-class question, because the rich have enough money and do not think about retirement or worry about it, and the poor have so little that retirement is an academic question.)

Whether one takes early retirement or retirement at the conventional time, takes it at a fixed age or at a flexible age, there is still a tremendous talent available to the church of Jesus Christ and the cause of Christ worldwide among those who have retired from some kind of job or industry and now have skills, talents, and abilities that can be channeled—and need to be channeled, both for their sakes and for the cause of Christ.

Harold Geist, in his book on retirement, says, "If people are to find a satisfying experience in retirement, there must be substitutes for the satisfying meanings of the job. In the main, these satisfactions are as follows: (1) a daily schedule, (2) a wide basis for many associations, (3) a sense of contribution, and (4) a definite position in society."[16] What Geist is suggesting is that order, significance, and contribution are vital for the well-being of the retiree. Planning to spend one's life sitting on a beach or staring out a window will lead to an early grave.

FACING DEATH AND ETERNAL LIFE

"Death always has been, and always will be with us. It is an integral part of human existence. And because it is, it has always been a subject of deep concern to all of us. Since the dawn of humankind, the human mind has pondered death, searching for the answers to its mysteries. For the key to the question of death unlock the door of life."[17]

With these words, Elizabeth Kubler-Ross begins her classic book analyzing the stages that both precede death for the one about to die, and follow death for friends and relatives who remain. Stage one, *denial*, brings with it the experience of shock. Stage two is *anger* with intense emotion. Stage three is *bargaining*, with the gradual realization of what is about to happen. Stage four is preparation or movement toward self-awareness and contact with others, but often coming out of an experience of *depression*. Stage five is *acceptance* with increased self-reliance. The experience of death must be faced by all until Jesus returns.

The church can be of significant help in providing love, support, and care for those who are both facing dying or the loss of ones who have died. Sometimes the most caring and loving thing we can do is simply to be friends during these times of special stress and be silent or weep with them. One of my students at Trinity Evangelical Divinity School, doing a doctoral program on counseling the bereaved some years ago, concluded that the bereaved do not need Bible verses they already know, but our care. Helping a person through times of trauma, as Kubler-Ross indicates, takes patience and selfless love.

A word of caution needs to be given. Kubler-Ross and others clinically analyze the subject from physical and emotional viewpoints, but do not touch the real heart of the matter in spiritual terms. Whether a person is young or old, if they go through the portal of death without a personal relationship with Jesus Christ, they go into a Christless eternity in hell. We must keep a sharp focus on the concept that for the elderly who know Christ as personal Savior, the preparation for death is a time of helping them to get ready to meet their Savior and Friend. For those apart from saving faith in Christ, we must do all we can to persuade

16. Geist. *The Psychological Aspect of Retirement*, pp. 27–28.
17. Elizabeth Kubler-Ross. *Death: The Final Stage of Growth*. (Englewood Cliffs, N.J.: Prentice-Hall, 1975), p. 1.

them to believe and receive the gift of life in Christ. Otherwise, they will meet Him—but as Judge—not Savior.

Three main diseases face the aging adult. They are diseases of the heart; cancer; and cerebrovascular problems, mainly strokes. Those three problems alone account for over 70 percent of the deaths of people 45 years of age and older. But whatever the cause, death is an event; it is a door through which one must pass from this life to the next. The Bible tells us that we "see in a mirror dimly, but then face to face." Death can occur at any age, but it is certain among the aged. Some key questions that must be grappled with in ministering to the dying are: Should they be informed of their condition? Should they be allowed to die at home, or be confined to a hospital? Should individuals who are existing on life-support systems be continued on those systems even though there is no expectation of recovery? Those are matters that need to be discussed with older adults; and after prayer and careful study of the Scriptures, decisions need to be made so that if a person is incapacitated, he will have the right of being cared for as he wants.

People have different reactions to the death of another. It largely depends upon the relationship they have with the dying person. The death of a stranger has a different impact upon a person from the death of a spouse, parent, child, or friend. The death of a relative who is living with you is considerably different from the death of a relative you have not seen for many years. But the situation also has a bearing: for instance, being told of a death is not the same as witnessing it. And the death of one who appears to be in good health is different from the death of one who has a lingering illness or has been going through excruciating pain. Most pastors and lay people are never really prepared to deal with this last event of life on earth.

Aside from the intense emotional experiences are the financial and legal responsibilities. Unfortunately, most Christians and others do not have wills. They have not made an estate plan and are thereby allowing the state government to dictate what is to be done with their children and/or assets. Wills seminars and estate planning seminars are becoming more common in churches and Christian organizations. Having a will and a proper plan for the estate that God has entrusted into the care of each of His children is a biblical responsibility.

Following the death of a child of God, those relatives and friends who remain need care and follow-up beyond the typical six-week period. A caring, supporting community needs to involve the loved ones in effective social and spiritual engagement.

MINISTRY TO AND WITH THE ELDERLY

In Titus we read that the aged men and the aged women have a responsibility in godly living and in godly teaching (Titus 2:2-5). The very things that we find described as responsibilities and privileges for all believers apply to the senior adults. They are to be involved in worship, instruction, fellowship, and outreach ministry. Many senior adults have the opportunity to continue to function and move about and should, therefore, take their rightful place as leaders and teachers in the ministry of the local church. Some of the choicest servants of God I know are those who are well beyond the retirement age and are continuing to serve in teaching and leading capacities. They have great stamina, enthusiasm, and adaptability to changing needs of the congregation.

That is not true of all senior adults, however. Some are more infirm and must have limited responsibilities. Still, everyone can be a prayer warrior, and as a partner in prayer can support the general ministry of the church.

The church must also be sensitive to the needs of the senior adults. Access routes to the church buildings should be equipped with proper ramps and railings so that individuals who have physical problems can have easy access to worship and study. The church should provide spiritual and social ministries geared specifically for the elderly and encourage their participation and support.

One church in northern New Jersey rents a bus every two months for a two-day outing for its senior club to visit tourist areas, Christian organizations, and ministries. In another retirement area in the East, there is a weekly prayer and Bible study fellowship time held in conjunction with a luncheon. In the Midwest, one large church has an active senior adult program for those who have special talents such as carpentry, plumbing, electrical skills, and other types of service; they help schools, churches, and widows or single parent families with practical chores at little or no cost. This service outreach causes them to be not only useful, but ministering in a very practical way. On the West Coast, there are churches that have pastors to the elderly, and some have even taken small groups of senior citizens on short-term missionary ministries. The only limit is the creativity and commitment toward this valued and valuable part of our community.

Senior adults continue to learn, and therefore many churches are having special seminars, Bible studies, and workshops for their senior adults to assist them in an ongoing, growing spiritual experience. One of the most exciting things in Christian education with senior adults is intergenerational learning. Having grandmothers and grandfathers mixing with primary department children or with senior high young people can be a most rewarding learning experience for both age groups. Having people of all ages sharing and interacting not only helps with understanding, but also develops maturity. There are some adults in the senior category who feel they have "done their bit" and now it is "time for the younger folks to take over." Too often this is taken at face value, and valuable talent is lost for the cause of Christ. A program must be developed so that the church can move forward, utilizing the talents and the skills of all the members of the Body, for they have all been placed there for a purpose.

A CHURCH PLANNING PROCESS

If a church is to revitalize its senior adult ministry, it must make a commitment to that end. A statement of purpose must be drawn up and ratified by the leadership of the church that spells out clearly what the ministry to senior adults is intended to do. Money needs to be allocated to support the program, and leadership must be dedicated and set aside to assist.

Once the purpose has been clearly stated and the support factors put in place, then clear goals should be established annually. Remember that senior adults are not little children in old people's bodies. They have much wisdom, talent, and can direct their own ministries if given support, encouragement, and resources. Select some key leaders from among your senior adults to head up, coordinate, and plan the program. More likely than anyone else they will be accurate in determining the goals toward which the organization of this ministry should head.

Once the purpose and goals have been established, resources allocated, and leadership set in place, a program needs to be designed and implemented. Some churches have a "home department," which is a monthly program to visit shut-ins by faithful senior citizens or others. Regular materials are taken to them, and their significant life events such as birthdays, anniversaries, Christmas, and Easter are remembered. In addition, some churches have recordings of their church services, and they are taken to shut-ins so that they can learn and worship.

Some churches have organized senior fellowships to provide the kind of program that would attract nonbelieving senior citizens to Christ. They involve social, recreational, and spiritual activities. Programming can include some of the topics discussed in this chapter, such as death and dying, retirement, and planning wills and estates. Perhaps some community leaders would be willing to come in and speak to the group, or travelogues or missionary speakers could be provided. Special holidays can always provide highlights with Thanksgiving dinners, a sweet-heart banquet, or a concert. Why not let the senior citizens help plan and direct the missionary conference for the church, together with the teenagers? That will provide both youth and experience, and involve both in the cause of Christ worldwide.

Loneliness, uselessness, and a lack of an orderly life are key problems many senior adults face, and Christians are not isolated from those experiences. A well-ordered and organized senior adult ministry will honor Christ and enrich the church.

Senior adults are a sizable and significant force in the latter part of the twentieth century. They have knowledge, experience, and creativity. God has declared that they are to be respected, allowed to be productive, and properly honored. Today, they are living longer and are capable of more positive living and useful ministry than ever before.

Our senior adults are also in need of understanding and help in physical, mental, emotional, and legal matters. The changes that occur within them and around them tend toward limitation at a time when they should be free to fulfill themselves in all kinds of personal and ministry ways.

The stage is being set. The cast is growing in numbers and talent. What we need now is a well-designed script that will call forth the best efforts of all involved. It is my prayer that the Bible-believing, teaching churches of today will rise to the occasion to do their best for the glory of God and the good of the *whole* Body.

1. The Scriptures speak of the glory, respect, and productivity of senior adults. In what ways can the local church provide opportunities for, and ministries to, senior adults so that those biblical principles will be practiced?

2. Over one-third of most local church congregations, it is estimated, are sixty-five years of age or older. How does that compare to your church? Why is the percentage of senior adults in church so much higher than the percentage of senior adults in society? What must the church do to address this obvious opportunity?

3. This chapter sets forth five factors that appear to be very important in the positive adjustment and adaptation of senior adults. Interview six or more senior adults and present a brief paper that challenges or supports those concepts.

4. Interview several funeral directors regarding the pressures and problems faced by the relatives of those who have died in old age. Is there a difference between the deaths of young and old? Between sudden death and lingering illness? How can the Christian leader of adults prepare people emotionally for this last great event of life? Financially? Socially? Spiritually?

5. What is your church doing to care for the variety of needs that senior adults have? Analyze your church program and identify its strengths and weaknesses. Lastly, outline a program for the elderly that will be biblically responsible and practically workable.

14

Meeting the Social Needs of Adults

Americans are spending as much on their leisure time as the federal government pays each year for our national defense. Our buying in the areas of sports equipment, recreational activities, and entertainment is in excess of 260 billion dollars per year. The amount has quadrupled since 1965, when 58 billion dollars was spent, and doubled since 1972, when 105 billion dollars was spent.[1]

Some researchers have observed that Americans are working harder at producing less and playing more. It seems that finding new and more exciting forms of recreation has become our new national pastime.

As Christians, our lives are to be totally committed to Jesus Christ. That means that we strive to make Jesus the Lord of all of our lives, including our leisure time and activity. Frances Clemens comments, "The Christian must gear his leisure to the committed way of life. With all of this valuable time at our disposal, it is important that we fill it constructively. . . . Leisure can be spent either constructively or destructively, in re-creation or de-creation. Recreation is the constructive use of leisure time."[2]

1. *U.S. News and World Report,* 26 July 1982, pp. 47–48.
2. Frances Clemens, Robert Tulley, and Edward Crill, *Recreation and the Local Church,* (Elgin, Ill.: Brethren, 1956), p. 22.

BRUCE R. MCCRACKEN is acting chairman of the Christian Education Department, Lancaster Bible College, Lancaster, Pennsylvania.

It may be helpful to define further the word *social*. Frank Hart Smith defines social recreation as

> Activity engaged in during one's leisure time; it is an activity which involves social interaction; and it is an activity which is primarily engaged in for enjoyment.
> Social recreation is people with people in a social setting. Social recreation is people talking, people laughing, people drinking coffee, people playing—together. Together is a big word in social recreation. It is one of the essentials in the whole concept of social.
> Social recreation . . . includes parties, fellowships, banquets, receptions, teas, picnics, social outings of all kinds.[3]

We are living in an age in which work weeks are being shortened from forty to thirty-five, and even thirty, hours. That is a far cry from the sixty-hour weeks people worked just fifty years ago. In addition, with retirement time increasing (see chapter 13 on senior adults), more time is available to more people. For the Christian, the proper use of all God's resources is a must. Since time is one of those precious resources given to us by God, then using our "free" time for the glory of God and the good of the Body of Christ is not an option with the Christian—it is a necessity.

Using leisure time constructively and creatively is, therefore, a concern of the local church. Persons responsible for planning ministry are forced to ask several questions. What are the social needs of adults? Should the local church try to meet those social needs? How can we best meet the leisure needs of our congregation? In exploring the answers to those and other questions, we will attempt to formulate a philosophy of social activities within the local church.

BIBLICAL RATIONALE

God created man for a variety of reasons, and not the least of them was fellowship. In Genesis 3:8-10 we read that God created a being that was capable of walking and talking with Him in a loving and open relationship. It would appear from this that one of the aspects of the nature of God is that He is a social Being. We, being created in the image of God, are also social beings. Our Creator has placed within us social needs. Those social needs are evidenced in the fact that, as human beings, we must communicate, laugh, and play with other people. The

3. Frank Hart Smith, *Social Recreation and the Church* (Nashville: Convention, 1977), p. 8.

Bible shows us that God designed fellowship to be an integral part of the lives of His people.

OLD TESTAMENT

In the Old Testament we are confronted with the challenge to minister to the social needs of the people of God. One clear evidence of this is the wise provision of an abundance of holy days (holidays) in the Hebrew calendar. Those days centered on the planting and harvesting of crops, the change of seasons, and historical events. All of the special days had religious meanings to the chosen people of God.

The three main festivals of the Hebrew calendar are the Passover with the Feast of Unleavened Bread, Pentecost, and the Feast of Tabernacles. Passover and the Feast of Unleavened Bread were to commemorate the nation of Israel's deliverance from their bondage in Egypt. The purpose of the Feast of Unleavened Bread, which directly follows the one-day Passover celebration, was to remind the Jews of the hardships suffered during their speedy exodus. Holy day offerings consisted of the first grains of the year.

Pentecost, or the Feast of Weeks, was instituted for the purpose of dedicating to God the first fruits of the wheat harvest. Tabernables, or the Feast of Booths, was to memorialize the wilderness wanderings. It also signified the completion of the grain, fruit, and grape harvests. We can see the calendar significance and the historical relevance in the correlation of these days to the various harvests.[4]

Many of the festivals lasted for extended periods of time, usually seven days. Work and toil were suspended as the people paused to make sacrifices and to worship. They also celebrated. The Old Testament is filled with illustrations of festivals that abounded in music, singing, dancing, and feasting. It seems that God not only wanted His people to enjoy Him, but to enjoy each other in social activities as well.

We can gain some further insight into the Israelites' social life by studying their words for *festival*. The most commonly used Hebrew term for these feasts was the word *mōʿēd* meaning a set time, or assembly, or a place of assembly. The other frequently used term was *ḥǎg* which comes from the verb "to dance." The two terms suggest that the divinely designated days were to be shared by all of the people and filled with not only worship, but with celebration, joy, and gladness. The Psalmist says,

4. Gleason Archer, *A Survey of Old Testament Introduction* (Chicago: Moody, 1974), pp. 242–43.

"He brought forth His people with joy and His chosen with gladness" (Psalm 105:43).[5]

NEW TESTAMENT

In the New Testament, we see our Lord involved in the lives of people. We see God, in the Person of Jesus Christ, desiring and enjoying the fellowship of His creation. In Mark 3:14 and John 3:22, Jesus calls the twelve disciples to be "with Him." This suggests that Jesus felt the need for companionship and social interation. Our Lord can be found in a number of social settings throughout the gospels.

John 2:11 tells us that Jesus performed one of His first (if not the first) signs at the wedding in Cana. To the Jews of Jesus' day, a wedding was a social event beyond question. It is interesting to observe that that particular miracle did not have to do with the healing of the sick, the raising of the dead, or the casting out of demons. The miracle demonstrated His power over all of creation as He provided the needed beverage for their continued social interaction. Having sufficient food and drink for such an occasion was an absolute necessity. Our Lord was as willing there to turn water into wine as He was to multiply the bread and fish to feed the hungry multitude, because without basic physical resources the effectiveness of social interaction and spiritual ministries is diminished.

Jesus took advantage of social activities and settings to teach. In Mark 2:15-17 we see Jesus being accused of eating with tax-gatherers and sinners. Jesus stated to the self-righteous scribes and Pharisees that "I did not come to call the righteous, but sinners." There are several lessons to be found in this story. The most obvious is that we, as Christians, need to be sharing our faith with sinners and not spending all of our time with saints. And second, social settings sometimes provide the best atmosphere for sharing Christ with nonbelievers. That is because of the freedom created in a relaxed environment and the friendliness fostered at social times.

Jesus, like all of us, spent many hours socializing around the meal table. In Luke 7:36-50, Jesus ate with a real sinner—a Pharisee! It was in his home that Jesus was anointed by the prostitute, and Jesus used the occasion to teach the host a lesson on forgiveness. Jesus taught Martha the need to be still while she was fussing to get His dinner ready in Luke 10:38-42.

5. Merrill F. Unger, *Unger's Bible Dictionary* (Chicago: Moody, 1961), s. v. "festivals."

After teaching about the perils of riches, Jesus called Zaccheus, the tax collector, out of the tree and went to his home. People complained again that Jesus was eating with sinners; but Jesus was teaching His followers that God is no respecter of persons and that the wealthy needed Him as well as the poor.

A social event was the setting for Jesus' farewell discourse to His disciples. It was during the Passover seder that Jesus announced His betrayal and His death and introduced the Lord's Supper ordinance. And again, Jesus initiated a men's prayer breakfast after His resurrection in John 21. That was another powerful teaching time. It was there that Jesus forgave Peter for his denial and commissioned him to the "feeding" ministry.

Luke tells us in Acts 2:42 and 46 that the early church devoted itself to four things: "And they were continually devoting themselves to the apostles' teaching and to fellowship, to the breaking of bread and to prayer . . . . And day by day continuing with one mind in the temple, and breaking bread from house to house, they were taking their meals together with gladness and sincerity of heart."

Those verses reveal the recipe for a successful and growing church. One of the main ingredients is fellowship—times together around the meal table in the homes of fellow believers. It would seem that the disciples carried Jesus' tradition of table fellowship into the life of the early church. The fostering of the "one mind" in this text may have come from the times of fellowship together in the homes. It may be that the gladness is missing in our churches today because sincerity of heart is absent. The text clearly shows that the two are not mutually exclusive.

We can conclude from this brief biblical rationale that social activities are indeed beneficial to ministry.

THE SOCIAL NEEDS OF ADULTS

Realizing that good programming is always built on the meeting of real and felt needs, it is important for us to ask the question, What are the social needs of adults? In chapter four, the overall needs of adults were presented, and it might be helpful to go back over that material again. This chapter presents the social needs of adults and then divides them according to age categorizations.

Although the amount of leisure time is growing for most adults, it is important to balance that fact with the realization that many young couples are extremely involved in the business or professional world. In attempting to get financially established, many couples have relatively little leisure time. It is also important to note that their social lives also revolve around their circle of business friends and associates.

Adults are involved in a very busy and, most often, productive life-style. The philosophy of self-actualization that says, "Be all you can be," is pushing the average person to the brink of exhaustion. Both men and women are actively pursuing careers and are greatly entangled in the web of the working world. The church has trouble ministering to the social needs of those adult members because they are generally too busy to socialize at a church function.

Another reason the church sometimes fails to meet those needs is because adults are perfectly capable of meeting and satisfying their own social needs. Adults are independent and have the financial and trans-portation resources needed to provide their relaxation. They usually own sporting equipment, recreational vehicles, camping gear, or any-thing else needed to have fun. Usually they possess all the physical capabilities needed to "do their own thing."

THE SOCIAL NEEDS OF YOUNG ADULTS

One of the most difficult age groups to effectively minister to both spiritually and socially is the young adult, aged eighteen to thirty-four. Needless to say, the sixteen-year age span accounts for much of the difficulty in identifying and meeting the needs of this group. The prob-lem is further complicated by at least five sub-cultures found within this age group. They are: college students, both single and married; single career young adults; and the married couples, with and without chil-dren. Each of the distinctions introduces a new set of needs that should be met by any church program.

The young adult possesses a wide variety and range of interests. That includes an enjoyment of many different kinds of social and recreational activities. Let us suppose that we have a group of fifteen young adults, each with at least three recreational interests. This menagerie of people represents at least forty-five different interests. If a church attempted to meet one of those needs per month, it could almost fill a four-year social calendar!

Two implications for the church social calendar become evident here. First, there must be a variety of social activities planned throughout the year. The church group that tries to get away with volleyball every Friday night will not experience the best results. A few of the remaining forty-four interests should be used. Second, planning of the social sched-ule should be participative. A group, or committee, of young adults should be responsible for putting together its own calendar. That will usually ensure a greater variety of events, because more than one person has input into what is going to be done. That sort of planning will produce a very positive by-product: leadership skills of the young adults will be strengthened.

Young adults are participators, not spectators. They enjoy being involved in the action and are not content just to watch. Their physical and mental prowess is at its peak. Vigorous activities sometimes satisfy their craving for physical and emotional release from the tensions of life. Highly organized competition is usually enjoyed.

Those factors suggest several areas of need within the social program of the church. Churches may consider participation in community athletic leagues. Softball, bowling, basketball, and various other church leagues abound in many areas. Young adults may also want to consider an intramural recreational program. That format would provide the degree of organization desired, yet combat competitiveness and rivalries with other church groups. Intra-church tennis, golf, ping-pong, basketball, volleyball, and other tournaments would be an asset to a young adult recreational program.

For example, one organization scheduled a ping-pong tournament. Singles and doubles competitions were set up. Winners were presented with an award plaque for their achievements. Another group planned an intramural two-on-two basketball tournament, with each team consisting of one fellow and one girl. The intramural atmosphere allowed players of lesser ability to have fun too.

As we have seen above, another benefit of an intramural program would be the increased involvement of church members. Many of the young adults who participated in the basketball tournament would never have played on an inter-church team. A church softball team can play only nine players at one time, though up to twenty might be effectively used on the team. An intramural league may involve several teams, which would increase the level of participation. That is important, because young adults would rather be active than passive on the athletic field.

The two-on-two basketball tournament mentioned above introduces another social need of young singles. Many young people are interested in meeting members of the opposite sex, and the church could capitalize on this need by providing well-planned social activities that help foster the desired interpersonal relationships. Many churches have "lost" young adults to the world because there was no other place for them to go to meet new friends. Churches may want to consider cooperating in doing social activities together in order to help Christian singles meet.

Young adults are transient. Following high school graduation, many leave home to go to college. Others depart to a new town or city in order to find a job. The close-knit relationships that were built during high school are shattered by distance. Bonds of friendship that have been built in church youth groups are also severely stretched, only to be retightened one or two times a year. Loneliness increases after the strong supportive ties of home have been cut. Those same feelings of transition are felt by newlyweds who move into a new apartment complex or community. The need for social fellowship and meeting new Christian friends is crucial at this point in the adult life. Churches need to be aware of their role in providing a place for young adults to cultivate new relationships.

In light of the present divorce rate, even among Christians, we should comment on the very similar need that young divorcees and/or widows and widowers may have as well. A significant number of divorcees leave the church.[6] Churches may want to rethink their role in recovering those young adults. Loneliness is one of the greatest sources of devastation in our society today. Building a social ministry within the church program will help meet many needs for friendship, love, and acceptance.

There are several financial factors to consider when programming to meet the social needs of young adults. College students and young married couples, especially those with children or buying a home, are usually less likely to be able to afford the activities of certain social events, whereas young career adults and young marrieds without children where both partners work are more capable of paying for social activities. On the whole, however, young adults are in their financial building years. Expensive weekend retreats, or other activities that would consume their budgets, should be considered carefully.

One church has developed a "scholarship program" for helping its young people attend special social events, conferences, or weekend retreats. Participants perform services for the church in return for admission to the desired activity. Chores such as polishing pews, waxing floors, vacuuming, typing, setting up rooms, and other odd jobs are assigned by the church custodian. The church contributes a set amount per hour towards the "tuition" of the individual. No cash is ever given to the individual; monies are paid directly to the sponsoring organization by the church.

THE SOCIAL NEEDS OF YOUNGER MIDDLE ADULTS

One could sum up the social and recreational needs of the young middle adult in two words—family oriented. Family life is usually at its

6. Charles M. Sell, *Family Ministry* (Grand Rapids: Zondervan, 1981), p. 32.

peak during these "prime of life" years. Homes are bustling with children who may range in age from one year through their middle teens.

In today's society it is very common for both the father and mother to be working outside the home. Mothers sometimes postpone employment until their children are old enough to begin school. Others entrust their babies to day care centers and preschools in order to reenter the job market. In the case of single parents, employment outside of home is usually not an option, but a necessity. Those factors produce a number of family needs revolving around what has become known as the "latch-key" child, or the child who comes home to an empty house after school. Several researchers are claiming that the increase in juvenile delinquency is being fueled by the resultant idle and unsupervised time at home.

How can the church minister to such various needs? What can the church social program do to build up the family's recreational times? In dealing with these questions, we must begin by explaining the need for family-centered ministry within our churches.

Too often the church has been guilty of stealing valuable family time. Church planners sometimes pride themselves in having an activity going on every night of the week for each and every age group within the church. That devastates family life. Many a well-intended church program has allowed (if not encouraged) parents to abdicate their family's social responsibilities, as well as their spiritual responsibilties, to the church. If you have trouble with what has just been said, ask yourself: How many times do we ascribe low spiritual commitment to Christ and the church to a family that is missing from Sunday school or church to be together for a weekend activity?

There are churches that honestly believe they can meet all of the needs of their families. That is not true. The church can, and should, help reinforce the family life of its members. Churches need to begin exploring better ways of helping parents develop home-centered recreation. That will mean several philosophical changes in our present church mentality.

First, the church can most help parents by meeting needs that parents have trouble meeting. We must recognize that the home is more important than the church in meeting people's social needs. The church can be a great help to families, but it must not seek to take over the task of managing a family. For example, churches may want to provide some after-school activities to help alleviate the latch-key child problem. With parental permission, children could be picked up at their schools and taken to the church or another recreational facility for an afternoon of fun and teaching. Churches may want to examine the possibility of using older teens for activity leaders. That kind of program would benefit all parties involved. The parents would benefit in knowing that their children are being properly supervised in a wholesome activity. They could pick up their children after work knowing that they were in good hands. The children would benefit by being involved in an activity that provides them with some fun and spiritual enrichment, rather than an afternoon filled with TV. The teenage assistants would grow in leadership skill and ministry awareness; and, of course, the church would also benefit because it has been given the opportunity of ministering to the parents, children, and teens. After-school specials could be an effective outreach into the neighborhood families. The church children could invite their non-Christian friends, the families could be contacted, and the church would have a natural opportunity to witness to them.

Second, the church can help families in their recreational activities by training parents. Leaders may schedule one family activity per month. For example, all the families in the church could be involved in making Christmas decorations at home to be used in decorating the church. Each family could make a tree ornament depicting a scene from the biblical account or a family tradition that is observed by that individual family. The ornaments could then be brought to the church and hung on the congregational tree. Each family could have one member explain the decoration, while another member places it on the tree. When the Christmas Eve service is completed, the families may take their ornament home to be enjoyed. That would benefit both the family in the thinking and creating of the ornament, and the church with beautiful and meaningful decorations.

Third, the church could rent a campground or Bible conference ground for families to use. Families could individually set up their own campsites and then cooperate in a corporate program of activities. The program schedule could include games, outings, and campfire devotions. Families would volunteer to plan several of the activities and lead them during the retreat. For example, the Jones family may volunteer to lead singing for the campfire devotionals. They would, as a family, select songs that each member enjoys. Three-year-old Susie may suggest "Jesus Loves Me" or "This Little Light of Mine." Ryan, age ten, may want to add "His Banner Over Me Is Love" (with motions, of course), and Daniel, fourteen, can offer several of his favorites. Those selections, plus Mom's and Dad's favorites, would give the Jones family a repertoire of songs that most of the other families know and enjoy. The Joneses may even plan and practice several special musical numbers to be performed at the campfire sessions. All can be encouraged and stimulated by the church in order to enrich family life and recreation.

Fourth, monitoring busy church schedules can foster family activities at home. Having different members of the family out to church on different nights of the week destroys the opportunity for the family to be together. Imagine if Father is out to men's fellowship on Monday night, Mother is at women's circle meeting on Tuesday, the children have their club meetings on Wednesday, the parents are gone on Thursday for choir, and Friday is a covered dish dinner. That busy church schedule can be compounded by the complexities of the average family's daily routine. Music lessons, concerts, plays, sporting activities, shopping, and a host of other vital events all diminish the hours families have together. By the time Saturday rolls around, everyone is too tired to do anything as a family. If you think this is an exaggeration, look at your church bulletin next Sunday. The church will have to grapple with those crucial problems. There are no easy answers. Some churches have attempted to consolidate their activities into one or two nights of the week. A church may schedule choir and other committee meetings from 6:30 to 7:30 on Wednesday nights; Bible study and prayer meeting would run from 7:45 to 8:45; and the youth and children's programs would meet simultaneously. That would be a first step toward family times at home.

Fifth, the church can build a program to train parents in developing home-centered activities with their children. It could be done in a mini-Sunday school or Wednesday night elective. The church may want to consider adding some of the books listed in the bibliography on family recreation to their libraries. Major publishing houses produce a variety of materials designed to help the parent plan and lead family recreational times. Churches can do much in facilitating family recreational activities.

Sixth, the church can offer assistance to single parents in helping them meet their family social needs. It is estimated that one out of every six children will lose a parent by divorce by the time they are eighteen.[7] The children lack the role model of father or mother after divorce shatters their family. Single parents are hungry for help in getting their sons and daughters together with other significant adults who will provide a good example for them to follow. Churches may want to ask families to "adopt" a single parent family. That would involve having family times together. The host family could include the single parent's family in their holiday times or special outings like picnics or trips to the zoo. Fathers and mothers could spend time with both their own children and their adopted sons and daughters. That would provide

7. Sell, *Family Ministry,* p. 21.

some positive role modeling. Such care and concern even on a social level can have a great impact on the lives of both single parents and their children.

THE SOCIAL NEEDS OF OLDER MIDDLE ADULTS

The social needs of older middle and younger adults differ, because the older middle adult is emptying his nest, but the younger middle adult is building his. The older adult usually has more leisure time, because his children have left home to begin college or to enter professional careers. They need social activities that will enrich their marriages. Years of parenting may have eroded the relationship between husband and wife. Many couples need to become reacquainted during this time. They also need fellowship with their peers. Lives that have been focused on the family so long may also have weakened friendships.

Physically, older middle adults are beginning to slow down; but they still enjoy a good active game as long as it is not overly strenuous. They also like to compete in mentally stimulating board or table games. Financially, they are more independent than their younger middle adult friends.

Couples' competitions may help meet their social needs. Husband and wife golf, tennis, or bowling teams may be formed into an intra-church league. Or churches may want to challenge other churches to a tennis or golf tournament. That is a friendly and fun way to meet new friends. Another by-product of that kind of activity is the interaction that takes place between husbands and wives, which can enrich marital relationships.

One Sunday school class of older middle adults in the Midwest planned a trip to Hawaii. Everyone had an enjoyable time on this corporate vacation. The lives of couples were enriched during that time to get away. Travel activity does not have to be as elaborate as a trip to Hawaii to be effective in meeting the social needs of these adults. We should note, however, that the older middle adult does usually have the time and money, from many years of employment, to enjoy getting away from everyday routines. From time to time, the same benefits could also be achieved by trips to the mission field. Visiting or helping missionaries can be a very profitable vacationing experience.

THE SOCIAL NEEDS OF OLDER ADULTS

The social needs of the senior saints are very similar to the needs of older middle adults. Only about 4 percent of older adults are physically incapacitated, but many are crippled by feelings of not being wanted or needed. They are usually handicapped by a reduced income of social security and company pensions. Loneliness is a common denominator in this group of adults and it is amplified through the death of a spouse. Needless to say, retirement has provided them with a great deal of leisure time that needs to be filled constructively.

Those factors suggest that the church can do much to support the social life of the older adult. One church in a suburb of Philadelphia has developed a program called "Lunch Fellowship." Each month, hundreds of older adults are involved in a covered-dish luncheon. They enjoy a good meal, a time of fun in celebrating birthdays with cakes and kisses, singing, special music, guest speakers giving brief devotionals. An activity like that not only meets social needs, but ministers to a variety of other needs. Loneliness is put aside for a few short hours; a warm meal fills an empty stomach; and someone has remembered their birthday! All of those things taken for granted by many of us are special social events for older adults.

Day trips are another popular social activity for this age group. Church buses could be filled with people and driven to parks, shopping malls, historic sites, and many other local attractions. It should be noted that those activities are not intended simply to occupy time. Many of these adults have significant contributions to make to the ministry of the local church.

In planning events for members of this age group, one needs to be sensitive to their financial plight. Churches need to think carefully as to how to help them afford some of their social activities. A scholarship program, similar to the one suggested earlier for young people may be one answer.

The Benefits of a Local Church Social Ministry

In deciding whether or not the local church should minister to the social needs of adults, there can be only one answer—Yes! Man is a social being and needs to have desires for fellowship and fun met in one form or another. We have already seen the importance of centering our leisure time on activities that are pleasing to God. The church has much to benefit from incorporating a recreational ministry within its program.

There are three benefits to examine, aside from the fun, that result from building a social schedule into your church calendar: socials will strengthen the teaching of the church, the outreach from the church, and the ministry within the church.

We have already seen in the life of Jesus that ministry to the social needs of adults enhances the teaching ministry to adults. Teachers are models. Larry Richards in *A Theology of Christian Education* lists seven keys to modeling. They are as follows:

1. There needs to be frequent, long-term contact with the model(s).
2. There needs to be a warm, long relationship with the model(s).
3. There needs to be exposure to the inner states of the model(s).
4. The model(s) needs to be observed in a variety of life settings and situations.
5. The model(s) needs to exhibit consistency and clarity in behaviors, values, etc.
6. There needs to be a correspondence between the behavior of the model(s) and the beliefs . . . of the community.
7. There needs to be explanation of life style of the model(s) conceptually, with instruction accompanying shared experiences.

These factors help us see that institution and modeling are not contradictory or mutually exclusive . . . . For God's Word to catch at our hearts and be most effectively applied for transformation, we also need an intimate relationship with the teacher.[8]

All those keys refer to the need for relationships between teachers and students apart from the classroom. The socialization theory of Richards suggests that more meaningful learning takes place outside the classroom than inside the classroom. It occurs in the everyday settings of life. Socialization can take place within a classroom setting if the teacher works at building meaningful relationships with his/her learners. Strong personal relationships strengthen the teaching/learning process.

Often, when teachers and preachers are seen in an informal setting they seem more like real people. Members of the class or church feel more at ease in a relaxed environment. Teachers may build strong personal relationships with their students during a social activity. Those relationships become a solid foundation upon which to build biblical content and application. Alert teachers will discover the needs that exist within the lives of their students. Addressing real needs becomes the key that opens learners to the power of the Word of God. The relationships built between students and teachers outside the classroom are also valuable inside the classroom. It is upon those friendships that free-

8. Lawrence O. Richards, *A Theology of Christian Education* (Grand Rapids: Zondervan, 1975), pp. 84–85.

flowing discussions and questions are launched. Social events can prove to be another vital instrument in the teacher's tool box.

According to the Great Commission, discipleship and evangelism are the two primary functions of the church. We have already seen how social activities can aid in the discipleship, or teaching, area of ministry. Let us now see how socials can assist the church in outreach.

Needless to say, a well-planned social will have the potential of attracting non-Christians. That is especially true in a situation where a number of husbands or wives may not know the Lord. Unbelievers are more apt to come to an informal gathering than they are an actual class or worship service. Socials offer an ideal introduction to the group. They can sense genuine warmth and friendship in a natural and nonthreatening environment.

Housewives can gather for exercise classes. Young adults might enjoy an evening of vigorous games. Senior citizens could organize a shuffleboard or checkers tournament. Sports and recreation activities are a natural for building the friendships that lead to evangelism contacts. All of those activities could easily be done in an average church. A large room or fellowship hall is all that is needed for the exercise class. A rectangle painted on the parking lot and some inexpensive volleyball equipment is all the young adults will need. Shuffleboard courts could be painted on a tile floor indoors, or on a smooth sidewalk or parking area.

Meeting the social needs of all adults can be a fun and profitable ministry. Many of the activities suggested in this chapter have been geared to specific age groupings. But there are certain activities that have universal appeal in meeting the social needs of adults. Some of these activities would include: seasonal celebrations or parties, fellowship hours, banquets, receptions, coffees, picnics, musicals, film or dramatic productions, and game nights.

Mancil Ezell states,

> Social recreation can greatly enrich the Christian life . . . No church need ever apologize for alloting a portion of its annual budget for social recreation. On the contrary, when a church does budget funds for social recreation, it shows concern and wisdom. Whether social recreation takes the form of all fellowships, parties, games, or banquets, it is a necessary ingredient in the abundant life for the growing Christian.[9]

9. Mancil Ezell, "Social Recreation: The Planning and the Promotion," in Smith, *Social Recreation and the Church*, p. 18.

We must realize that in ministering to the social needs of adults we are helping to minister to the whole person. That is because each individual is a physical, spiritual, emotional, and social being. In order to be effective in ministering to one area of a person's life, we must work with the total individual.

1. Develop a one-year social calendar for each of the four adult groups discussed in this chapter. Be sensitive to the specified needs mentioned and any seasonal or church-wide activities that may be involved in the planning process (e.g., missionary conferences, annual conferences, etc.) Be sure to include:

a. Two or three socials that would attract nonchurch members, or outreach-oriented activities.

b. Three or four (one per quarter) activities that could be used to strengthen the bonds of friendship between Sunday school teachers and learners.

c. An activity that would help singles meet other Christian singles.

d. Several family-centered activities.

e. Mixer socials for young couples—a block party, for example.

2. Brainstorm ways of adding social activities to the church calendar without increasing the number of evenings away from home. Ask questions like:

a. How can we add a social element to our adult Sunday school class?

b. What social activities could we incorporate into one regular Sunday morning or evening program? Be creative!

3. Brainstorm ways of training parents to plan social activities for their families. Remember the Christmas ornament idea? You may want to consult the following publications for help.

Dad's Only newsletter, P.O. Box 340, Julian, Calif. 92036.
Family Ministry by Charles M. Sell (see bibliography).
Family Life Today magazine, monthly publication of Gospel Light, Ventura, Calif. 93006
The Christian Family Growing Together, published quarterly by David C. Cook Publishing Co., 850 N. Grove Ave., Elgin, Ill. 60120.

4. Read chapter 3 of Frank Hart Smith's book as listed in footnotes and outline the process of planning and promoting social events.

5. Research the various feasts and celebrations of the Israelites. How was their social activity related to their spiritual growth and development?

PART FOUR

FAMILY MINISTRY

William L. O'Byrne

15

A Biblical Understanding of Marriage

What does the Bible teach regarding marriage? As evangelical Christians, we ask that question assuming that the notions conveyed by the biblical writers are, in fact, true. Francis Schaeffer calls them "true truths."[1] What the Bible informs us to be the nature of God, or of man, is truly what God or man is like.

As the Bible itself often testifies, its depiction of God is not exhaustive; for how could the infinity of God be thoroughly revealed in finite words conveyed to finite creatures? Yet, the Bible's revelation of God and His ways to humanity, though not exhaustive, is thoroughly adequate. Evangelicals emphasize the full adequacy of the Bible to communicate to mankind the ways of God, so that we may be informed, inspired, and inclined to trust God and follow Him in loving obedience, thus understanding His purposes in creation and achieving the blessings reserved for those who follow the "owner's manual"—the Bible.[2] "All Scripture is God-breathed and is useful for teaching, rebuking, correcting and training in righteousness, so that the man of God may be thoroughly equipped for every good work" (2 Tim. 3:16, NIV). God influenced the

1. Francis A. Schaeffer, *The God Who Is There* (Downers Grove, Ill.: Inter-Varsity, 1968), p. 151.
2. For a most thorough treatment of divine revelation by a contemporary evangelical, see Carl F. H. Henry, *God, Revelation, and Authority*, vols. 1 and 2 (Waco, Tex.: Word, 1976).

WILLIAM L. O'BYRNE is associate professor of Christian education at Houghton College, Houghton, New York.

recording of the revelations and events of His relationship with mankind so that what was recorded was historically and spiritually accurate, adequate for mankind's needs. Thus, evangelicals choose to call the Bible by the term that best conveys the qualities of truthfulness, authority, and divine control: The Word of God.[3]

In examining marriage and family in the Bible, we shall discover numerous assumptions, practices, and customs. The concept of Levirate marriage, for example, may be traced throughout the pages of the Bible from the first reference in Genesis (38:8) to the Sadducees' questioning of Jesus in Matthew (22:23–30). However, we are not concerned here with a sociological, psychological, or even historical examination of marriage or family, but rather a theological one. Precisely what are God's intentions or purposes for marriage and family, irrespective of social, political, and geographical factors?

This treatment will be essential, not exhaustive, and thus an *introduction* to a theology of marriage and family. The basic questions include: What are God's purposes for marriage? Does Scripture give a control or model within which marriage and family may be understood and evaluated? Finally, is there a continuity for marriage and family from the Old Testament through the New?

GOD'S PURPOSES FOR HIS CREATURES IN MARRIAGE

ACT ONE: CREATION

The grand epic style of early Genesis demands that our treatment of creation be graphic and dramatic. We are not approaching mere history, but colossal events. God is speaking! God is acting! Therefore, it is fitting to envision creation as a drama. Act 1 is a review of creation in seven scenes, or days. God is center stage bringing order out of chaos, separating light from dark and waters from clouds, arranging the face of planet earth. By His command life begins on the land and in the waters. Soon creatures of every sort swim and creep, fly and run. Then, with a deliberation drawing special attention, God speaks: "Let Us make man in Our image." Man and woman are created. So ends Act 1.

ACT TWO: LIFE IN EDEN

Between curtains, God removes Himself to the wings, so that as the drama continues, those created in His image are central. The act 2

3. Ibid., 2:13.

curtain rises. There, center stage, stand Adam and Eve, or "Man" and "Out of Man." Unique to all the other creatures of Eden, they have required the Creator's special attention. First, they were created through the conspiring of the Godhead: "Let *us* make man . . ." They reflect the diversity yet unity of their Creator: Father, Son, and Holy Spirit. Next, created in God's image, they are rational, moral, emotional, and personal beings conscious of their selfhood, conscious of their relationships with one another and with their Creator. They are communicators who by a faculty unique among the creatures are able to form words in their minds before speaking and through language to share thoughts with one another. They can reflect on the beauty of a sunset or the appeal of a fruit, qualify a creature with a name, and even contemplate their own limitations. Their minds can "see" what their eyes do not see, "hear" what they do not hear, and "speak" what they do not speak. Further, they share a prerogative on which the others could not even act, for they could not even think it, the ability to say No to their Creator. They are choosers, deciders from the very start, so very much like their Creator. Further, they are capable of giving and receiving that which the other creatures cannot: love. Brute instinct drives the lioness to suckle and defend her cubs, but those on center stage may choose to elevate another's needs above their own.

But they are not finished yet; they have a mission, namely, to manage God's garden in His stead. Theirs is the stewardship of planet Earth. And from the wings, their Benefactor promises blessing. They are recipients of that prototype benediction uttered by the First Celebrant: "And God saw all that He had made, and behold, it was very good." So there we find Adam and Eve without need of costume, initiating the drama of humanity guided by a simple script. Little could they imagine what would follow all too quickly.

At the very outset, then, it is apparent that those two were created to be mutual helpmates—to complement one another, to share life, to share God's fellowship, to engage in the proliferation of human life on earth.

ACT THREE: THE ENEMY

To grasp fully the script of Genesis 3, it is necessary to examine a scenario not revealed in Genesis, nor the rest of the Pentateuch, but in the prophets Isaiah and Ezekiel. How did such a malevolent creature as the serpent ever slither his way into the script?

How you have fallen from heaven,
O star of the morning, son of the dawn!
You have been cut down to the earth,
You who have weakened the nations!
But you said in your heart, "I will ascend to heaven;
I will raise my throne above the stars of God,
I will sit on the mount of assembly
In the recesses of the north.
I will ascend above the heights of the clouds;
I will make myself like the Most High."
Nevertheless you will be thrust down to Sheol,
To the recesses of the pit.

(Isaiah 14:12-17)

This passage alludes to Lucifer, Son of the Morning! Thus, Isaiah opens the curtain on a spiritual drama that must have occurred prior to Genesis 3.

The fallen angel Satan has engaged Almighty God in a battle of cosmic dimensions. Revelation 12 informs us that fully a third of the "stars of heaven," or angels, were party to Satan's insurrection. Michael and his angels will fight against and prevail over the dragon and his angels and thus the cosmic spiritual war will eventually come to an end. However, until that final scene, the enemy will spare no effort to tempt even those creatures made in God's image to join his rebellion. In fact, Satan will consider the enrollment of mankind on his side the greatest victory against the Godhead. If he can inveigle man's mind, heart, and will to reject God's script and accept his revision, he will achieve temporary victory: creatures created in God's image will repudiate their Designer and choose the ways of God's archenemy. What a victory! The stage, the actors, the script—all controlled by him.

The marriage relationship is the focal point of the enemy's attack against God. Adam and Eve, husband and wife, are tempted and together fall. Every creature created in God's image had rejected their designer! The serpent was completely effective. Though rarely mentioned, is it not significant that the marriage relationship of so many of the patriarchs and Old Testament leaders was the source of severed relationships and of spiritual failure? Abraham's deceit concerning Sarai, his breaking of the "one flesh" relationship with her to rush God's will for his progeny; the lack of unity in Isaac and Rebecca's relationship, which allowed favoritism to blossom into deceit and robbery; Jacob, whose lessons in favoritism pitted brother against brother with the result that a family was divided; David's lust, which ultimately led to adultery and murder and the withholding of God's favor resulting in his inability to construct God's house; Solomon's eventual fall because he adopted pagan marital practices; the errant sons of priest Eli and prophet Samuel; all show how the marriage relationship can be Satan's point of entry.

ACT FOUR: GOD'S COUNTERATTACK

The entire scenario of the Bible may be conceived as the struggle of Satan to repudiate God and to enlist God's creatures into his rebellion. God, however, chooses lovingly to influence His creatures to opt for His ways and defeat the enemy. In fact, God's curse of Satan turns out to be His second blessing of mankind:

> And I will put enmity
> Between you and the woman,
> And between your seed and her seed;
> He shall bruise you on the head,
> And you shall bruise him on the heel.
> (Genesis 3:15)

The antagonism between God and Satan now enlarges to encompass all of God's creatures. "The creation itself also will be set free from its slavery to corruption" (Rom. 8:21). All mankind, the progeny of the woman, will exist in tension with Satan's forces ("seed") until one of the woman's offspring strikes the death blow to the serpent, though not without severe wound to Himself. Thus the *proto euangelium,* the first heralding of the gospel, announces the climax of the battle and God's glorious victory through the Seed, the Man, Jesus Christ.

MARRIAGE'S PURPOSES: MIRRORING, MULTIPLYING, AND MANAGING

MIRRORING THE IMAGE OF GOD

What then are God's basic purposes for mankind in the marriage relationship? First, man and woman in the complementary relationship of marriage are reflectors of the image of God. Neither a man nor a woman by themselves adequately communicates God's nature. God is Creator. We are creators. God, in the diversity of the Trinity, conspired to create man in His image. A husband and a wife conspire in the marital relationship to create children. They enter into a communion of love, of giving and receiving. They mirror the unity yet diversity of their Creator.

Although any human bears the image of God, it is apparent that maleness alone, or femaleness alone, cannot adequately display that image. Humanity is not complete without both sexes: "Male and female He created them" (Gen. 1:28). Further, they were created to become a union (Gen. 2:24). The diversity as well as the unity of the godhead is symbolized in the husband-wife relationship. Harmony is achieved musically by the sounding of two or more tones at one time; a husband and wife living and loving in godly harmony more perfectly mirror the unity in diversity of the godhead than either one singularly.

It is noteworthy that the ancient Chinese notion of the *tao* hints at a similar conclusion. The *tao* includes the law of the bipolarity of nature: *yang* and *yin*, "light and darkness, heat and cold, male and female.[4] Pantheists that they were, for Taoists God was identical with nature, and though nature—and thus God—was impersonal, it was clear that both male and female were essential elements in godness. It appears that God's light in general revelation permeated some of the darkness of man's rational processes among the Chinese, contemporaries of David— about 1000 B.C.

Carl F. H. Henry refers to the theological significance of marriage, but does not expand on the subject when he states: "In recent years more emphasis has been placed on physical aspects (of the divine image) as well (e.g., sexual differentiation in unity as symbolic of a dynamic love relationship; and surrogate-rule over nature)."[5] Clearly, a theology of marriage is needed to delve into those implications. As Henry intimates, the very existence of the Godhead as a *relationship* speaks loudly to the significance of the husband-wife relationship as a symbol of the nature of God. It likewise speaks contrary to the current unisex vogue, which blurs not only the biological dimensions of sexuality, but the whole range of historical meanings as well.

MULTIPLYING GODLIKENESS THROUGH FAMILY

The husband-wife relationship is designed to multiply a specific quality—godlikeness. To be sure, the image of God is severely marred by sin. On this side of Eden parents must both model and guide their offspring in righteousness so that they will most fully mirror their Creator and help defeat the enemy. Israel was commanded thus to perpetuate righteousness in what has become known as the *Shemá*.

4. Laurence G. Thompson, "Chinese Religion," in Frederick J. Streng, Charles L. Lloyd, Jr., and Jay T. Allen, eds., *Ways of Being Religious* (Englewood Cliffs, N.J.: Prentice-Hall, 1973), p. 204.
5. Henry, 2:124.

> Hear, O Israel! The Lord is our God, the Lord is one! And you shall love the Lord your God with all your heart and with all your soul and with all your might. And these words, which I am commanding you today, shall be on your heart; and you shall teach them diligently to your sons and shall talk of them when you sit in your house and when you walk by the way and when you rise up. And you shall bind them as a sign on your hand and they shall be as frontals on your forehead. And you shall write them on the doorposts of your house and on your gates. (Deut. 6:4–9)

This ancient prescription for parents contains five elements.

1. There is a call to the entire nation, to every parent (implicitly, every Israelite would become a parent), to perpetuate godliness.

2. The foundation of Israel's religion was an intense affection for the Lord. While the Hebrew *aheb* (affection, love, like) is a general term, the subsequent modifiers serve to raise the quality of that love to an intensity that is supreme; all of one's heart, soul, and strength is to be focused on commitment to the Lord.

3. Beginning with such an all-encompassing love for God, it follows that His laws would be "on your heart." Those laws, then, are not mere external religious observations, or even important moral prescriptions. Rather, their observation is a tangible means of expressing devotion to God: Because He is so loved, His intentions become the organizing hub of our lives.

4. It logically follows that if one's love for God is so inclusive, and obedience to His commands is a demonstration of the quality of one's love, then as givers of life to children, parents will leave no stone unturned in endeavoring to transfer their love for God to those growing God-imagers. To "teach" or "impress" (NIV) those noble laws of our glorious God upon our children is the only path to follow.

5. The method of such teaching will therefore have to match the importance of God's laws. If a curriculum is relatively unimportant, its method of instruction may be more casual, sporadic, even occasional. But if that curriculum is the summum bonum, the highest good, then the instructional method must be intense, persistent, intimate, and pervasive, applying to every nook and cranny of life.

Such is the tone of the *Shemá*. Conversation is the primary technique; everyday experiences are the classroom: while sitting at home, walking down the road, preparing for sleep, and upon awaking. Virtually every occasion of life becomes the classroom of the Lord. Why? Because the Lord has blessing in His heart for His people. His law is the tangible means of His people living at peace with one another—righteousness simply means 'right living.' So, on the horizontal level of human relations, God's law is the vehicle for harmony, success, and prosperity (Josh. 1:8-9). Vertically, it is a means of "reality testing"—it demonstrates a follower's love for and faith in his God.

The method has two other techniques: (1) tied to forehead and wrists, God's law is ever present, modifying every gaze, tempering every deed, and (2) posted on gates and door jambs, it identifies the occupants of that home (to others and to themselves) as lovers of God through devotion to His gracious commands.

The tragic subsequent history of Israel reveals gross inconsistency in the application of the *Shemá.*

> There arose another generation after them who did not know the Lord, nor yet the work which He had done for Israel. Then the sons of Israel did evil in the sight of the Lord, and served the Baals, and they forsook the Lord, the God of their fathers, who had brought them out of the land of Egypt (Judg. 2:10-12).

How could such a travesty occur? One obvious answer is that parents did not love the Lord their God, nor revere His commands, and thus did not transfer a love of God and His Word to their children. They utterly failed to mandate or model the multiplying of godliness to their descendants.

MANAGING GOD'S CREATION

A third responsibility for mankind is the management of God's creation. As God's surrogates, Adam and Eve were given a measure of authority over the other creatures and the natural resources of vegetation, land, and waters. David, the psalmist, echoes God's ancient mandate given in Genesis:

> What is man that you are mindful of him,
>   the son of man that you care for him?
> You made him a little lower than the heavenly beings
>   and crowned him with glory and honor.
> You made him ruler over the works of your hands;
>   you put everything under his feet.
>   (Psalm 8:4-6, NIV)

Further, in the instructions for parents to lead their children in the observation of God's law, that authority extends even to society. God instructs the children of Israel to regulate society through the family structure: children, parents, clan, tribe. God warned Israel that adoption of the governing model in the surrounding nations, namely, elevation of a man to the position of king, would have dire results. Central government would mean taxation and conscription, the two woes of free peoples even to the present.

Such a ruling mandate was not merely sociological, nor even political, but moral. By living according to God's laws and teaching children to do the same, each family, clan, and tribe would maintain a dynamic social and spiritual order. Good human and spiritual relations would ensure peace and prosperity, not to mention the protection of God from all manner of temporal and spiritual calamity, including control of disease, epidemic, and crop destruction (Deut. 7:12–16).

THE CONTROLLING MODEL: COVENANT

Central to Israel's relationship with the LORD was the concept of covenant. Though not explicitly labeled "covenant" in the early Genesis chapters, it first appears in God's interaction with Noah regarding the building of the ark and the ensuring of safety to him and his family. The tenor and implications of covenant permeate Genesis chapters 1, 2, and 3. In Genesis 1, God gives man the responsibility of reproduction and dominion over creation, with His assured blessing. The covenant elements in the second chapter include man's placement in the garden, his responsibility for naming the creatures and caring for the garden, the provision of a "suitable helper," and the proscription not to eat of the tree in the center of the garden. God's response, implicit throughout the text, was to be one of continued communion with Adam and Eve and one that provided for their needs.

The reason for marriage is clearly covenantal: "for this cause a man shall leave his father and his mother, and shall cleave to his wife; and they shall become one flesh" (Gen. 2:24). Throughout its history, Genesis enunciates the norm of children arriving at maturity (being independent enough to leave home), establishing an integral relationship with their spouses, and developing relationships characterized by unity.

Genesis 3 introduces the covenant breaker. The serpent attempts, and succeeds, in causing Adam and Eve to break covenant with God. In response, God allows the covenant breakers to live, but with three modifications: (1) their lives will be short-lived—death will eventually overtake both; (2) the environment will resist their attempts at control, making the job much harder; and (3) a negative spiritual influence will overshadow their lives—Satan will incessantly attempt to detour them from peace and a proper relationship with God. Certainly, those new elements in the revised covenant would jeopardize the earlier one: leaving parents will ever be problematic and the permanence of the marriage relationship will continually be threatened by egocentrism. The original formula for marital unity will be forever qualified.

From a legal perspective, a covenant is much like a contract. It is a legal bond in which each party is obligated to certain claims of the other. Elements of a covenant include: (1) agreement between two or more persons; (2) conditions—that is, how each party is intended to perform; (3) the expected results for each party; and (4) the security that comes from an assurance.[6] The whole life of Israel must primarily be comprehended through covenant; covenant is Israel's axis and source of equilibrium, its gyroscope.

God initiated the covenant for His creatures' benefit. Mankind receives blessing from God as a result of compliance with the terms of covenant. God's intention is mankind's good. Certainly, a creator has a claim on that which he creates; an inventor has the right to receive value from what he has invented. God holds the patent on mankind. He has a claim on His creation. Covenant is God's means of exercising claim on His creatures, especially those creatures created in His image. God knows how His "imagers" function best and how they will receive optimal blessing. Covenant is God's way of communicating His responsibility and concern for His creatures.

Covenant may be conceived as follows (see figure on p. 222): (1) Out of His grace God initiates a relationship with Israel, promising to bless, if (2) Israel will obey His guidelines affecting all areas of life. This reciprocating verticle line of God's blessing and man's obedience becomes the axis around which the entire nation revolves. (3) God's input does not fail because of who He is, Almighty God. Man's response is the qualifier. As long as loving obedience is man's response, God will respond with spiritual, moral, social, and material health and prosperity for every person, couple, clan, tribe, and the entire nation. The covenant apparatus may be likened to a child's toy, a top with a spiral shaft proceeding vertically from its center, topped by a knob or handle. By pushing down on the handle the spiraled rod extending down into the center of the top's mechanism causes the top to revolve. The handle is then lifted so that the next downward power stroke may be applied. The reciprocal action of thrusting downward then lifting for the next thrust causes the top to spin on its axis. The axis and the verticle rod are identical. So it is with God and Israel. God's downward power animated Israel and will continue, conditioned only by Israel's upward response of loving obedience. Obedience brings blessing and protection. Conversely,

6. *Wycliffe Bible Encyclopedia*, s.v. "Covenant."

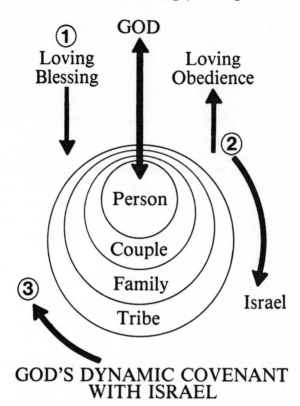

GOD'S DYNAMIC COVENANT
WITH ISRAEL

results in withheld blessing, and thus vulnerability to the Enemy's onslaught.

Marriage and family are central to Israel's covenant relationship with God, as previously demonstrated. Old Testament writers, kings, prophets, and scribes all conceived of marriage in terms of covenant.

> [Wisdom] will save you from the adulteress,
>   from the wayward wife with her seductive words,
> Who has left the partner of her youth
>   and ignored the covenant she made before God
> [*or:* the covenant of her God, NASB]
>   (Proverbs 2:17, NIV)

Both readings convey the covenantal relationship of marriage, whether it be a marriage covenant made with her husband, or having been married under covenant in its broad sense applying to all Israelites. Hosea's marriage to an adulterous wife (Hos. 1:2) depicting God's love and mercy toward "adulterous" Israel demonstrates God's persistent love even through broken covenant. God says, "For I delight in loyalty rather than sacrifice, and in the knowledge of God rather than burnt offerings. But like Adam they have transgressed the covenant; there they have dealt treacherously against Me"[7] (Hosea 6:6-7). There we see an intertwining of the concepts of marriage and covenant; marriage is *a* covenant within *the* Covenant of God with Israel.

Most striking is the interplay of covenant and marriage in the prophet Malachi. Describing Judah's unfaithfulness to the Lord, the prophet points out that Judah broke the covenant "by marrying the daughter of a foreign god" (intermarrying with pagan women), and by breaking faith with the "wife of your youth . . . though she is your partner, the wife of your *marriage covenant*" (Malachi 2:11, 14). There we see a direct biblical linking of the two terms, specifying marriage as covenant. The prophet continues:

> Has not the Lord made them one? In flesh and spirit they are his. And why one? Because he was seeking godly offspring. So guard yourself in your spirit, and do not break faith with the wife of your youth. "I hate divorce," says the Lord God of Israel. (Mal. 2:15-16, NIV)

The implications of these statements include, first, a reiteration of the "one flesh" concept of the ancient Pentateuch. A husband and wife are not two separate beings affiliated merely through a relationship maintained if mutually agreeable. They constitute an integral, unique entity brought into existence *by the Lord*. As children of Israel's covenant with the Lord, their marriage is itself an expression of covenant—initiated by God, witnessed by families, and contracted together. Second, the prophet rhetorically seeks the rationale for such oneness—why is it necessary? The answer is that in order for their offspring to be godly, they must have both parents declaring and living a joint expression of faith in the Lord. Godly offspring are trained by *both* parents, who model and instruct godliness through their respective personalities, relationships, responsibilities, and roles, as well as through informal and formal spiritual activities. Third, Malachi identifies the locus of man's decisions: his spirit. His injunction urges a man to protect that "control center" so that moral attacks will not cause him to sever his unity with his wife.

---

7. Although the first three chapters of Genesis do not include the word *covenant* (Hebrew, *berith*), it is noteworthy that by Hosea's time it was clearly established that Adam's relationship with God was within "covenant." By New Testament times, Paul instructed that the Old Covenant was initiated by Adam and the New Covenant by Christ (Rom. 5:12-21).

The prophet records the Lord's response to divorce as "hate." The Covenant Lord God of Israel categorically repudiates marital infidelity, which jeopardizes the unity requisite to raising a new, godly generation.

SUMMARY OF OLD TESTAMENT TEACHING

The Old Testament presents a clear picture of the source, purposes, and implications, of the man-woman relationship. For the patriarchal period, as for Israel under the law of God, and extending even through the last words of the prophets, the marriage relationship in and as covenant formed the hub and source of human and spiritual blessing for God's people. God's blessings on all mankind would result from the descendants of Abraham; children born of the union of Abraham and Sarai and nurtured in their home would be the means of God's blessing reaching worldwide. The ancient *Shemá* of the law was to be the model for the eons of Israel's history. Through children taught diligently in the ways of God, righteousness would flourish in every family, clan, and tribe; righteousness would infuse Israel and spread to the Gentiles. The family would be the vessel from which godliness would be poured into children's lives, and they in turn would bring blessing to mankind.

THE SAYINGS OF JESUS

Some have argued that the Old Covenant and New Covenant are radically different and even opposed to one another. But it is evident that Jesus' message and ministry maintained the primary message of the Old Covenant, that God is seeking a people who will enthusiastically enter into contract with Him: "Love the Lord your God with all your heart, and with all your soul, and with all your strength, and with all your mind; and your neighbor as yourself" (Luke 10:27). Further, Jesus purposely clarified His intent not to abolish the covenant, but to "fulfill" it (Matt. 5:17).

Jesus' fulfillment of covenant drove right to the heart of the matter, dealing not with mere external observation of regulations, but with the quality of the person who loves God and treats his fellow men and women accordingly. Whereas ancient and then modern practices put the onus for adultery on the tempting woman, Jesus shifted the emphasis to the instigator:

> You have heard that it was said, "You shall not commit adultery"; But I say to you, that everyone who looks on a woman to lust for her has committed adultery with her already in his heart . . . Everyone who divorces his wife,

except for the cause of unchastity, makes her commit adultery; and whoever
marries a divorced woman commits adultery. (Matt. 5:27-28, 32)

The force of Jesus intensification is to support the law fully by pointing
to its touchstone, man's heart. Jesus clearly speaks the language of both
Jeremiah and Malachi regarding marriage. The issue is internal, not
external: "Rend your heart and not your garments" (Joel 2:13).

In his response to the testing of the Pharisees regarding divorce, Jesus
bases His argument on the primordial Genesis prescription, and echoes
Malachi: "They are no longer two, but one flesh. What therefore God
has joined together, let no man separate" (Matt. 19:6). The marriage
covenant produces a new entity in God's eyes; it is instigated by God
and is thus inviolable by man. Divorce is a work of the Enemy.

Clearly, then, Jesus intensifies the covenant, maintaining the Old
Testament theology of marriage while prophetically calling Israel to
return to a heart relationship with God, and with one's spouse, in love
and fidelity.

FIRST CORINTHIANS 7

Although some critics characterize Paul as "male chauvinist," stern
and inflexible, it is noteworthy that of all the biblical writings reflecting
on marriage he is the major biblical apologist for a warm, loving relationship between husbands and wives. The apostle Peter strikes the same
tonality, though briefly, in his first letter (3:1-7). To grasp Paul's theology
of marriage, one must grapple with two passages: 1 Corinthians 6 and
7, and Ephesians 5:21—6:9.

In all exegesis the question of applicability is crucial. Is a certain
teaching, instruction, or message intended to be a universal truth, normative for all Christians everywhere, or a particular truth, applicable
only to those to whom it was written? Tempering Paul's discourse in
1 Corinthians 6-7 is his own qualifier: "In view of the present
distress . . . " (7:26). Another modifying clause appears in various forms
six times in 7:17-24: "in which he was called." With that expression,
Paul asserts the rule of continuity of situation for those who are Christ's.
What is a person's state when he becomes a Christian? He "should
remain with God in that condition in which he was called." Whether
circumcised or uncircumcised, slave or freeman, virgin or married, stay
that way! Again tempering his instruction are statements such as "the
time has been shortened," "for the form of this world is passing away,"
and "I want you to be free from concern." Given the hostility of the
pagan world to Christianity, plus Paul's persuasion concerning Christ's

imminent return, he sets down practical principles for Christians: it is better not to marry both "for your own benefit" and to serve the Lord unhindered.

Yet, even in that situation, Paul is flexible. If one's constitution is strongly disposed to marriage, possibly for those who are already "engaged" and eagerly anticipating marriage, it is better, says Paul, to get married than to be sexually frustrated. His general counsel is to reject marriage, but his particular counsel depends on the emotional and spiritual constitutions of the persons in question. The principle of individual differences applies: If you do marry, "you have not sinned." Thus, Paul gives practical and general counsel, modified to make allowances for individual differences. Clearly, he is not proscribing marriage or giving out arbitrary restrictions. Some persons may have the "gift" of celibacy; others not.

The following are Paul's universal injunctions concerning marriage:

Paul stresses monogamy. Clearly, Paul operates within the ancient prescription of Genesis 2:24, reinforced by the prophets and Jesus. Other pauline passages support monogamy, for example, the requirement for an elder or deacon to be "the husband of one wife" (1 Tim. 3:2, 12; Titus 1:6).

Paul considers the ongoing meeting of one another's sexual needs as normative for Christians: "Stop depriving one another" (7:5). The use of the word "duty" (7:3) is perfectly consistent with the definition of *agape* love. Each spouse has the duty from God to meet the other's needs. That duty is founded on the principle of mutual authority. In marriage, Paul teaches, each spouse has authority over the other's body (7:4). The exercising of such authority is predicated on the spiritual nature of marriage and on affection and sensitivity, not on the right of demand.

Interruption of sexual relations between husband and wife must be based on mutual consent. For Paul, unilateral withholding of sexual love from one's marital partner is clearly wrong. Surely, in the everyday ups and downs of marital relations, partners will disagree, neglect responsibilities, react in haste and anger, and attempt to "get back" at one another. But for Paul, the withholding of sexual affection was unacceptable.

Healthy sexual relations are a deterrent to infidelity. Paul indicates that a reason for temporary cessation of sexual relations may be spiritual devotion. A couple may decide to "fast" sexually. The decision to do so must be unanimous. However, after the prearranged spiritual retreat, the couple must resume normal sexual relations, just as persons would resume their normal diets. Paul stipulates: "Come together again lest Satan tempt you because of your lack of self-control" (7:5). Paul knew human nature very well. The sexual desire is intense, and Satan's temptations work to abnormalize the normal.

The subsequent injunctions concern divorce, but also reveal Paul's view of marriage. First, Christian spouses must not divorce. That is a general principal addressed to both husbands and wives (7:10-12). If they break that command, they may not marry another, but should seek reconciliation. Second, believers who have unbelieving spouses must remain with them. Children of such a relationship are not to be considered "unclean" spiritually, because one of the parents is a Christian, or spiritually "clean." Precisely what Paul means by "unclean" is not clear, but it is clear that his emphasis is on the evangelization of the unbelieving spouse by the believer. But such is not an adequate argument for seeking to marry an unbeliever: "Do not be bound together with unbelievers; For what partnership have righteousness and lawlessness, or what fellowship has light with darkness?" (2 Cor. 6:14). Third, if the unbelieving spouse determines to separate himself by divorce, then divorce is permissible for the Christian: "The brother of the sister is not under bondage in such cases" (1 Cor. 7:15). "Is not under bondage" refers precisely to the marriage bond. The question of remarriage of the Christian so divorced by an unbeliever has been the subject of much discussion in recent Christian works.[8] Paul affords no help in solving the problem. Fourth, marriage is lifelong commitment for the Christian, terminated only by the death of a spouse, after which marriage to another Christian is possible (7:39).

Those, then, are the marriage regulations that Paul enunciates for the Christian church. He stipulates that some of the regulations come by revelation ("not I [commanding], but the Lord," whereas other regulations are equally authoritative for the Corinthian church, but do not represent revelation for all time ("I say, not the Lord"). At the close of the passage, Paul affirms that in giving his judgment regarding a woman remaining single after a Christian spouse's death, he does so with the Holy Spirit's approval. It is apparent that Paul affirms his written instructions to the church to be in perfect tune with God's will, because when they are, they will also harmonize with the best interests of our humanity—created by the Creator.

EPHESIANS 5:21—6:9

We turn now to the major Pauline passage on Christian marriage. Although much contemporary discussion centers on the sociological

8. See J. Carl Laney, *The Divorce Myth* (Minneapolis: Bethany, 1981), p. 160.

notion of "roles," it may be well to avoid jargon from the social sciences. Paul was not so much concerned with social roles as with spiritual attitudes resulting in a certain *quality* of behavior displayed by Christians, irrespective of their roles within a given social system. In order to appreciate his intent, we must discover the contextual soil in which the discussion grows.

THE CONTEXT

In both Ephesians and Colossians Paul deals with the three most common human relationships of the first century: husband-wife, parent-child, and master-slave (Eph. 5:21—6:9; Col. 3:18—4:1). The Colossians passage is a shortened version of the Ephesian treatments, so we will isolate the Ephesian passage. In typical Pauline fashion, the first half of Ephesians is theological and the second is practical. Paul's practical section begins with his prayer that the mutual love among the members of the church at Ephesus will increase: that they be "rooted and grounded," "comprehended," and "know" love that is beyond human ken (3:17-19). Somehow, that love is bound up in the mystery of the filling of God's creatures with Himself. Mystical? Yes. But also practical: lives authentically in tune with God will exude a practical concern for the needs of others.

That such love is not merely an emotional state is clear because Paul immediately delineates the *behavior* expected: humility, gentleness, patience, unity, and service (4:1-13). Practical stuff this Christian love of the brethren! Next, Paul moves into a discussion of the contrast in living between the darkness of the godless Gentiles and the light of those in Christ: "I say this therefore, and affirm together with the Lord, that you walk no longer just as the Gentiles also walk, in the futility of their mind" (4:17). In closing his section contrasting godly and ungodly living, he employs a bridge to the practical treatment concerning human relations. It is important to grasp the significance of the passage:

> Therefore be careful how you walk, not as unwise men, but as wise, making the most of your time, because the days are evil. So then do not be foolish, but understand what the will of the Lord is. And do not get drunk with wine, for that is dissipation, but be filled with the Spirit, speaking to one another in psalms and hymns and spiritual songs, singing and making melody with your heart to the Lord; always giving thanks for all things in the name of our Lord Jesus Christ to God, even the father; and be subject to one another in the fear of Christ. (5:15-21)

In this transition, Paul uses five Greek participles to describe the life of the wise believer filled with the Holy Spirit: speaking, singing, psalming, giving thanks, and submitting. Speaking to one another and submitting. Speaking to one another and submitting to one another are man-directed, whereas singing, psalming, and giving thanks are God-directed.

Paul clearly directs Christians to submit to one another. He is urging a spirit of deference growing out of believers' concern for their brothers in Christ. Believers are to be very important to one another as brothers and sisters. Although each member of the body has its function (gift), and although there is a ranking based on experience, reputation, and gifts within the church (elders, deacons, etc.), the attitudes that underly the actions of even the highest leaders must be Christlike. The Christian's goal should be the "fruit of the Spirit" (Gal. 5:22–23) and an "attitude . . . which was also in Christ Jesus" (Phil. 2:5).

Although the attitudes of believers are to be focused on doing that which is loving towards fellow believers and not lording it over them, there must still be the exercise of leadership, including assigning responsibilities, making decisions, and teaching novices. A teaching elder, for example, "submits" to a novice by treating him lovingly, yet spurring him on toward growth. Following Paul's example, an elder may correct doctrinal and practical errors and even rebuke where necessary. However, his focus must be on lovingly helping the novice on toward maturity. He may discipline a wayward member, but it must be accomplished with a humble spirit; "we are members of one another" (Eph. 4:25).

With the foregoing as context and foundation, Paul expands on the attitudes that Christians should possess and display in their various human relations: husband-wife, parent-child, and master-slave.

THE WIFE: SUBMISSIVE SUPPORTER

Though husbands and wives are equals in essence, created in the image of God, conspiring in the Fall yet one in Christ and in renewal in the Holy Spirit, Paul enunciates rankings for them that must prevail for the maintenance of both spiritual and social harmony. Certainly Paul could have chosen neutral language to convey the Christian wife's attitude if he intended mutual submission of husbands and wives. That he employed the term *hupostassō,* which connotes ranking in military language, is indicative of Paul's intent. The godly wife who appreciates the spiritual worth and calling of her husband under God's grace will respond to him appropriately. Paul's use of words and argumentive or rhetorical analogies makes his intention quite clear, as the following chart demonstrates.

Verse	Statement of Biblical Text	Rhetorical Function
22	"wives, be subject"	statement of thesis
22	"as to the Lord"	supportive analogy
23	"for the husband is the head of the wife"	primary support of thesis
23	"as also Christ is the head of the church"	supportive analogy
24	"as the church is subject to Christ"	supportive analogy
24	"so also the wives to their husbands"	statement of thesis
24	"in everything"	intensification

Several contemporary apologists for the "mutual submission" concept divert Paul's clear language and analogies so that modern meanings can be read into Paul's language,[9] but Paul's historically understood intent will remain. Contrary to some current presentations, Paul was not demanding a wife's stoic deference to a husband's godlessness nor her demure silence (eyes heavenward in a gesture of trust in God!) as her husband makes decisions detrimental to the moral or physical welfare of the family. Paul's instruction to wives was simply that they must acknowledge the essential leadership of their husbands, who are accountable to God for their wives and families.

A contemporary illustration may prove helpful. In military service the rank of the company commander or commanding officer (usually a captain) is one grade higher than the executive officer (usually a first lieutenant). Although the commanding officer (C.O.) possesses the highest rank, the executive officer performs tasks and exercises authority virtually as high as the C.O. They are in constant communication, the "exec" acting as the commander's council or advisor. To the troops, the variation in authority between the two officers is not too important. But the C.O. is accountable to the battalion commander for his company. Following Paul's use of *hupotassō,* the wife submits to her husband as the executive officer submits to the commanding officer—but with council and advisor responsibilities. The husband is accountable to God (analo-

9. For differing views on the subject of headship, see: Patricia Gundry, *Heirs Together* (Grand Rapids: Zondervan, 1980), p. 192, in which she states: "I do not see the New Testament usage of the word *head* awarding husbands authority or leadership positions over their wives as a God-given office men are to occupy in marriage" (p. 116). A similar view is presented in Peter DeJong and Donald R. Wilson, *Husband and Wife: The Sexes in Scripture and Society* (Grand Rapids: Zondervan, 1979). For a contrasting position see: James B. Hurley, *Man and Woman in Biblical Perspective* (Grand Rapids: Zondervan, 1981); and W. Peter Blitchington, *Sex Holes and the Christian Family* (Wheaton, Ill.: Tyndale House, 1980).

gous to the battalion commander) for those placed in his care and for their performance.

Urged by the issues of our contemporary world and personal lives, we could wish that the Holy Spirit would have nudged the apostle to be more explicit and to open up the subject with examples, illustrations, and detailed guidelines for applying the text to our milieu. Still, there is much we can deduce. There is no inference in Paul's writing here that a husband and wife do not have an intimate give-and-take relationship. Could the Paul of the New Testament fly in the teeth of the freedom and latitude of the "excellent wife" of Proverbs 31? Hardly. Would he demand the female to cower in the marriage relationship? Would Paul disavow a concerned wife's serious discussion with her husband over family and relational needs? Could he berate the evident gifts of Prisca (Aquilla's wife), or God's call of Deborah? Never.

From Paul's continual concern for the outward testimony of God's people (that they live as creatures of light rather than darkness) and from his concerns for orderliness in the worship of the Corinthian church, it may well be that Paul was concerned with the opposite problem. Consider the typical pagan wife of cosmopolitan Corinth, overly style-conscious, vying with men for wealth, power, and status, wheeling and dealing in the most profane manner, even swapping dirty stories with the men, and striving against her husband for rule of the domicile. Such must never be even remotely associated with a godly wife. Paul's urgings to the Roman church apply: "Do not be conformed to this world, but be transformed by the renewing of your mind . . . I say to every man among you not to think more highly of himself than he ought to think" (Rom. 12:2-3).

THE HUSBAND: LOVING LEADER

From Paul's injunctions to husbands, it is patently clear that wives are in no respect doormats or chattel slaves in cowering subjection to their husbands. It would be contradictory for a husband here described to expect his wife's lock-step subservience or groveling deference.

> Husbands, love your wives, just as Christ also loved the church and gave Himself up for her; that He might sanctify her, having cleaned her by the washing of water with the word, that He might present to Himself the church in all her glory, having no spot or wrinkle or any such thing; but that she should be holy and blameless. So husbands ought also to love their own wives as their own bodies. He who loves his own wife loves himself. (Eph. 5:25-28)

A thorough exegesis of this passage is not appropriate in this brief overview, but several obvious factors must be cited. The example or model for the Christian husband is the Lord Jesus Christ. The following chart simplifies the explanation:

Verse	Christ's Action/Attitude Toward Church	Purpose
25	love and self-giving	to make her holy
26	cleansing by washing with the word	to present her to Himself: radiant, without stain, holy and blameless
29	feeds and cares for	edification

Each of Christ's actions on behalf of the church result in the betterment of the church: the church is loved, cared for, cleansed, and fed. The Christian husband is to focus on the needs of his wife, unselfishly. The expression "gave Himself up for her," hearkens back to Christ's teaching that love involves the elevation of other's needs to a position equal to or higher than one's own, and that ultimately the greatest love is to lay down one' life for another. A husband who has such high regard for his spouse cannot abuse or take advantage of her. The outcome of such Christlike husbandly treatment is a wife who knows she is wanted and cared for, who is fostered, encouraged, and built up—a person who knows she possesses eminent worth in the eyes of her spouse.

Significantly, the godly husband's attitudes and actions towards his wife's edification are not uni-directional. Paul informs the Ephesian church that the actions of the loving husband are *reflexive*, they bounce back. Christ's efforts on behalf of the church, while nourishing and perfecting it, are also to His own advantage. As the church is cleansed and accomplishes great things for her Master, the Master is blessed. Similarly, a Christian husband whose objective is the enriching of his life partner, cannot help but benefit from a happy, loved wife who is the object of her husband's sincere affection.

All efforts to squeeze Paul's teachings into this or that contemporary social mold, or to strain at socially acceptable role models for men and women in any given society, pale into insignificance in the brilliant light of the Christ-love that radiates from a husband and wife who live in the Spirit. This, then, is Paul's Spirit-directed model for a husband-wife relationship that is mutually edifying and glorifying to God. It leaves plenty of elbow room for differing gifts, and abilities, as long as *agape* love is the holy oil both lubricating and illuminating the relationship.

Without hesitation, Jesus and the apostles maintained the Old Testament's high covenantal view of marriage as an institution and relationship established by God and dissoluble only by Him. Though Jesus emphasized the kingdom of God as the archetypical model of God's developing and ultimate relationship with man, its worthy concommitant figure was the household of God emphasized by the apostles. In fact, the marriage analogy is so persistent and appropriate that John's apocalypic vision of the victory of Christ is anticipated through the imagery of a wedding ceremony and banquet.

> Hallelujah!
> For our Lord God Almighty reigns.
> Let us rejoice and be glad
> and give him glory!
> For the wedding of the Lamb has come,
> and his bride has made herself ready.
> Fine linen, bright and clean,
> was given her to wear.
> (Revelation 19:6–8, NIV)

The marriage image is so powerful that John's angel guide instructs him specifically to record a commendation: "Blessed are those who are invited to the marriage supper of the Lamb" (Rev. 19:9).

However, even in the late chapters of John's Apocalypse the marriage imagery is not exhausted—even with the uniting of the bride-church with the Bridegroom-Lord. John's vision records the culmination of this epoch of heaven and earth's history, their "passing away." In their place is a new heaven and earth. The new earth is described as the "holy city, new Jerusalem," presented by God in such glory that John is compelled to use the only language appropriate for such a sight: "I saw the holy city, the new Jerusalem, coming down out of heaven from God, made ready as a bride adorned for her husband" (Rev. 21:2).

To be sure, in that new heaven and earth giving and receiving in marriage will have run their temporal course, being no longer necessary, as Jesus instructed the Sadducees: "In the resurrection they neither marry, nor are given in marriage, but are like angels in heaven" (Matt. 22:30). But during these earthly eons the coming together of a man and a woman is ordained by God, with the intentions of human joy, love, and fidelity, intimacy, and the conception, birth, and nurture of offspring who will be vehicles for God's promulgation of righteousness. We modern lovers of God through His Son, Jesus Christ, tossed about on the waves of social change, do well to keep our eyes on that pole star of marriage and family presented in God's Word, for it is so evidently God's will for His offspring.

1. Discuss how the image of God may be considered to be more perfectly reflected in the marriage of a man and woman than in either male or female alone.

2. What three purposes of God for the marriage relationship can be found in the creation of mankind in Genesis? Discuss or explain each.

3. Given the Genesis 2:24 rationale or foundation for marriage, discuss the implications of each aspect: leaving, cleaving, and one flesh. Does "cleave" have more than one meaning in English? Using Malachi 2:15 in conjunction with Genesis 2:24, discuss whether or not the "one flesh" expression should exclusively refer to sexual relations.

4. What are the four elements of a covenant, and how are they fulfilled in God's covenant relationship with Israel? Use scriptural evidences for each.

5. What scriptural evidence would you martial to demonstrate that marriage was conceived by the Israelites as a covenant within the Covenant?

6. In reflection on the sin of Lucifer (see Isa. 14 and Ezek. 28), what is the relationship between his personal downfall and the nature of his temptation of Eve? Why would Satan's success in the temptation of mankind be a feather in his cap?

7. All of God's creatures except humans must conform to God's decrees—they can do nothing else. Why, then, is mankind's loving obedience to God so very significant? Discuss your answer with scriptural support.

8. Defend this statement with scriptural evidence: "The relationship between marriage in the Old Testament and in the New Testament is one of continuity." Use the teaching of Jesus for your major argument.

9. In the military, when a noncommissioned officer salutes one of higher rank, he gives recognition to the authority behind the rank. His salute implies nothing regarding the intelligence, character, or ability of the individual person in ranking uniform. How might this analogy apply to Paul's view of wifely submission?

10. Using the text of Proverbs 31, argue the position that the role of women in the Old Testament was confining and suppressive. Or, argue the opposite.

11. The term *reflexive* was used here to describe the result of the attitudes and actions of the Christian husband described in Ephesians 5. Explain how Christ's work in behalf of the church and a Christian husband's response to his wife deserve the term.

16

Preparation for Marriage and Family

The family has for decades been a subject of increasing concern on the part of clergy, educators, doctors, legal authorities, and politicians. Journalists also have found the family "hot copy." Immediately after World War II, many who sensed the social and moral pulse of the nation began warning of the threat to our families' corporate health. Elton Trueblood in the early 1950s included concern for the family in his classic *Your Other Vocation*. He even included a chapter calling for "Recovery of Family Life," in which he indicated that "many parts of our civilization are in danger of widespread decay, but no single danger is more serious than that of the decay of family life."[1] Surely, he was prophetic. In the more than thirty years since that writing, the deterioration of the family has been evident in the increasing rate of divorce, the resulting broken homes, and frightening statistics concerning the general moral and spiritual collapse of the American populace.

In the mid-nineteenth century, 75 percent of Americans lived in rural settings, largely on farms. Children were an important part of the farm work force, as were grandparents and others outside the nuclear family. As a result, family life was characterized by working together, firm discipline, close bonding, and a continuity of roles and values.

1. Elton Trueblood, *Your Other Vocation* (New York: Harper & Row, 1952), p. 81.

The Industrial Revolution brought migration to urban centers and a separation of money-making work from the family, as fathers left home to work in factories. The negative effects on nurture, discipline, and relations within the family can hardly be overstated. Children hardly saw their fathers. Families were no longer working together to survive. Discipline, closeness, and values became difficult to maintain.

Today we are still feeling the effects of that great change. Marriages are hard to hold together; divorce has risen dramatically, even within the church. Families that do stay together are generally not very closely knit. Discipline is difficult to maintain; values are difficult to inculcate in children. And today, fully half of the mothers of school age children are employed; in most cases, that will only compound the problems.

Still, Americans believe marriage and family to be important institutions. The family is the foundation of society and of the church. George Gallup, Jr., reports that "the majority of American women see marriage, home, and family as the ideal life-style for them." The report goes on to indicate that 75 percent of American women stipulate that "marriage and children are among the important elements that would create the ideal life for them now and in the future."[2] Because of the pivotal importance of marriage and family to Christian faith and life, clergy and religious professionals continually express concern in books, articles, seminars, and media interviews. The first woman in the Supreme Court of the United States, Associate Justice Sandra Day O'Connor, reaffirmed the historic and critical position of marriage at her Senate confirmation hearing in 1981, when she said, "Marriage is far more than an exchange of vows. It is the foundation of the family, mankind's basic unit of society, the hope of the world and the strength of our country. It is the relationship between ourselves and the generation to follow."[3]

Of far greater importance, however, than statements of professionals and statistics is the fact that Christian children increasingly are raised in broken homes, forced to choose between parents, and are reared by step-parents who often have figured largely in the breakdown of their parents' marriages. The sheer volume of negative factors against healthy emotional and spiritual development in such situations is staggering.

Often, the church merely preaches two or three half-hour sermons on the topic throughout the year. An occasional film series or class on

2. George Gallup, Jr., and David Poling. *The Search for America's Faith* (Nashville: Abington, 1980), p. 43.
3. Justice O'Connor expressed these thoughts at the Senate Judiciary Committee hearing on her confirmation in Washington, D.C., September 9, 1981, reported in *The New York Times,* 10 September 1981, p. 10.

marriage or family is becoming more popular. At its worst, in many churches "concerned" people speak in hushed tones after a service: "Did you hear about Charlie and Sarah?" "Yes, isn't it terrible—and they're supposed to be Christians too!"

Increasingly, young people caught between the jaws of contemporary peer pressure and the natural excitement and stimulation of discovering themselves as maturing social-sexual beings find it difficult to integrate biblical teaching and family and church expectations with the thoughts and physio-emotional responses they are experiencing. What every church needs is a means of guiding its members in the areas of marriage and family *throughout their lives,* beginning in early childhood.

Thus, the church must focus on people *as they are maturing* with an on-going program tuned to their developing physical, intellectual, emotional, social, and spiritual needs. It dare not merely provide premarital counseling six months before couples marry. This chapter, therefore, will present material to help Christian education leaders in the planning of a program to prepare growing Christians for marriage and family from their preschool years onward—into adulthood.

CHARACTERISTICS OF LIFE-RELATED MARRIAGE AND FAMILY EDUCATION

Before a discussion of the actual elements of the church's approach to lifelong marriage and family education, it is necessary to describe the general nature of such a program. That is, what factors will serve as guidelines for the development of such a program?

INTEGRATION

Achieving a balance of emphasis between marriage and family life topics is crucial for a program that will meet the needs of the children and adults. This would be a worthwhile subject for research and development in Sunday school curricula. Although all major evangelical publishing houses include lessons that treat marriage and family in varying degrees, I am unaware of a concerted effort to thoroughly integrate sex education, family life, self-esteem, marital preparation, and the like into curricula.

GRADING

An integrated program must be geared to each group's stage of development. That is difficult in the publication of materials to be used nationwide, because from community to community the stages of development differ depending on numerous societal factors. In churches where there are trained educators, there must be an effort to adapt materials to the known maturity of the community and group.

CONTEXTUALIZATION

James F. Engel in his work on communications cites Eugene A. Nida in defining contextualization: "Our real objective . . . is not a change of content . . . but rather a fitting of the same content into such culturally meaningful forms as will be fit vehicles for the communication of the message."[4] For Nida the message of God's Word is the independent variable with the particular cultural norm serving as the dependent variable—a kind of code that must be identified and appropriately employed so that the message is meaningful. In Lois LeBar's model, the Word of God (living and written) remains the independent variable while a pupil's life situation (society within a culture) and current needs, plus essential personal experiences, become the code to be deciphered for effecting changed lives.[5]

For our purposes here, the point is that teachers and Christian education workers in a given church must know their pupils so well that the entire teaching vehicle will be on the right road—meshing with the images, experiences, and needs of the specific group with whom they are working. Thus, personal involvement is the key to contextualization. LeBar's expression "Begin where they are" is crucial. Contextualization within any given group is thus dependent on a personal relationship between the teacher or leader and the individual pupils. One can not *begin* where they are unless one *is* where they are—in a personal relationship. A teacher or worker whose life is intertwined with that of his pupils can be effective, because he knows where each person in his group is. He knows their characteristics, needs, experiences, problems, joys, sorrows—the whole gamut of factors that affect their attitudes and actions.

CONTINUITY

Living in an age of change and innovation in which variety tends to be elevated to the status of a virtue, a Christian education program that has as its goal the meeting of marital and family life preparational needs

4. James F. Engel. *Contemporary Christian Communications: Its Theory and Practice* (Nashville: Nelson, 1979), p. 272.
5. Lois E. LeBar, *Focus on People in Christian Education* (Westwood, N.J.: Revell, 1958), p. 206.

must possess the characteristic of continuity or perpetuity. Year after year, relentlessly, church educators must insure that maturing persons grapple with the biblical content and personal application regarding the one relationship that most people undertake—marriage. Marriage and family are so much the testing ground of our Christian experience and faith, that any whole-person or holistic program must have marriage and family subject matter as much a part of it as the presentation of the plan of salvation. That may sound extreme, but "working out of our salvation" is nothing less than integrating the life of Christ in us. Such integration takes place first in our thought lives and next in our relationships and stewardship. Marriage and family are the hub of human life. A well-designed program of Christian education will provide a significant amount of curricular space for family life topics.

Materials must be chosen that address the actual needs of students. For example, one of the finest little books on sex education for prepubescent children is Ken Taylor's *Almost Twelve,* first published in 1968 and by September of 1982 was in its twenty-fifth printing. In the intervening fifteen years, however, children's readiness for sexual information, as well as their rate of physical maturation, has progressed to such a point that *Almost Eleven* or *Almost Ten* would be apropos.

BIBLICAL FOCUS

The Scriptures must be considered by curriculum writers and teachers alike as the only rule of faith and life. What has been given by God through the biblical writers is normative for mankind, for knowledge of God and His ways and for principles of living that glorify God. God's Word is the bedrock of curriculum.

An ongoing program founded on the absolutes of God's Word will focus operationally on a personal faith testable in the context of human relations. Christian marriage and family concepts center on the evidence of one's relationship with God reflected in one's relationships with others. After hearing the lawyer's summation of the law's requirement for eternal life, Jesus commended him: "You have answered correctly." However, Jesus was not satisfied with mere recitation of the truth—as surely true as it was. He required that the theory become incarnational: "*Do* this and you will live" (Luke 10:28). Again, there must be balance: knowing, believing, and incorporating the truth into experience.

PERSONNEL

The quality and sincerity of the perople who teach and lead the children, youth, and young adults is crucial. Jesus instructed that a pupil, "after he has been fully trained, will be like his teacher" (Luke 6:40). The modeling dimension of teaching is paramount—and inevitable. Students will reflect the quality of the lesson material of the teacher *and* the teacher's attitude towards the material and toward life. As in any area of ministry, the persistent need is *maturing leaders.* That is, the Christian education board, or pastor, elders, deacons, or whatever governing body whose responsibility includes personnel, must assess that prospective teachers or leaders truly walk with Christ, have a command of God's Word, and are beyond reproach ethically and morally. Do they know how to teach or lead? Do they possess a love for the age group with which they work? Beyond those factors, teachers should also have marriages that work. It would be well to require personnel to be involved in marriage enrichment seminars and denominational and regional evangelical efforts to deepen marriages and foster godly family lives. It seems best to have units regarding marriage and family to be team taught by couples; it helps students to have one of their own sex whom they respect up there teaching.

TOWARDS A PERSPECTIVE ON MARRIAGE AND FAMILY PREPARATION

Theoretically the subjects of marriage and family may be dichotomized, but in reality they are inseparable. Virtually every person is born into a family of at least father and mother. Most children know their grandparents, but whether or not they do, they are influenced by their grandparents' parenting of their parents. Even a person's view of marrige is based largely on the marriage that he witnessed in his own parents. In the work of William Westley and Nathan Epstein, which examined 170 college students and 88 families, it was apparent that marriage quality and the emotional health of the children are closely correlated.

> Our most important finding was that children's emotional health is closely related to the emotional relationships between their parents. When these relationships were warm and constructive, such that the husband and wife felt loved, admired, and encouraged to act in ways that they themselves admired, the children were happy and healthy.[6]

Conversely, how a person comes to identify himself in his own family, and in his spouse's family, and how he perceives others' acceptance and expectations will seriously affect his marital relationship.

6. William L. Westley and Nathan B. Epstein, *The Silent Majority* (San Francisco: Jossey-Bass, 1970), p. 158.

Thus, an integrated and unified program of marital preparation will include the *family.* The following elements needed to constitute a program must be thoroughly integrated into the curriculum following the basic characteristics previously listed: integration, grading, contextualization, continuity, personnel, and biblical focus.

SEXUALITY

Wary as many evangelicals may be of "sex education," children need to form Christian opinions and convictions concerning what they are as sexual beings created by God and how they should relate to their own as well as to the opposite sex. Their sexuality will be a filter through which they appraise all of life's relationships and view themselves. Because all knowledge is cumulative, if the formative steps are faulty or outright fallacious, each successive step will be flawed. Casebooks are full of examples of children raised in homes that were sexually either repressive or overt but malevolent. As Lester Kirkendall concludes in his landmark study of 200 college-age men, "Extremes of sanctimony and lasciviousness confuse people and make objectivity impossible and inconsistency certain."[7]

As prevalent as sex information has become through public and private schools, libraries, newsstands, television, and theatre, Christian parents are still struggling with providing godly, balanced sex education for their children. While leading numerous seminars in evangelical churches on the subject of marriage and family, I have asked Christian people to respond with raised hands if they thought their sexual preparation by their parents was "adequate," let alone "excellent." Out of nearly 1,500 registrants over a period of two years, only a handful have replied positively. With their own children the pattern continues. In a more formal sampling during the teaching of a course on the Christian Education of Youth at a Christian liberal arts college, I devised an instrument to anonymously record the sexual development of class members. Out of thirty-five students in the class, twenty-nine (83 percent) indicated that they came from Christian homes. Of those, only four (13.79 percent) registered *any* parental sex education. Through personal counseling with various class members—over Cokes in the student lounge—it was apparent that several of the students' current problems with the opposite sex related to the inept brand of sex educa-

7. Lester A. Kirkendall, *Premarital Intercourse and Interpersonal Relations* (New York: Julian, 1961), p. 235.

tion they received. What Lois LeBar called for back in the sixties still has not become the norm in evangelical church education in the eighties:

> With sex gone berserk in our day, sex education must integrate questions of sex into the larger problems of the freedom of the individual, development of personality, satisfying interpersonal relations, and the home as the unit of society.[8]

Obviously, such an integrated program will require a graded approach, with units that regularly treat sex education topics but are not necessarily labeled Sex Education. Eventually, in church school classes for parents, the topics will be integrated into the curriculum to help parents become their own children's sex educators. Rex Johnson's twelve-session elective course for adults may be employed to guide parents in the godly *what* and *how* of their children's sex education.[9]

FAMILY

Essential to a Christian grasp of marriage is an appreciation of the biblical conception of family. O. R. Johnston says that the essential dimensions of the married state are "protection, home-making, economic support, sexual access and responsibility for children."[10] Integrated with biblical doctrines of the nature of God, man, redemption, and sanctification will be discussions on how God best communicates His person through His Son, who comes from God and is the "express image" of the Father. A child's earliest and most lasting knowledge of God's person and work and how to live the Christian life comes from his parents.

Again, marriage and family education occurs initially and primarily in the child's own family. Church and school may employ the best methods and materials and the finest modeling teachers, but as the diagram below indicates, the initial factor in a person's concept of marriage is the family he grew up in. The relationship between the parents, as well as their personalities and views, project a concept of "mythology" of their family. As children are born into the unit, their presence modifies the family and increases the complexity of the relationships. Early in a child's life, grandparents and other relatives may figure large in the child's self-concept and his view of what it is of which he is a part. By trial and error he learns to influence the other individuals in the unit—and thus the unit as a whole.

8. LeBar, p. 168.
9. Rex Johnson. *At Home with Sex* (Wheaton, Ill.: Victor, 1979).
10. O. R. Johnston, *Who Needs the Family?* (Downers Grove, Ill.: InterVarsity, 1979), p. 41.

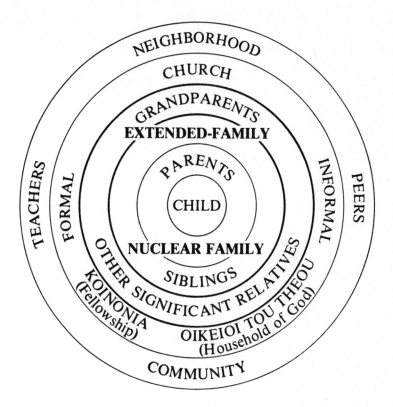

The second major factor for families that are strongly religious is the church. Many evangelicals enjoy far more satisfying relationships with church families than with blood relatives. Thus, a child may be enculturated in a Sunday school class among other children whose parents are friendly, if not quite close. Periodic visits in the homes of those "family" members serve to test a child's view of himself, his parents, and his family. Homogeneity in belief systems, values, attitudes, and life-style serves to reinforce the parents' view. Good times and pleasures shared with the other families also serve as positive reinforcement of the "family mythology." Further, the child's relationship with Sunday school teachers and the minister helps to inform him of his identity and shape his outlook. Less personal initially, but nonetheless influential, may be the immediate community or neighborhood. As children play with neighbors, visit in their homes, observe other parents in their relationships with spouses and children, their knowledge of the range of relationships expands.

School is the next factor. Here the child's scope of relationships broadens, with impact on his view of himself, his parents, siblings, and the whole galaxy of meanings he attributes to persons, places, things, and ideas.

Yet throughout his formative years, and then again when he is married, a person finds his personality continually enacted on the stage of family. It is the pole star either towards which he is moving or from which he gets his bearing.

COURTSHIP

As has been discussed quite regularly in the field literature since the early 1970s, the 1960s have been called the turning point of the "second sexual revolution." The "first sexual revolution" occurred towards the close of the eighteenth and beginning of the nineteenth centuries, witnessing a change from family involvement in spouse selection to what might be termed *affective selection.* That is, young people began to choose their mates on the basis of romance—how a boy and girl emotionally related to one another. "Falling in love" has been culturally effective only since the mid-nineteenth century. The second revolution, however, is characterized by rejection of pressures from traditional social sets, whether family, community, or peer-group, and by the separation of sexual relations from lifelong monogamy.[11] Increasingly, through numerous means, the message is getting out that parents, church, and community should have no say in who a young person dates or mates—be it in or out of wedlock. In our humanistic age, sexual needs are becoming on a par with all other human needs, which may be satisfied as one likes.

How the church is to help its children (alas!), youth, and adults through the modern malaise is the critical issue. As Christian young people approach courtship, leaders will want to prepare them to make intelligent, spiritual evaluation of their new social and physio-emotional awarenesses. Materials must be selected that help young people examine the marriage versus singleness question, dating and marriage expectations, degrees of intimacy, standards of sexual expression, and related topics. Those subjects should be discussed continually from the perspective of kingdom living as expressed in Scripture, with an ultimate concern of glorifying God through one's dating, courtship, and marriage. The method must involve the young people in discussion and discovery

11. See Edward Shorter, *The Making of the Modern Family* (New York: Basic Books, 1975), pp. 79–119.

as much as possible. That will encourage a group openness for honest grappling with feelings, images, pressures, and attitudes. At various stages, parents may be involved with the young people in study groups, not as spies but as helpers to guide young people through the experiences in Christian love. Such a group process will also aid in establishing group norms that will serve as caring boundaries for behavior.

SELF-IMAGE

The psalmist David asks a question that men have asked in numerous ways since creation: "What is man . . . ?" (Ps. 8:4). Young people today are asking the question, not so much from an abstract philosophical perspective, but personally: Who am I? The question has become a sort of rite of passage into adolescence, yet unfortunately, it haunts many people into their young adult and even mature years. In college bull sessions the question is ubiquitous. The sources of the question are legion.

Transcience is one factor in the self image quest. The average length of residence of American families has dwindled to but three-and-one-half years. Regional allegiances are eroding. Just about the time a young person has made good bonding relationships within a community, the family moves to Albuquerque or Des Moines.

Divorce and broken homes prove to be continual sources of the question. Children caught in the middle of parents' squabbling and hatred witness parents in combat and ultimate separation. Invariably they wonder if they were the cause of the parents' broken marriage. So often, the only answer they can imagine is positive. They bear the pangs of the misplaced guilt, digging emotional holes from which it may take a lifetime to climb out—if ever.

The question of David, however, must be completed. He did not stop with the simple interrogation. "What is man?" but went on with clauses relative to God's action on man's behalf:

> . . . that You are *mindful* of him
> . . . that You *care* for him
> . . . that You *made* him a little lower than the heavenly beings
> . . . that You *crowned* him with glory and honor
> . . . that You *made* him ruler over the works of Your hands
>
> (Psalm 8:4-6)

David's inquiry was not pensive searching for self-identity, the existential question, as much as it was a rhetorical means of standing in awe of God, amazed at His esteem for mankind. David had the firm conviction that he was the object of God's thoughts, concern, exaltation, and giving of responsibility. Christian young people and adults must learn and believe who they are in Christ Jesus. The home and the church must conspire in their young people's search for identity lest they lose the dignity that is rightly theirs through Him, with whom they are seated "in the heavenly places" (Eph. 2:6).

Dr. James Dobson speaks to the socio-psychological results of rampant human feelings of inferiority.

> Teenagers are by no means alone in this personal devaluation. Every age poses its own unique threats to self-esteem . . . little children typically suffer loss of status during the tender years of childhood. Likewise, most adults are still attempting to cope with the inferiority experienced in earlier times.[12]

Those who work closely with young people and young adults know that lack of self-value is the culprit that leads so many to seek approval through acts that, ultimately, are selfish, ugly, and dehumanizing—acts that assert that man is not made in God's image. In a state of wretchedness, weighed down with guilt and self-rejection, the neurotic sinner thinks, "See, I'm right: I'm not worth much. Look what I've done. Look at the mess I've made of my life and others'. God shouldn't love me. God couldn't love me. God doesn't love me!" In such a condition young people are swept into marriage by rebellion, social pressure, sexual overexposure, pregnancy, rebound, and escape—all symptomatic of a self unaware or unbelieving of God's unconditional love.

Throughout the curriculum of the church, from childhood through senior citizens, there is the need for a full-blown biblical anthropology that practically relates the sinful nature of man to the rebirth of *imago dei* through faith in Jesus Christ. Though the likeness of God is marred through the Fall, it is not, Humpty-Dumpty-like, destined for ultimate ruin, because God has acted in His Son to put all the pieces back together again! In many and varying ways that theme needs to be studied, discussed, preached, and lived. The quality of church *koinonia* or "body life" helps to put practical meat on the bones of this theology. It is through positive human relations that people experience a sense of self-worth, reinforcing the truths tentatively held at first, then firmly grasped, and affecting the quality of their Christian life.

---

12. James Dobson, *Hide or Seek: How to Build Self-Esteem in Your Child* (Old Tappan, N.J.: Revell, 1979), p. 19.

As Christian educators, we naturally believe that that process must start in the home and be reinforced early in a child's church experience. It is thus that a biblical curriculum must be complemented by leaders who truly believe and respond to people as if they were important to them. Acceptance will characterize such leaders. Informal, private conversations with young people will focus on youth feelings, needs, aspirations, joys, and sorrows. Leaders will be available for counsel, to bring the strength and hope of God's Word, incarnate through their sincere friendship, to the needs of children, youth, and adults.

MARRIAGE

This subject has been kept to last in this list because of the climactic effect of the wedding ceremony on all that has gone before. The practical culmination of the process described above takes place when a young man and woman who have developed a biblical sense of who they are in Christ, the significance of their sexuality, and the importance of family in God's master plan for human life, and have succeeded in godly courtship, finally stand before God, the church, and the pastor pledging their love and fidelity to one another "until death do us part." Yet, though they are at the end of one process, courtship, they are at the beginning of that which, God willing, will last many times the few years of their courtship experience.

In his practical tool for teaching about marriage, H. Norman Wright shows readers the pillars of marriage.[13] Those pillars include: marital goals and expectations, needs of spouses, handling change and crisis, decision making, resolving conflict, prayer, and forgiveness. Other subjects could include an examination of the biblical roles of husband and wife in light of contemporary society. Marital sexuality has been treated by several competent Christian medical professionals and others, some of whose works are listed in the resource appendix. Paramount, of course, is the subject of love, to which Dwight H. Small addresses *How Should I Love You?*[14]

The following chapter will consider premarital counseling and classes in some detail, but for our purposes here, the entire curriculum in this marriage and family track should acquaint the young person, during his later teen years, with the rewards and problems of marriage. In today's more open society, in which subjects such as sexuality are common fare in the media, the church must take advantage of the setting to present a

13. H. Norman Wright. *The Pillars of Marriage* (Ventura, Calif.: Regal, 1979).
14. Dwight Hervey Small, *How Should I Love You?* (San Francisco: Harper & Row, 1979).

distinctively Christian approach to marriage. Amidst so much popular discussion of non-traditional life-styles and with many writers stumping for open marriage and contract marriage, I was gratified, as well as amazed to find a decidedly Christian perspective on marriage in a popular woman's periodical, from a Christian writer, Alan McGinnis, whose prior writings *The Friendship Factor* and *The Love Factor* have been widely circulated. Now, in *The Romance Factor,* excerpted for a *Good Housekeeping* article, McGinnis says:

> There are even many psychologists and marriage counselors who tell us that an occasional affair can be beneficial to marriage.
> But despite these efforts to make husbands and wives regard fidelity as outmoded, our instinct to pair off with only *one* person has very deep roots in almost every society. Human beings form meaningful bonds with one another because we apparently function happily in one-to-one relationships of commitment and trust.
> Hence the Bible's clear-cut proscriptions against extramarital sex, and the history of church support for monogamous marriage. The Scriptures take an unequivocal position: It is always a sin to commit adultery.[15]

That should provide motivation for Christian educators not to react defensively to the world's obvious bias towards darkness but to press the cause for the light with all the fine materials available at our disposal, recognizing that "greater is He who is in you than he who is in the world" (1 John 4:4).

Preparation for Christian marriage and family life becomes all the more important as the hostility of a godless age increases. Curricular materials must clearly and persistently address the issues and integrate the topic throughout materials for all ages. Proper teaching on self-worth, sex education, and the courtship and marriage questions from a distinctly biblical perspective must permeate our families and churches.

The following chapter seeks to set forth an approach to meeting those needs through a total church ministry. Effort must be expended to meet this vital challenge. Our children and youth are depending upon it.

15. Alan Loy McGinnis, "How to Stay Happily Married," *Good Housekeeping,* September 1982, pp. 119–92.

FOR FURTHER STUDY

1. For what reasons is it necessary to implement a long-term marriage and family preparation program in the church, starting with pre-schoolers right on through young adulthood?

2. What qualifications should one possess to minister most effectively as teacher or leader of a marriage and family program in the church?

3. Discuss the use of the Bible in teaching pre-pubescent children (ages 9–11) regarding the relationship of parents to their children. Isolate an appropriate Scripture segment, identify the family principle contained therein, discuss the elements of the age characteristics of the children that would best integrate with the principle, and suggest a lesson approach, activity, and application.

4. What relationship exists, if any, between the emotional tone of the husband-wife relationship and the emotional health of their children? Suggest a biblical example.

5. Present three reasons sex education should or should not be part of the children and youth curricula of the church. Support your reasoning with Scripture portions, employing grammatical-historical interpretation.

6. Discuss the notion of self-concept in relation to the biblical doctrine of anthropology.

17

A Family Life Ministry Program

How are we to translate all these ideas and motivations into action? A program with the characteristics listed in chapter 15 will require more than a unit on marriage and family in the next quarter of our Sunday school. The following elements are necessary to implement our perspective.

PROGRAMMING ELEMENTS

MARRIAGE AND FAMILY LIFE COMMITTEE

Depending on the size of the church, the family life project may become the responsibility of the Christian education board or committee, a minister of family life, or be assigned to a special committee of the Christian education board designed specifically for the purpose. Such a committee is to be a permanent standing committee that will oversee and maintain the marriage and family program throughout and work in cooperation with the various agencies of the church. As in all new programs, but especially because of the potentially incendiary nature of the subject, this committee's work must be highly visible, open to input from everyone and proceeding step by step with prayer for God's guidance.

Although it is not within the purview of this chapter to chronicle every aspect of such a committee, there are several important steps it should take. First, the committee must develop a "Statement of Intent" based on the mandate given it by the Christian education board. A well-written prospectus should be constructed specifying the needs, aims, methods, materials, organization, administration, and evaluation of the program with adequate biblical support. The prospectus should be condensed into a letter sent to the congregation that outlines the committee's intent and invites, warmly, input from all members. Several open meetings of the committee, with refreshments, may be beneficial for getting people talking about the subject. Ever and always, commitment to Jesus Christ must be held high, so that members recognize the spiritual purposes of the program. It is not a social-psychological experiment but the means of building spiritual values into our children, their marriages, and families.

Second, the pastor should be asked to keynote the committee's existence and the forthcoming program with a series of sermons on marriage and family from the perspective of their centrality to the biblical revelation and God's plan for His people.

Third, the committee will spend hours reviewing materials for each age level, insuring that both the approach to Scripture and the perspective fit with the church's standards. Further, the commmittee will have to decide whether to work with present personnel from each agency or establish a few couples who would, on a visiting team basis, periodically visit agencies to work with the pupils in the several subjects. In many churches the specialized team approach may work best, because except for some progressive curricula, regular teachers or leaders would have to work with other than the regular materials. Such a team approach would also give the team time to gather materials during one quarter, refine areas and methods from the experience of a previous teaching period, and constantly upgrade their approach.

CHURCH OR SUNDAY SCHOOL

The most logical agency for implementation is the Sunday school. Amidst all the curricular material that is published, there must be room for a progressive series of units on sexuality, family, courtship, self-esteem, and marriage. Materials of this sort are more available for junior and senior high and above than for children. Major publishers do employ occasional lessons that treat the subjects, but with materials that are arranged according to a study of a book of the Bible, and unless writers are sensitive to the subject-needs that we are outlining here, they usually opt for traditional topics.

There are, however, materials geared to children, youth, and adults that may be used as substitute or complement on a three-year cycle. The summer of 1982, Concordia Publishing House released their updated Concordia Sex Education Series, prepared by the Lutheran Church-Missouri Synod. The courses consist of books, filmstrips, and cassettes, enough materials for one unit of up to twelve sessions, depending on the age level. Following this plan, every three years a student could have a unit dealing with sexuality. Coordinating between departments is, however, in order: if materials on sexuality are used during a child's first year in the primary department and during his last year in the junior department, there would be a hiatus of five or six years between exposures.

Materials abound for use by youth and adults, mainly as elective courses. The major publishing houses, denominational and independent, offer courses that usually run for one quarter, with a paperback text, a leader's guide, and duplication masters and/or transparencies. Once again, it is necessary to stipulate that teachers of those courses be mature Christians with the ability to personally communicate the love of Christ through their working with people respectfully, tactfully, and with a sense of humor.

YOUTH GROUPS

Boy-girl relationships engage a major portion of adolescents' waking and dreaming hours. Still, use of materials should be closely coordinated with the Sunday school staff so that "overkill" does not occur. In the less formal youth programs, young people may conduct their own research projects by developing a questionnaire with which they poll their friends on sexuality, marriage, family, self-esteem, courtship, and other related topics. Films, filmstrips, cassettes (see James Dobson's cassettes, *Preparing for Adolescence,* in the reference section), interviews with doctors, nurses, Christian psychologists, social workers, as well as the pastoral staff, will prove informative and authoritative, yet realistic.

In the more informal setting of the youth group, young people socialize more freely, divide into cliques, sub-groups, or pairs, and test ways of acting and the quality of relationships. In this context, it is possible to evaluate their progress in social maturity through observation. Group teaching methods such as brainstorming, role playing, discussing, and many others may reduce the threat of the subject matter, creating the atmosphere in which young people are free to be as honest as the social context and their maturity allows. Mark Senter indicates,

> The youth group is left then with two primary responsibilities: fellowship and ministry. It is on these two functions that the youth group should focus.
> Perhaps the best way to describe the youth group is as a laboratory for the Christian life.[1]

In a laboratory, experiments often have to be scrapped and tried again with numerous modifications. The failure of an experiment to verify a theory is considered a normal occurrence. So too with youth groups. Young people will form relationships, test what it is like to develop a friendship with this or that person, terminate one friendship, begin another. Under the loving guidance of mature leadership these may be the most positive group experiences: where love and acceptance, and opportunity to test, are normative.

RETREATS AND CAMPS

It is often said that one week at camp accomplishes as much as three months of Sunday school. Whether that is true or not, it speaks for the concentration of time, the day and night involvement, and the captive audience. If a retreat program was planned on an ongoing basis, emphasizing specific themes for each year on a three-year cycle, subjects such as love, courtship, and marriage could appear regularly as part of the youth curriculum. Christian specialists could be brought in, as well as films, tapes, and extended content sessions—all of which would be precluded in Sunday school or youth group.

WORKSHOPS AND SEMINARS

Denominations and Christian organizations are sponsoring Christian marriage and family programs of from five to twenty hours duration. These are for single adults or married couples and may be held at a church, camp, or retreat center, or, as with Campus Crusade's Family Life Conference, at regional meetings in hotels or motels. These programs vary in emphasis from those that are interaction-intensive to those that emphasize lectures.

Although pastors may present excellent sermons on family life and sexuality, or even teach or guide a class, the benefits of an outside

1. Mark H. Senter, III, "Youth Programs," in *Youth Education in the Church*, ed. Roy B. Zuck and Warren S. Benson (Chicago: Moody, 1978), p. 269.

specialist are enormous. First, he lives with the subject matter day in and day out. He is constantly reading, discussing, writing, in conferences, and possibly counseling in the field of marriage and family. What he brings, then, is fresh to the audience, and usually he is able to answer the broad spectrum of questions people ask. Quite often, such visits from specialists help people with special needs to identify them and recognize that seeking professional help is normal. Some specialists may even adapt their materials to congregational needs; through prior discussion with the pastor or director of Christian education, the specialist can learn of the needs of the group and thus may tailor-make his presentation.

Increasing, specialists are putting their materials on film, video cassette, or audio cassette. James Dobson's *Focus on the Family* film series has been used quite effectively worldwide. This series employs a booklet for follow-up study by parents, which may be purchased with the film for a very nominal fee. Unfortunately, many groups fail to utilize that tool, and simply view the films as they would listen to a sermon. Once the "message" is over, its time to go home. That has become a bad habit connected with film viewing in the church, to the point that films are not used educationally but as an audio-visual sermon—or worse, as entertainment.

LIBRARY OR RESOURCE CENTER

The plethora of materials available today is both bane and blessing. There is much material that is excellent and worthy of church libraries; but how to choose appropriate materials within one's budget is a serious dilemma. Many churches are encouraging members who have books that they have read to donate them to the library so that all members of the church may have opportunity to gain the input. Creative teachers and youth workers utilize the library for their pupils' research, having different persons read and report to their classes. The bibliography of this book should prove helpful to church librarians as well.

A VISIBLE CHURCH POLICY ON MARRIAGE

Given the persistently high rate of divorce and remarriage, it is incumbent on a church that is serious in its commitment to biblical marriage to communicate its perspectives and procedures to its people on a continual basis. A church should have a viewpoint or philosophy of marriage and standards regarding marriage and remarriage that are known by the congregation. Many ministers experience frustration because so many people seeking church weddings have no idea how the church and the wedding are related. Often people call the pastor and ask, "Do you perform weddings?" Certainly a pastor performs wedding ceremonies, but that is not what the inquirer means. He means, "Will you perform a wedding service for someone who is not a member of your church?" Often those persons have visited the church to "spy out the land" for their or their children's wedding. If the architecture and decor of the church are pleasing, it may become even a weekly request.

Initially, a policy will need to be constructed by the pastor and elders or other church leaders. Such a policy will require much study and discussion between leaders so that a mutually agreeable statement can be produced. Of course, some denominations have stated policies already, precluding the long, hard preparatory work. But the work is worth it. First, such a time can draw leaders together personally, as they engage in what they know is important work for the betterment of the church and its marriages and families. Second, having a policy is a time-saver and a means of avoiding uncertainties—at least, some of them. Third, a policy sets a standard, providing guidelines and a unified perspective. It will provide the pastor with a security net so that he will not be tempted to make accommodations. Fourth and finally, it will help insure fairness and even-handedness in treating people; a pastor or board may for example feel forced to accommodate to a wealthy or long-time church family. Naturally, the policy should include the need for the pastor to clear all weddings through the board, so that there are no surprises.

The church policy may be condensed into an attractive booklet and made available to everyone in a literature rack in the church narthex, or foyer. Ushers, deacons, or pastor may then simply refer inquirers to the booklet. The booklet may be entitled: "Your Wedding at First Church." The content of the booklet may include the following:

1. A warm, friendly introduction expressing the church's praise to God for marriage and the joy of helping Christian people to plan a worshipful ceremony that will be testimony to all who attend.

2. A statement on the biblical foundation of marriage: its purposes, essential qualities, and the qualifications of those intending Christian marriage. At this point, the church requirements regarding the spiritual condition of marital candidates and divorce/remarriage should be clearly stated.

3. Requirements for premarital counseling should be outlined clearly to the candidates. How many sessions with the pastor are required? What tapes, books, questionnaires, and so on are a part of the program?

4. Regarding the ceremony itself, a statement should reflect the fact that a wedding ceremony is a service of worship to Almighty God; that

certain elements in the vows are required by the church; that musical and poetical materials used must clearly reflect a godly perspective on marriage rather than popular, romantic, or even erotic notions.

5. Finally, the practical arrangements should be clearly delineated: use of facilities, decorations, reception hall, kitchen, fees for musicians and custodian, and so on.

The utilization of a wedding booklet should clearly communicate the appropriate information and tone to members, who should already know the policy, as well as to persons who are unchurched but want to get married in a church for sentimental or traditional reasons. It may also become the springboard for communicating the gospel to persons who are coming to church for purposes other than worship.

THE PASTOR AND MARRIAGE PREPARATION

PREACHING AND TEACHING

The declaration of the "whole counsel of God" is, of course, the responsibility of every Christian minister, whether in a church that adheres to a liturgy and follows the Christian year, or in a congregation that worships spontaneously. With numerous seasonal, doctrinal, practical, and biblical emphases that should be the subject of preaching, it is incumbent on a pastor to devise a preaching plan for at least the year ahead and better, two or three years hence. The months of May and June are particularly suited for preaching on marriage and family, containing as they do Mother's and Father's Days and Children's Sunday. Because June is traditionally a month for weddings, such an emphasis is appropriate. Actual weddings, marriage reaffirmations, and even a wedding demonstration, could complement a preaching series. Dialogue sermons could include an "engaged couple" asking questions of the pastor, thus helping him present God's Word on marriage. A "married couple" could engage the pastor in dialogue regarding the purposes of family and family relations.

Churches with regular Sunday evening services might find films appropriate as teaching tools to heighten interest and interaction. A crucial point: films, filmstrips, and audio and video cassettes are educational devices that should be used appropriately, not as ends in themselves. An introduction to the teaching aid should be employed to help the audience anticipate the issues, paradoxes, problems, or ideas presented through them. What should viewers look for? What is at issue, for example, between a father and son depicted in the film? Is the film's portrayal realistic or idealistic? How does the father feel? What emotions do you detect in the son? Some programs are designed for stopping the cassette or film and having discussion before progressing.

Possibly, at the close of a cassette, questions should be distributed and small groups gathered in different areas of the hall or building for discussion or study. Groups may regather at an appointed time for sharing of conclusions or questions. For example, during a demonstration wedding, the action could stop after each segment with explanation by the minister as to what is next in the ceremony and its spiritual significance. Questions may be asked, discussion encouraged, and even Bible discovery can take place on the spot during this "stop action" technique.

RAPPORT

A crucial aspect of the pastoral role involves the quality of his relationship with his people—especially the young people considering marital preparation. During more than twenty years of active ministry, I have observed the style of many clergymen. Some are aloof and remote, though trying to be friendly. Some have gifts in the area of scriptural exposition, but tend to be impersonal or judgmental. Generally, young people do not seek out such clergy for fear of censure or exposure. Certainly, if pastors are not involved with their young people in various informal settings, they will project an image of authoritarianism. Even pastors of "super churches" must take the time to visit Sunday school departments, not for observation, but for informal question-answer sessions.

Crucial to pastor-youth relations is what Young Life Campaign has termed "winning a hearing"—the trust factor. Occasional informal involvement in recreational or athletic programs helps young men appreciate the manliness of their pastor. Whether or not he is a great athlete is not at issue. Is the pastor a warm, friendly human being whom they can trust? Does he sincerely like people? Does he love them? If those questions are answered in the positive, it will insure a pastor's rapport with his young people, and thence their openness to seek him out generally as well as in times of need. Another rapport-builder is humor. Pastors must learn to laugh at their own foibles, to admit humanity. In those ways, a pastor's genuineness will be evident and will be a calling card for those in need. One pastor has reflected,

> I see my task as personalizing the gospel of our Lord Jesus. So I push aside the tables and the lectern and sit on a chair in a circle with my students (whom I refer to as friends), as I eat popcorn and drink Pepsi in their living

rooms or around the fireplace at the retreat center, as we go off on field trips to the funeral home and other places. We interact with each other, as persons, in a learning community.[2]

Planned sessions where the pastor speaks on love, courtship, and marriage should be a part of the youth program at least every two years, so that he has exposure to all young people who are consistently a part of the church youth program. Content is important, but just as significant is the establishing of an ongoing rapport with the young people so that as they approach engagement and marriage they will sense that he is open and available to help in their second most important decision of life.

PREMARITAL COUNSELING

Probably the most visible evangelical approach to premarital counseling is the work of H. Norman Wright, associate professor of psychology at Biola University and Talbot Theological Seminary. Wright's *Premarital Counseling* (Moody, 1980, rev. ed.) is a manual for pastors and other Christian workers who prepare young people for marriage. I have adapted and re-ordered his list of goals according to a spiritual-relational hierarchy:

1. *To build an in-depth and ongoing relationship with the couple.* Without this first step, ministry becomes impersonal. A pastor wants to know the persons with whom he works, their personality differences, attitudes, images, likes and dislikes, and temperaments. In that way, the candidates for marriage will always know that he is available to listen and help sincerely, not merely as a part of his job.

2. *To help the couple grow spiritually.* This will be the foundation for personal, marital, and eventually parental growth. The pastor has unique opportunities, especially in one-to-one sessions, to probe the spiritual depth of each, leading them in Christian discipleship. Such spiritual growth relates to the marital relationship and to parental modeling and teaching.

3. *To create the atmosphere in which a couple may vent their anxieties regarding marriage.* Even contemporary young people, who have been exposed to more information on sexuality, relationships, and marriage than probably any other generation, have concerns relating to roles, performance, and expectations that need to be brought to the surface, discussed, and resolved.

2. Richard Rehfeldt, "The Road to Educational Ministry," in *The Pastor's Role in Educational Ministry* (Philadelphia: Fortress, 1974), p. 37.

4. *To minimize surprises.* Unexpected attitudes, expectations, or experiences invade a relationship with anxiety and distrust. The more one spouse knows about the values and background of the other, the fewer surprises are possible.

5. *To give positive teaching and correct faulty impressions or information.* This can be in regard to marriage, finances, relationships to in-laws, sex, and family. The books that the counselor has the applicants read are a major source of valid information.

6. *To help the couple arrive at a final decision regarding marriage.* Engagement breaking is not regarded today as negatively as it was even twenty-five years ago. Though a couple's engagement may signal to the community their intention to marry, it is not a fait accompli. As a deeper relationship develops, one or the other, or both, may recognize that sufficient factors are not present to provide the inner security necessary for a stable marriage, and the engagement will be broken.

7. *To make arrangements for the wedding ceremony and reception.* Many pastors today are assisting candidates in the creation of ceremonies that are distinctive, thoroughly Christian, and reflective of the tastes of the couple. Traditional practices and local customs are discussed from such simple decisions as color scheme to the more complex ones concerning designing a wedding reception that will reinforce the wedding testimony.

COUNSELING FORMS

For more than a decade I have generally followed a six-session format in premarital counseling that varies slightly from Wright's model: first session with the couple, second session with each partner, an hour each; and each of the following sessions with the couple. I have sometimes varied it, with the second and third sessions also being separate. The sessions are usually weekly. Assignments given each partner to complete prior to the next session range from working on a questionnaire, to a structured discussion on a given topic, to the reading of a book or listening to tapes. It is also advised that between three and six months after the wedding, the pastor or counselor arrange a seventh session as a follow-up for evaluation and enrichment.

CONTENT

Implicit in the purposes for premarital counseling listed above is the need to discern the attitudes and values of the prospective marriage partners towards two ends: (1) to comprehend the relationship and the interacting of the two personalities in order to predict the success of the marriage; and (2) to lead the pair through the creative and reflective process of projecting themselves ahead into the marriage relationship in order to help them anticipate marriage and family life, so that adjustments may be made in their own attitudes and expectations. If prospective partners are not compatible, often premarital counseling and testing will reveal this, allowing the couple both time and the setting for adequate discussion and, if necessary, the breaking of the engagement. Often the counselor will have to break through the romantic aura of the relationship to help the prospective partners confront the realities of their personalities and expectations—even to the point of having to recommend a "holding pattern" in the relationship, or outright breaking of the engagement.

Of course, the counselor is in a critical position should a cessation of the relationship be deemed necessary. Only after objectively dealing with all the data learned through the counseling process—including test scores—and after sincere prayer for guidance and tact, should a counselor recommend breaking off an engagement. This is ticklish business for the premarital counselor, because if the persons are members of his church or their families are, he may feel compelled not to jeopardize his standing with those families and thus withhold his honest evaluation. One who does not speak the courage of his convictions soon finds himself the easy pawn of church power structures and inevitably experiences a loss of self-esteem. The initially more painful way of integrity is ultimately best, for we who minister in Jesus' name must answer to a Master whose "Well done, thou good and faithful servant" is the validator of our ministry.

Content areas for premarital counseling are generally considered to include the following:

Spiritual orientation. A consistent Christian orientation to marriage cannot accommodate to the marriage of a Christian to a non-Christian: "Do not be bound together with unbelievers" (2 Cor. 6:14). There can hardly be an ingredient in a relationship as crucial as the partners' view of ultimate reality, their love and commitment to God in Christ and their expression of that commitment in daily and church life. Such an orientation must affect the utilization of time, values relating to talent, money, and possessions, and the quality of human relations. If a couple is at odds concerning those values, the incompatibility is so pervasive as to nullify any attempt at circumvention, be it hoping that things will work out or that the non-Christian will become a sincere believer. This may sound like a hard line in light of the contemporary trend to ignore "religious" differences. However, in focus here is an intended marriage partner who is a committed believer in Jesus Christ as Savior and Lord.

We are not considering two nominally religious persons for whom religion is merely a social and cultural involvement.

Obviously, two persons whose religious beliefs are nominal may value church involvement because of the reinforcement of good morals, especially when it comes to the perceived needs of their children. If should be noted, however, that many young people whose interest in religion was minimal throughout later teens and early twenties and even into the first years of marriage, suddenly experience spiritual resurgence when children come to the relationship. That syndrome is perfectly understandable because the presence of children awakens in parents a sense of responsibility, reminds them of their formative years, and usually carries with it certain considerations for grandparents who expect at least minimal religious observations for their grandchildren. Although the church should think creatively about how to disciple such parents, that in no way ought to reflect on the stance of the church regarding mixed marriage.

The Christian counselor or pastor will meet sincere Christian young people who have "fallen in love" with non-Christians and believe that through marriage they will be able to lead the spouse to spiritual commitment. Experience is a sad invalidator of such a notion, in support of the spiritual principle cited earlier. Further, pastors will be confronted by nominal Christians who are even willing to make overt religious affirmations just to get the pastor to perform the service. One particularly knotty relationship is that of a sincerely committed Christian with one who is immature spiritually. Similar to the Christian-non-Christian dyad, the more mature believer often thinks that he will be able to draw the other partner into a deeper Christian commitment. Experience confirms that the likelihood of such spiritual mentoring is indeed slim. First of all, if one spouse suspects that he or she is the object of the other's proselytizing, he will resist being changed by the other. That will serve only to introduce into the relationship another factor for tension. What occurs often, however, is that either the more committed partner remains staunch, resulting in religion becoming a cause of dissension throughout the life of the relationship, or the spiritually mature partner capitulates for the sake of peace and lives a defeated Christian life.

Communication. Many fine works provide detailed treatment of communication in marriage (see Chapter 19). I will simply say that marriage partners must learn to speak the truth in love (Eph. 4:15). It has only been in the past decade or so that stress has been laid on both partners communicating their feelings with one another in perfect candor. In so many relationships partners "gunny sack" hurts, slights, and irritations. If they had the boldness to talk with their spouses in love, marriage partners could keep hidden agendas at a minimum. Counselors will want to help prospective marriage partners learn the skills for effective communication.

Conflict Resolution. Whenever any two persons live together in a relationship having the proximity of marriage, conflict will be inevitable. Conflict is a fact but not necessarily an evil. Different tastes in food, architecture, colors, and music are conflicts, but they need not become contentions. The key to keeping conflicts merely differences that are appreciated by both parties lies in the personalities of the partners and the means by which they compromise. Communication techniques will figure large in the process, but one's temperament and the degree to which the issue is tied to one's self image will greatly affect the outcome. Writers and counselors today speak of *resolution of conflict* not merely as a general term referring to the settling of an argument, but as a special method for reaching a conclusion that is fully acceptable to both parties, in contrast to the typical methods—win, lose, withdrawal, or fifty/fifty compromise—in which thoroughly mutually agreeable settlement is rare.[3]

Finances. Financial concerns make their way to the top of a couple's priority list early in marriage. Partners who come from differing socio-economic settings find themselves continually in arguments over how their monies should be allocated for expenses, whose money should be used for what, and how much should be set aside for savings. Premarital counseling will help them discuss the pros and cons of various budgetary methods and zero in on the method they will use as their marriage begins. Many current books provide programs for helping couples start their marriages on optimal financial footing.

Sexual Relations. With the contemporary overkill in the area of sexuality, no one can exist in Western society without being made continually aware of sexual issues through print, video, and film media. Still, many couples enter married life virtually ignorant of the pervasive degree to which their sexual relationship will affect their overall relationship. The pastor/counselor will use a simple questionnaire to allow the couple to test their own understanding of sexuality. He will recommend books, encourage open discussion, and suggest medical counsel regarding birth control. From a biblical perspective he will lead the couple to appreciate the positive dimension of sex from God's point of view. That will be a liberating revelation, should the couple not have had exposure to contemporary biblical materials on sex in marriage.

3. H. Norman Wright, *The Pillars of Marriage* (Glendale, Calif.: Regal, 1979), pp. 145–60.

Roles. Will the prospective couple carry on the sex roles of their parents or drastically alter them? Who will cook, wash dishes, change the oil in the car, take out the garbage, run the vacuum cleaner, do the laundry, balance the checking account? Thorough structured discussion of those kinds of expectations will help the couple know one another much better than the usual haphazard role struggles of early marriage.

In-laws. During the early stages of romance, a couple rarely thinks about in-laws. However, as the relationship matures, it becomes quite apparent that a young person marries not just a spouse but his or her whole family. Attitudes, actions, values, and histories all conspire to create an overwhelming amount of familial baggage that every person brings to marriage. How one responds to his spouse's family, and they to him, impinges most directly on the happiness of the couple—even when they think they are all alone. The counselor will help each partner verbalize his thoughts about his own and his spouse's family, and teach them to positively relate to both.

Children. Few young people learn how to be parents except by the informal method of remembering and reproducing to a greater or lesser degree the styles of discipline practiced on them by their parents. During the stage of premarital preparation the counselor will help the couple focus on the number of children they desire, the spacing between children, the type of living conditions optimal to family, and the roles of both parents in children's development. The methods and materials of Christianizing their children will at least be introduced so that adequate spiritual preparation may take place for rearing godly children.

Goals. An old saying states, "If you aim at nothing, that is precisely what you will hit." Although many Americans still maintain a kind of we'll-deal-with-that-when-we-have-to mentality, marital relations specialists are finding that when a couple sets goals together and together work to achieve those goals, their relationship then takes on a tone of mutual anticipation, cooperation, achievement, and evaluation. A kind of "mile marker" approach gives the couple both things to look forward to and to look back on as achievements—together. That kind of "fore and aft" mooring provides strong anchoring for the relationship during the waxing and waning of emotional tides and the inevitable battering of periodic relational storms. Areas of goal establishment could include: finances, time together, house acquisition and improvement, interaction with children and relatives, vacations, spiritual growth, Bible study, service for Christ in and out of church, relations with neighbors and community, and sex life. One primary principle of married life comes to the fore at this junction: All actions affecting one's spouse must be discussed together and a unanimous decision reached. There must be no unilateral decisions.

Undoubtedly, one or another marriage counselor will add to, delete from, or reorganize this list of areas for premarital counseling. Nevertheless, the counselor must have a game plan clearly established in his file so that his preparation of every couple for marriage covers all the bases. Without such a plan, the counselor's time and energy are insufficiently focused to produce the required result: the best possible preparation for marriage within the time allotted.

GROUP PREMARITAL COUNSELING

Such a program as outlined above, with the six counseling sessions, areas to be discussed, and tapes and texts to be coordinated, may seem a formidable juggling act for a busy pastor counseling several couples during a typical springtime. Therefore, an alternative to counseling one couple at a time is group counseling. With as few as three or four couples and up to fifteen, weekly sessions may incorporate all the materials previously cited and involve each couple in a group dynamics approach to marital preparation. Though the method is not as personal as private counseling, there is a trade-off in that couples discussing the topics together help form a kind of consensus, which helps in the firming of commitment and forces verbalization of ideas in a context in which glib answers are rarely tolerated. Further, following their weddings, couples so counseled may continue to fellowship together, forming a support group. The possibilities for follow-up and group marital maintenance during the early stages of marriage could prove crucially helpful. Wright outlines such sessions in detail.[4]

With marriage and family forming the primary social context for the promulgation of our Christian faith, ordering human social life in holiness, and human intimacy, it is incumbent on the church not to leave instruction in those areas to chance. There must be a unified, integrated, contextual, and biblical approach to marriage and family that the church updates and refines generation after generation, to prepare its members for those relationships in which the seed of Christian faith is planted,

4. H. Norman Wright, *Premarital Counseling* (Chicago: Moody, 1981), pp. 173-79.

nurtured, and allowed to flourish. This chapter has outlined an elementary approach for meeting those needs. Be assured that the laboratory of our Christian faith is first and foremost our most intimate relationships, in marriage and in the family.

1. Describe the courtship patterns of the young people of your hometown community. How should knowing those factors affect your church's approach to helping young in the areas of relationships with the opposite sex, dating, courtship, and marriage?

2. If you were to present a prospectus to a church for the hiring of a minister of family life and counseling, what reasons would you martial to warrant such a post?

3. Review one or more units of the Concordia Sex Education Series (1982), identifying age group characteristics of which the writers and illustrators were cognizant. Specify the characteristcs and show how the text and/or illustrations agree. Select at least six characteristics and examples. If per chance they should not agree, demonstrate why.

4. Present at least three reasons a church should have a visible policy regarding marriage.

5. Evaluate your own home pastor (anonymously) concerning his relationship with your church young people, indicating why young people would or would not seek him out regarding problems of family, dating, courtship, or marriage.

6. Prepare a dialogue sermon in which the pastor converses with an "engaged couple" about their intended wedding. Write out the entire script—including props, if appropriate.

18

Marital Maintenance

It happens to everything: the mainspring of the clock on the mantle unwinds in eight days; the fuel cells in the atomic reactor lose their ability to produce thermal energy; the automobile engine requires regular maintenance, or sooner or later it will become inoperative. Even the universe appears to be slowing down, according to the principle of entropy.

Human relationships have their own kind of entropy. Boy meets girl. They share similarities in socioeconomic backgrounds, religion, education, and personality; they become emotionally involved; they get married. For a while things go well as each works hard to continue to persuade the other that he/she was a worthy choice. But eventually the relationship experiences a series of predictable crises. Almost invariably the partners drift apart. It could be called marital entropy.

J. Richard Udry demonstrates eight stages in a typical American marriage:[1]

1. Beginning marriage (before children).
2. Oldest child an infant.

1. J. Richard Udry, *The Social Context of Marriage,* 3d ed. (Philadelphia: J. B. Lippincott, 1974), p. 205.

3. Oldest child a preschooler.
4. Oldest child an elementary school child.
5. Oldest child a teenager.
6. Oldest child living away from home; other children at home.
7. All children living away from home.
8. Husband retired.

By the time a marriage arrives at stage 4, a couple has experienced approximately ten years of marriage. The relationship has been strained numerous times: a wife's pregnancy, the birth of a child, altered life-style because of the child, increased costs, a husband's struggle to establish himself in his occupation, uprooting for employment promotion, and many other factors provide rich soil for the seeds of relational instability. These typical marital epochs occur for the Christian couple as well as the rest of society.

Unfortunately, for the most part couples are not given the prognostic nor diagnostic tools to anticipate the effects of the stages of their marriages; nor do they develop sufficient sensitivity to detect when the relationship begins to experience inertia. Therefore, it is imperative that the church thoughtfully evaluate its programs and emphases so as to help its married couples to be aware of their relationships, and provide both the workshop and the tools to keep the relationships in smooth running condition.

THE CAUSES OF SEPARATION AND DIVORCE

SOCIETAL CAUSES

Any of Udry's eight stages may contain factors that will lead to tension. In addition, David Knox lists seven societal causes of marriage disintegration, that is, factors growing out of our American culture that work against marriage.[2]

Changing family functions. The family used to be the hub of the lives of the family members, organizing meals, clothing, recreation, religion, education, and welfare. Increasingly, our American way of life has developed specialized agencies that have assumed traditional family functions. With fewer reasons for persons to find their integration at home, couples are not forced into mutual dependency.

2. David Knox, *Exploring Marriage and the Family* (Glenview, Ill.: Scott, Foresman, 1979), pp. 519-20.

Employed wives. To a great extent today, wives are no longer dependent on their husbands for food, shelter, and clothing. Both men and women often find themselves in employment that increasingly places them with members of the opposite sex for six to eight hours a day. Marital infidelity and ultimately divorce can result either from discouraged spouses relating their problems to sympathetic members of the opposite sex, or the outright design of someone to "catch" a new partner.

Reduction of religious and moral sanctions. Knox says, "Marriage is often viewed in secular rather than sacred terms."[3] Even though churches disapprove of divorce, they seldom take a public stance. When the church sheepishly acquiesces to divorce, another social means of control erodes.

The increasing divorce rate. As divorce becomes more frequent, greater numbers of people are exposed to relatives and friends who are divorcing or divorced. Acceptability of behavior is often determined by frequency—that is known as "statistical morality." Our populace increasingly sees divorce as normal. With societal sanctions reduced only to occasional gossip or wrist-slapping, divorce is less socially undesirable and hence is seen as, mistakenly, the easy way out of a counterproductive relationship.

Mate selection. The motivation for marriage has changed greatly since the notion of romance permeated our culture. "Falling in love" has replaced security as the motivation for marriage. Although the pleasures of romance may keep a couple together for a while, it will not enable couples to make the adaptations necessary for a long-term marriage.

The happiness goal. The world of the 1980s is characterized by an overwhelming desire and search for pleasure. Lured by the pleasures of romance, couples often marry without adequate evaluation of the responsibilities inherent in marriage: employment on a steady basis, providing for children, schedules that militate against spur-of-the-moment excursions, social obligations. Unprepared for the responsibilities, seemingly shackled by obligations, emotionally distraught because expectations have not been met, couples often opt for divorce. All too often, they simply start the old cycle all over again with a different partner; it has been estimated that 42 percent of second marriages end in divorce.

Liberalized divorce laws. As Udry points out, "one of the most fundamental reasons for the high divorce rate of Americans is the fact that divorce is less socially stigmatized today than ever before."[4] Civil laws generally reflect popular social trends, and so we have increasingly liberal divorce laws. Citizens who feel caught in the trap of a bad

3. Ibid., p. 520.
4. Udry, *The Social Context of Marriage,* p. 404.

marriage are thus encouraged to take the exit approved by society rather than seeking help for restoration or healing of the relationship. California's divorce rate jumped 49 percent in 1970—the same year that state put the no-fault divorce laws in the books.[5]

PERSONAL CAUSES

The tenor of society may pave the way for divorce, but any divorce must include causes that are particular to the couple in question. These may include:

Negative behavior. This can include drinking, yelling, physical abuse, sexual unfaithfulness, inappropriate use of sex, spouse-parent power structures, and nagging. One or more of those symptoms can overpower whatever positive supports the relationship may have, leading a spouse to seek safety or freedom.

Boredom or satiation. Some relationships get locked into such a routine that spontaneity is lost. Often this happens when both partners are employed full-time and come home tired and frayed. So a routine of eating supper, doing chores, and watching television until bedtime ensues. Without adequate breaks in the routine, eventually one spouse (or both) realizes that their life is stagnant. Instead of cooperatively planning variation, one may see the other as the source of the stagnation and, given inadequate commitment to the relationship, may seek a change in partner to bring the desired change in life-style.

Infidelity. Emotionally healthy persons desire a relationship with others that is positive, encouraging, warm, and supportive. In the absence of what one believes to be the adequate amount of the above, a partner may seek other persons to provide them. A seemingly warm, compassionate, and caring co-worker may appear to be the means for receiving what a wife thinks she is not receiving from her husband, or vice versa. As indicated earlier, contemporary society places people together in close interpersonal relationships on the job, in social clubs, churches, and in urban and suburban settings through neighbors. Add to that a casual attitude toward sexual gratification, and infidelity becomes easy and common.

Acquiescence. For whatever reasons, an immediate cause for divorce is that one spouse wants a divorce, and the other, though apparently happy with the marriage, agrees, ostensibly because the other spouse wants it. The rate of such divorces is staggering: 40 percent of divorces include

5. Knox, *Exploring Marriage and the Family,* p. 520.

one partner who does not really want the divorce but acquiesces to the desires of the other.[6]

Given the spreading epidemic of divorce among Christians and the clear biblical teaching regarding the spiritual roots of marriage and its central role in multiplying godliness through descendants, what can the church do to help Christian married couples develop strong and lasting marriage relationships? First, we shall examine the areas of emphasis to be included in any program, and then we shall delineate the types of experiences currently being offered and suggestions for further implementation.

What kind of material should be utilized to help couples build strong marriages? The programs currently being offered through books, seminars, encounter groups, and film series have five basic themes.

IDENTIFYING THE PROBLEMS

"Forewarned is forearmed" may be said to be the philosophy of those who approach marriage maintenance.

Marriages are initiated for a great variety of reasons. Researchers have isolated numerous reasons given by interviewees, but they fall into about eight general categories: romantic feelings, sexual attraction, social pressure, escape from a bad home life, premarital pregnancy, rebound, rebellion against parents, and emotional responses of guilt or pity. Sooner or later, a Christian couple will have to face the reasons for their marriage and work through the guilt and anxiety that may be there. Once such admission is achieved, a couple may work on rebuilding or stabilizing the marriage.

From a Christian perspective, couples need to know and appreciate God's utilization of the circumstances of their marriage for the shaping of their individual and corporate lives.

> And we know that in all things God works for the good of those who love him, who have been called according to his purpose. For those God foreknew he also predestinated to be conformed to the likeness of his Son, that he might be the firstborn among many brothers. (Rom. 8:28–29, NIV)

The Bible often speaks of suffering as the precursor of maturity or spiritual success. Paul uses the athletic metaphor of disciplining his

---

6. Knox, p. 522.

own body as a form of suffering that, when taken full course, produces the champion runner (1 Cor. 9:24-27). God uses the experiences of life to hone the fine cutting edge of our Christian lives. Thus, the principle is to allow God to use the experience—not to reject His chastening—for our perfecting and His ultimate glory.

Couples also need to understand how their expectations regarding marriage were developed. Our media play a major role in informing young people what to expect from marriage. Hollywood and Madison Avenue conspire to communicate to the populace all of the *things we deserve* from the marriage relationship: fantastic sex, sprawling suburban homes, two cars in the garage, vacations on Caribbean islands or fashionable ski slopes. As a result, people often compare their actual mates and possessions with the artificial world view they have acquired. Too quickly they learn that the real world involves ample portions of drudgery. Soon, they are disillusioned; then a scapegoat must be dragged out and blamed for the failure. Rather than seeing that the hopelessly unrealistic view of life is to blame, the spouse is castigated: he doesn't make enough money, or she is frigid and not providing the anticipated romantic "high." Often the end of the scenario includes some sort of escape from the truth of the real world: alcohol, entertainment, drugs, purchases, vacations, or illicit love affairs as the disillusioned search for a new "dream girl" or "Prince Charming" who will afford them all their expectations.

The fallacy of the fifty-fifty relationship is also to blame. That is, there is a pernicious myth that states that all relationships may achieve balance simply by a fair apportioning of the various tasks pertaining to the relationship. Approval is given when the partner does his or her share. Each person strives to do his or her part, demonstrating to the other love and esteem! But living as we all do on this side of Eden, few of us truly strive to do our very best, we tend to respond to our spouses proportionally to the degree that we think they deserve it—we act as judges. Plainly, the fifty-fifty relationship does not work. The myth is promulgated by the universal need for balance but is woefully unrealistic because of man's egocentrism. We tend to focus on the weaknesses of our spouses, strangely enough, not on their strengths.

Certainly, the mature biblical view sees marriage as a serving and giving relationship on the part of both parties—100-100. Each has the good of the other at heart. When a spouse's emotional transmission to the other includes encouragement, building up, appreciation, a sense of worth, and warmth, the spouse tends to reflect that emotional tone.

It is apparent that in the glow of romance couples do not enter marriage appreciating the reality that human life also consists of sufferings and trials. Even without unusual problems, the process of bearing and raising children carries with it pain, heartache, and responsibility. Christian couples must learn to work through their problems and crises in a mutually supportive manner, avoiding blame and recrimination. Any time either partner senses emotional distance in the relationship there must be open discussion, communication of trust, and a willingness to admit wrongs and seek forgiveness. Forgiveness must be freely and sincerely given, not withheld or bartered.

COMMUNICATION

The quality of the husband-wife relationship may be safely said to hang on the ability of each partner to speak the truth in love. But communication includes much more than lovingly honest words. Sven Wahlroos defines communication as "any behavior that carries a message which is perceived by someone else."[7] Jesus' expression of the golden rule touches the same pulse: "Just as you want people to treat you, treat them in the same way" (Luke 6:31). James's "Prove yourselves doers of the word, and not merely hearers" catches the same idea. Our actions are communicators as well as our words. Many couples have not learned to be open in their communication with one another, either because of previous training or because of personality and disposition. Teaching communication should then be a part of the church's program for maintaining marriages.

David and Vera Mace, founders of the marriage enrichment movement, have been influential in numerous conferences, seminars, and writings on marriage for the past thirty years. They outline three essential elements for a happy marriage: (1) a commitment to growth, seriously entered into by husband and wife together; (2) an effective communication system and the skills to use it; and (3) the ability to accept marital conflict positively and resolve it creatively. The Maces identify four styles of communication, as delineated by the following chart:[8]

Style	Identification	Description
I	Transmissive	Passing on information in a generally unemotional manner—widely used in everyday conversations concerning events of the day, etc.

7. Sven Wahlroos, *Family Communication: A Guide to Emotional Health* (New York: New American Library, 1974), p. 4.
8. David and Vera Mace, *How to Have a Happy Marriage* (Nashville: Abingdon, 1977), p. 30.

II	Manipulative	The use of blame, command, the "putdown," and sarcasm to elevate the user and denigrate the receiver.
III	Analytical	Rational, diagnostic, and intellectual; usually ignores the fact that problems have an emotional core.
IV	Affective	See below.

Affective communication is foreign to the usual forms of discourse to which we are subjected day by day. A newspaper may use the transmissive style when reporting events, an advertiser will use persuasion to get us to purchase his product, and a scientist will be as objective as possible. However, in a relationship as intimate as marriage—and also in the close ties of family and immediate friends—we are sharing life with others; we are inextricably bound to others. Although the Maces do not mention it, the biblical concept of *koinonia* probably comes closest to defining the setting in which affective communication may take place. The apostle Paul uses the term in connection with the quality of relationship that exists between believers who all share the Spirit of God (Phil. 2:1). John employs the word referring to the quality of mutuality possible among those who "walk in the light" of Christ (1 John 1:7). Again, the term *agape* (love) is intertwined with *koinonia* in describing the kind of relationship that exists among believers in Christ.

Affective communication has at its root the principle that "individual happiness comes only through shared happiness."[9] Those are radical words to a world full of people rushing to gobble up all the pleasure possible for themselves. Affective communication involves the freedom to relate to one's spouse precisely how one feels at the moment, be it neutral emotions or strong sentiments. The point is that because of the quality of the relationship persons may honestly express their feelings and be vulnerable to each other. The simple theory here is that the other person cannot respond appropriately—in a positive, helping, and caring manner—if he is unaware how his partner truly feels. The frank expression of feelings is one of the most direct means of expressing *trust* in one's spouse, because implicit in the honest expression of feelings is the knowledge that the recipient will not reject, ridicule, or hurt when he is privy to one's honest emotions. If partners hide their true feelings or modify them so as to make them acceptable, the relationship will be based on illusion, or worse, outright dishonesty. To the degree that

9. Ibid., p. 86.

couples have not learned to trust one another with their honest feelings, true intimacy evades them.

It is crucial to affective communication, moreover, that spouses express their feelings (1) without attacking or blaming, (2) without self-defense, and (3) without ridicule. For example, a wife could express her honest feelings (that is, what she is actually feeling at the moment) in either a positive or negative manner:

> "Charlie, I'm scared to death when we go around these curves so fast!"
> "Charlie, I'm scared to death when you take these curves like an idiot!"

In the first example, the wife limits her expression to her actual emotions. In the second example, she pinpoints the fact that Charlie is to blame and resorts to name-calling. Once couples have been trained in affective communication and have both become committed to its utilization, several things become apparent: First, it speaks the language of love; "Your needs are more important to me than anything else"; Second, it provides peace of mind, because no one worries that the other is camouflaging reality. Third, it contributes to self-understanding, leading to emotional maturity, rather than game-playing and traps. The Bibliography includes several helpful tools on communication.

CONFLICT RESOLUTION

The subject of conflict resolution is closely linked to communication, because it is through certain techniques of communication that conflicts between persons are treated.

Conflict will always arise between two people, because we all have different habits, tastes, preferences, values, standards, convictions, thought patterns, self-images, views of the opposite sex, and religious experiences. Also, certain experiences common to most marriages will almost always precipitate differences of opinion. The birth of a first child brings into focus possible differing ways of caring for infants. A second child adds fuel to the fire of conflict. During a marriage's early years, when a husband is working long hours to establish himself in his career, his absence brings irritation. When children have complicated schedules necessitating various times for pick-up, eating, and bedtime, homemakers may feel like chauffeurs—without any tips! And when puberty arrives a whole new set of problems descend on the marriage relationship and escalate conflicts. Each one of those common marriage experiences has the potential for dozens of occasions when opinions clash. What better place to learn to anticipate the conflicts of married life than in classes within the church, with persons who share common faith in Christ and a desire for God's will in their lives?

But conflicts may also be the source of positive input to a marriage. A conflict highlights the need to learn to appreciate and care for one's spouse all the more. By working through conflict, couples may develop their skills in human relations for working with people in general. And by observing mother and father positively resolving conflict, children may learn to do so as well.

How may conflicts be resolved? It is possible in most conflicts for one or the other person to either win, yield, or withdraw. But there cannot be sincere mutual caring in a relationship if each conflict results in a win/lose dichotomy. So typically we speak of compromise—each side giving somewhat, each side receiving somewhat—as the means of pleasing both sides. But a closer look at typical compromise reveals various subtle mechanisms at work. Someone once said that "a compromise is a deal in which two people get what neither of them wanted." Sometimes compromises are achieved through one partner giving in *this* time, and the other partner giving in *next* time. But unless precise records are kept it is impossible to keep the score straight. Further, just as with the fifty-fifty concept of marriage, it is almost impossible to deal fairly with an issue because of the various means we humans have of getting our own way. Compromise appears to be the most humane way of handling conflict, but often there is subtle manipulation and only apparent compromise.

The approach that many marriage specialists employ today may simply be termed *resolving*. The resolution of a conflict occurs when both parties honestly can conclude they are happy with the outcome. There is no tearing of the relationship; rather, the process of resolution has actually brought the coupole closer together. Thus, resolution results in and reveals a high degree of relational concern. People resolving conflicts express greater concern for the condition of their relationship than for individual ego inflation. Through the process of resolving, the needs of both parties are met optimally.

Resolving technique can be outlined as follows. First, both parties must agree wholeheartedly that maintaining their loving relationship is more important than winning or having their way. Second, both parties should agree that there may be more than only one way of looking at the question at hand. In other words, neither party entertains the egotistical idea that he is the sole repository of wisdom, or that his perspective is the only one. Third, each partner must sincerely want to understand the other's reasoning and the related emotions. Therefore, each member will wholeheartedly listen to the partner's full explanation of his position, trying to vicariously appreciate both the reasoning and the emotion. Fourth, no derogatory remarks nor deprecations are allowed whatsoever. Fifth, imperatives and inclusive generalizations such as "You must do . . ," "I will have . . ," "You always want . . ," and "You never do . . . " must be entirely omitted. Sixth, resolving technique involves "I" statements rather than "you" statements. For example, "I feel lonely, ashamed, or afraid," not "You make me feel lonely, ashamed, or afraid." Resolution aims at ridding the discussion of any negative elements, any words or gestures that might be interpreted as being in the "attack mode."

Several special techniques have been developed for helping resolve conflicts in human relations settings such as business, education, government, and marriage and family. Several of the works that specify them are listed in the Bibliography. However, overriding all of the good techniques must be openness to the needs and feelings of one's spouse. Christian love epitomizes such openness because it considers others' needs first, works towards unity, and desires that which pleases God.

PARTNERSHIP DISCIPLESHIP

Although many of the current books and programs used in evangelical circles for marriage enrichment programs employ valid psychological and human relations principles in helping couples deepen their relationships, many are weak in centering marriage partners on Jesus Christ. That must be the primary criterion for any program employed by the church.

Many Christian marriage partners have individual devotions, Bible study, personal worship, and prayer. But only through a *shared spiritual life* can couples optimally grow together. Couples need to be guided in learning how to have spiritual times together.

The objectives of such times include, first, *mutual acknowledgement of dependence upon the Lord.* When an owner of a business can bow in prayer with his spouse, seeking the Lord's direction for their lives as well as for the business, that is a sign that such a person's spiritual priorities are rightly ordered. It is extremely difficult to carry on sham with God, with one's spouse, or with one's self while all three are in spiritual communion. Second, *mutual intercession* is both humbling and encouraging. It helps to have spouses pray for each other aloud. Of course, caution must be taken here that a spouse does not preach through the vehicle of prayer: "Lord, You know how weak Bill is. Don't allow him to be tempted to . . . " Third, *mutual growth:* as couples pray together openly, seeking God's direction for themselves and their children, they are able to observe God's actions, His answers to prayer. In so doing they grow together in faith. Fourth, *mutual love:* through a shared worship or devotional life couples are drawn together in greater unity.

The setting and method of partnership discipleship will vary depending on life-style. For many couples who both work full time outside the home, finding a fifteen- to thirty-minute period together may prove difficult. Still, ingenuity can find time that complacency never can. One couple who see very little of one another except on weekends keep a prayer diary along with their Bible on the kitchen table. A daily Bible reading guide spells out the passage to be read for the day. Each jots down notes, questions, or observations from the text for the other to read when it is his turn for devotions. Their common prayer list, Bible reading, and notes keep them together spiritually all week until the weekend, when they can have a substantive spiritual time together. Other couples may find that a shared devotional is possible almost every day. One Christian worker whose office is a scant hundred feet from his apartment has a second cup of coffee with his wife after the children are off to school. Together they read a chapter a day aloud, progressively, through the Scripture. They also spend time communicating their concerns about the children and various areas of their relationship. In that way they can bring all of their needs before one another and the Lord. The daily time has welded their relationship.

GOALS

Many counselors and clinical psychologists have found that stagnant relationships result from couples' not having goals or objectives toward which both could work. It is generally agreed that goals provide emotional drive and a sense of satisfaction when the object is achieved. For couples, a sense of mutual drive and mutual satisfaction results from setting goals, working towards their achievement, and realizing the objective. The combination of those elements helps to keep married couples working together and experiencing mutual satisfaction.

In his workbook for couples, *The Pillars of Marriage*, H. Norman Wright refers to the importance of goals as cited by Cornell Medical Center psychiatrist Ari Kiev:

> With goals people can overcome confusion and conflict over incompatible values, contradictory desires and frustrated relationships with friends and relatives, all of which often result from the absence of rational life

strategies. . . . Observing the lives of people who have mastered adversity, I have repeatedly noted that they have established goals and, irrespective of the obstacles, sought with all their effort to achieve them. From the moment they've fixed an objective in their mind and decide to concentrate all their energies on a specific goal, they begin to surmount the most difficult odds.[10]

The areas in which goals may be appropriate often are overlooked. Couples may work together to establish, for example, financial goals. Given a couple's income and priorities, what amount of money should be saved, for what purpose, by what time? Maybe a couple who are currently living in an apartment are concerned about purchasing their own home and the building of equity. Other goals may include a monthly "special event." In order to have special time together, a couple may plan periodic activities, place them on the calendar, and together have the joy of anticipation each month. Goals involving recreation, vacations, communication, Bible study, prayer, witnessing at work or in the neighborhood, and many others could be suggested.

Many other subjects could be part of a marriage maintenance emphasis of a local church, including subjects relating to family. Suffice it to say that there are numerous topics for study and discussion that will help couples to keep their relationships in focus—not only for maintaining and preserving what they have, but also for growing together.

A CHURCH PROGRAM FOR MARITAL MAINTENANCE

Once the various emphases involved in marital maintenance are perceived, methods and materials must be chosen and organization and administration must be put in place. The precise organizational approach is not germane to this writing, but several elements should be considered.

SMALL GROUP INVOLVEMENT

Rather than large, impersonal colloquiums treating the various subjects relating to marital maintenance, the most effective work takes place when five to eight couples meet together informally on a regular basis. Although that may take place in the context of a Sunday school class, the limitations tend to outweigh the benefits. A Sunday school class is usually one hour long, involves people who are dressed formally, and because of schedule (worship service, nursery, or choir service) and

10. Ari Kiev, *A Strategy for Daily Living* (New York: Free Press, 1973), cited in H. Norman Wright, *The Pillars of Marriage* (Ventura, Calif.: Regal, 1979), p. 52.

location (classroom) tends not to be casual enough for relaxation. A two-hour session with coffee, set in a family room or living room, is usually best.

The group should begin by committing to a certain number of weeks for the specific course in question. Try very hard not to allow any outside activity to invade the commitment to those hours. A mature, qualified Christian couple who act as co-leaders are the resource and catalyst for the group. Various evangelical publishing houses produce materials that are designed or adaptable for such groups. Scripture Press has published a "Family Concern" series under the Victor Books label, which may be used as home study programs or for Sunday school classes. Each of the eight courses includes a leader's guide. The same is true with Gospel Light's Regal Books, which has published paperbacks by H. Norman Wright for the same use.

SEMINARS AND CONFERENCES

Often it is easiest to get couples to join a small group when they have just finished a large group program dealing with marriage and family. For most people, any idea that their marriage relationship will be placed on public stage for dissection is anathema. The small group may be threatening for that reason. However, a church or area-wide marriage lecture or seminar is far less threatening. Currently there are several national organizations that present large group conferences. Various interesting film series are also useful for presenting married people a few entertaining and non-threatening experiences and instilling a few principles. Often, those programs start people thinking seriously about their relationships.

CRISIS INTERVENTION

One of the greatest needs of the church today as it faces an epidemic of divorces is a mechanism for detecting problems and providing encouragement and counsel where needed. In any given church the scenario often runs according to the following pattern. A couple is having problems. Either both members keep it quiet or one of them—usually the wife—shares something of the problem with a confidant. If the confidant is a spiritually mature person, it will result in prayer with and for the couple. But, it is very difficult to keep marital difficulties hidden from a group as close-knit as the church. Soon, everybody is talking about the problems the couple is having. The pastor may even be on the pipeline of information. Sometimes he feels he must act, and mustering up the courage, with much prayer, "enters in where angels fear to tread." Or, the husband or wife will come to see him for counseling; often it is very hard to get the other party in to see the pastor. Most often, the church assumes a "holding pattern," wondering what is going to happen.

But many churches have recently developed mechanisms for aggressive, caring responses to couples who are having marital difficulties. The key is trained couples who reach out to couples in distress through a direct method of visitation, counseling, and prayer. Such couples receive training through a regional or local counseling seminar (often in the local church), and work in close collaboration with the pastor. Their volunteer ministry usually takes place during evenings. Each partner of the helping team works to develop a personal relationship with the same-sex spouse of the troubled couple. They work out a week-by-week follow-up either with the couple or individually. They also seek spiritual solutions by becoming prayer partners with the couple. Though their work is usually confidential in that other church members usually do not know with whom they are working, they are responsible to the pastor or an elder in charge of the church's caring ministries.

WEEKEND RETREATS

In many churches, the adult fellowship sponsors adult retreats for various purposes—even for the rather general purpose of "fellowship." Groups select a retreat center, find a speaker (often not giving direction as to the content desired), publicize the event, and head for the hills. Given a weekend away, plenty of good food, mild recreation, game periods, the usual scenic beauty of the country, and an inspiring speaker (usually anyone except the pastor whom they hear week after week), adults return with glowing reports of the wonderful time they all experienced.

However, marriage and/or family enrichment weekends are increasingly finding their way into adult fellowship agendas. Such programs contain not merely several sermons from a speaker. Instead they have lectures, group discussion, individual evaluation and study, and time for couples to work through checklists, questionnaires, and times of intimate discussion, Bible study, and prayer. Such a setting, away from the routines of home, is ideal for working on goals. Many denominations are including marriage and family specialists in their national staffs just for the purpose of preparing materials and itineraries to member churches for such weekend programs.

BOOKS AND PERIODICALS

One of the most consistent means of helping marriages maintain stability and grow is the church library and/or Christian bookstore. Throughout the past decade, hundreds of evangelical books on virtually every aspect of marriage have come to the fore. Although some are oriented toward pastors and marriage and family professionals, most are aimed at married couples—for wives, for husbands, or both. Some church libraries in conjunction with adult Sunday school classes have sponsored five-to-ten-minute book reviews as part of the adult department opening program each week, or as part of the actual class. In that way an enthusiastic reader—preferably a man, to encourage men readers—relates a few highlights of the volume, maybe even a poignant illustration. Thus, as people read the various works on marriage and family and share them with their spouses and others in the church, there is a marital maintenance program operating in the church. Further, there are a few periodicals on the market today which are designed specifically for the family and marriage and are written from a distinctively Christian perspective.

The need in virtually every church for a means of helping married couples to cope with the special pressures of contemporary life on marriage is patently obvious. Charles R. Swindoll in his popular marital maintenance volume sees an analogy in four respects between remodeling a house and keeping a marriage in good repair.

1. It takes longer than you planned.
2. It costs more than you figured.
3. It is messier than you anticipated.
4. It requires greater determination than you expected.[11]

Although the above may be true for most married couples, it is certainly valid for any church seriously seeking to minister effectively to the needs of its married couples. To understand the social and personal pressures that springboard into divorce and to plan programs and recruit and train personnel to realistically, personally, and biblically help marriages grow, will probably take longer, cost more, be messier, and require greater determination than most programs of the church. But the results will be worth the effort: growing marriages, children raised

11. Charles R. Swindoll, *Strike the Original Match* (Portland: Multnomah, 1980), p. 10.

in maturing Christian homes, the solidarity and stability of the local church, and a whole host of people more sensitive to the needs of their brothers and sisters in Christ. It will be the practical outworking of Jesus' command and at the same time provide a powerful witness to the community as well.

> A new commandment I give to you, that you love one another, even as I have loved you, that you also love one another. By this all men will know that you are my disciples, if you have love for one another. (John 13:34-35)

1. Isolate one of the societal or personal reasons for divorce cited by Knox in this chapter, and expand it into a research project. Include statistical data where possible, and endeavor to discover several aspects of the problem and their possible causes. For example, what legislation in states other than California has helped pave the way for easier divorces?

2. How is it possible that specific marriage goals, designed and written down by a couple, become a source of nurture for their marriage relationship?

3. This chapter cited Udry's eight stages of a typical marriage, but there are undoubtedly many other experiences shared by married couples that have the potential for tension. Develop a list of crises experiences and arrange them in as much of a chronological order as possible. Wright's *The Pillars of Marriage* will prove a helpful resource.

4. Do you think that the fifty-fifty reciprocal performance relationship is practically possible? Cite reasons for your conclusion.

5. Examine the subject of personal suffering in its relation to spiritual growth. Cite biblical examples relating to both Jesus and Paul—both from their experiences and from their teachings.

6. Explain the style and purpose of *affective communication*. Consciously practice this mode of communication for several days as a personal communications experiment. Report your findings.

7. Consider Mace's proposition, "Individual happiness comes only through shared happiness" and see if you can discover biblical support for the notion. Some passages to consider include: Romans 12, Philippians 1 and 2, and Philemon.

8. Although this chapter did not isolate "witnessing" as a means of keeping a Christian couple growing together, reflect on the idea of a "shared spiritual life" in relation to a couple's communication of Christ to others, and suggest ways in which a couple may share in learning to witness, actually witnessing, and involving other Christian couples in the process.

Bibliography

This volume is intended to help the reader gain an introductory understanding of the Christian education of adults from a biblical viewpoint. The following list of resources should provide a base for further study.

Orientation to Adult Christian Education

Baldwin, F. *"Lifelong Learning" and Publication Policy.* Washington, DC: Lifelong Learning Project, U. S. Department of Health, Education and Welfare, 1977.

Bergevin, Paul. *A Philosophy for Adult Education.* New York: Seabury, 1967.

Brameld, Theodore. *Philosophies of Education in Cultural Perspective.* New York: Holt, Rinehart and Winston, 1955.

Brookes, Warren T. *The Economy in Mind.* New York: Universe, 1982.

Ceperley, Gordon. *A Promised Land for a Chosen People.* Collingswood, N.J.: Friends of Israel Gospel Ministry, 1978.

Drazin, Nathan. *History of Jewish Education.* Baltimore: Johns Hopkins, 1940.

Eavey, C. B. *History of Christian Education.* Chicago: Moody, 1964.

Gaebelein, Frank E. *Christian Education in a Democracy.* New York: Oxford U., 1951.

Gallup, George, Jr., and David Poling. *The Search for America's Faith.* Nashville: Abingdon, 1980.

Gangel, Kenneth O., and Warren S. Benson. *Christian Education: Its History and Philosophy.* Chicago: Moody, 1983.

Getz, Gene A. *Sharpening the Focus of the Church.* Chicago: Moody, 1974.

Groome, Thomas H. *Christian Religious Education*. San Francisco: Harper & Row, 1980.

Hesburgh, Theodore, Paul A. Miller, and Clifton R. Wharton. *Patterns for Lifelong Learning*. San Francisco: Jossey-Bass, 1974.

Kaluger, George, and Meriem Kaluger. *Human Development*. St. Louis: C. V. Mosby, 1979.

Knowles, Malcolm S. *History of the Adult Education Movement in the United States*. Huntington, N.Y.: Krieger, 1977.

Koop, C. Everett, and Francis A. Schaeffer. *Whatever Happened to the Human Race?* Westchester, Ill.: Crossway, 1983.

Lawton, M. P. *The Psychology of Adult Development and Aging*. Washington, D.C.: American Psychological Association, 1973.

LeBar, Lois E. *Focus on People in Christian Education*. Westwood, N.J.: Revell, 1968.

Lindeman, Edward C. *The Meaning of Adult Education*. 1926. Reprint. Montreal: Harvest House, 1961.

Merriam, Sharon B. *Themes of Adulthood Through Literature*. New York: Columbia U., 1983.

———, ed. *Linking Philosophy and Practice*. San Francisco: Jossey-Bass, 1982.

Naisbitt, John. *Megatrends: Ten New Directions Transforming Our Lives*. New York: Warner, 1982.

Novak, Michael. *The Spirit of Democratic Capitalism*. New York: Simon & Schuster, 1982.

Powell, John. *Why Am I Afraid to Tell You Who I Am?* Niles, Ill.: Argus Communications, 1969.

Powers, Bruce P., ed. *Christian Education Handbook*. Nashville: Broadman, 1981.

Schaeffer, Francis A. *How Should We Then Live?* Westchester, Ill.: Crossway, 1976.

———. *A Christian Manifesto*. Westchester, Ill.: Crossway, 1981.

Stokes, Kenneth. *Adult Life Cycle*. New York: W. H. Sadlier, 1982.

Thompson, Norma. *Religious Education and Theology*. Birmingham: Religious Education Press, 1982.

Toffler, A. *Future Shock*. New York: Random House, 1970.

———. *The Third Wave*. New York: William Morrow, 1980.

Towns, Elmer L. *A History of Religious Educators*. Grand Rapids: Baker, 1975.

Ulrich, Robert. *A History of Religious Education*. New York: New York U., 1968.

———. *Universal Jewish Encyclopedia*. New York: Universal Jewish Encyclopedia Co., 1948.

Wynne, John P. *Theories of Education*. New York: Harper and Row, 1963.

Young, Warren C. *A Christian Approach to Philosophy*. Grand Rapids: Baker, 1954.

Ziegler, Warren L. *The Future of Adult Education and Learning in the United States*. Syracuse, N.Y.: The Educational Policy and Research Center, 1977.

TEACHING ADULTS

Adams, William A. *The Experience of Teaching and Learning.* Washington, D.C.: Psychological Press, 1980.

Aldrich, Joseph C. *Lifestyle Evangelism.* Portland: Multnomah, 1981.

Beechick, Ruth. *A Biblical Psychology of Learning.* Denver: Accent, 1982.

Bruner, Jerome S. *Toward a Theology of Instruction.* Cambridge, Mass.: Belknap, 1966.

Cross, K. Patricia. *Adults As Learners.* San Francisco: Jossey-Bass, Inc., 1981.

Culver, Elsne Thomas. *New Church Programs with the Aging.* New York: Association, 1961.

Davie, R. H., ed. *Foundations of Lifelong Education.* Elmsford, N.Y.: Pergamon, 1976.

Draves, William A. *How to Teach Adults.* Manhattan, Kans.: Learning Resources Network, 1984.

Engel, James F. *Contemporary Christian Communications: Its Theory and Practice.* Nashville: Thomas Nelson, 1979.

Gangel, Kenneth O. *Twenty-Four Ways to Improve Your Teaching.* Wheaton: Victor, 1971.

Grattan, C. Hartley. *In Quest of Knowledge.* New York: Arno Press & *New York Times,* 1971.

Gress, James E., and Purpel, David E. *Curriculum: An Introduction to the Field.* Chicago: U. of Chicago, 1949.

Gross, R. *The Lifelong Learner.* New York: Simon & Schuster, 1977.

Havighurst, Robert J. *Developmental Tasks and Education.* 3d ed. New York: David McKay, 1972.

Heinich, Robert, Michael Molenda, and James D. Russell. *Instructional Media.* New York: John Wiley, 1982.

Hyman, Ronald T. *Ways of Teaching.* 2d ed. Philadelphia: Lippincott, 1974.

Kidd, J. R. *How Adults Learn.* New York: Association, 1959.

Klevins, Chester, ed. *Materials and Methods in Adult and Continuing Education.* Los Angeles: Klevens, 1982.

Knowles, Malcolm S. *The Modern Practice of Adult Education.* New York: Association, 1972.

———. *The Modern Practice of Adult Education: Andragogy Versus Pedagogy.* New York: Association, 1970.

———. *The Adult Learner: A Neglected Species.* 2d ed. Houston: Gulf, 1978.

LeBar, Lois E. *Education That Is Christian.* Westwood, N.J.: Revell, 1958.

Long, Huey B. *Adult Learning: Research and Practice.* New York: Cambridge, 1983.

Marlowe, Monroe and Bobbie Reed. *Creative Bible Learning for Adults.* Glendale, Calif.: Regal, 1977.

Mason, Harold C. *The Teaching Task of the Church.* Winona Lake, Ind.: Light and Life, 1960.

May, Philip. *Which Way to Educate?* Chicago: Moody, 1972.

McKeachie, Wilbert J. *Teaching Tips.* 7th ed. Lexington, Mass.: D. C. Heath, 1978.

Packer, J. I. *Evangelism and the Sovereignty of God.* Downers Grove, Ill.: Inter-Varsity, 1961.
Petersen, J. *Evangelism As Lifestyle.* Colorado Springs: Navpress, 1980.
Richards, Lawrence O. *Creative Bible Teaching.* Chicago: Moody, 1970.
————. *A Theology of Christian Education.* Grand Rapids: Zondervan, 1975.
Seidel, Robert J., and Martin Rubin. *Computers and Communication, Implications for Education.* New York: Academic, 1977.
Tidwell, Charles A. *Educational Ministry of a Church.* Nashville: Broadman, 1982.
Tough, A. *Why Adults Learn: A Study of the Major Reasons for Beginning and Continuing a Learning Project.* Monographs—Adult Education #3. Toronto: Ontario Institute for Studies in Education, 1968.
Walker, John. *Learning Comes of Age.* New York: Association, 1956.
Watson, David. *I Believe in Evangelism.* Grand Rapids: Eerdmans, 1976.
Wilbert, Warren H. *Teaching Christian Adults.* Grand Rapids: Baker, 1980.
Zuck, Roy B. *The Holy Spirit in Your Teaching.* Wheaton, Ill.: Scripture Press, 1963.
————, and Warren S. Benson, eds. *Youth Education in the Church.* Chicago: Moody, 1978.
————, and Robert E. Clark. *Childhood Education in the Church.* Chicago: Moody, 1975.

ADULTS IN THE CHURCH

Anderson, R. E., and G. G. Darkenwald. *Participation and Persistence in American Adult Education.* New York: College Board, 1979.
Bartholomew, Laurella. *Ministering to the Aging: Every Christian's Call.* New York: Paulist, 1979.
Bengston, Vern. *The Social Psychology of Aging.* Indianapolis: Bobbs-Merrill, 1976.
Bower, Robert K. *Administering Christian Education.* Grand Rapids: Eerdmans, 1964.
Boyd, Bob M. *Recreation for Churches.* Nashville: Convention, 1967.
Brown, Harold O. J. *Death Before Birth.* Nashville: Nelson, 1977.
Bruce, A. B. *The Training of the Twelve.* Grand Rapids: Kregel, 1971.
Claasen, Willard. *Learning to Lead.* Scottsdale, Pa.: Herald, 1963.
Clemens, Francis, Robert Tulley, and Edward Crill, eds. *Recreation and the Local Church.* Elgin, Ill.: Brethren, 1956.
Cristoff, Nicholas J. *Saturday Night, Sunday Morning.* San Francisco: Harper & Row, 1978.
Cumming, E. M., and Henry, W. *Growing Old.* New York: Basic Books, 1961.
Elliot, Elizabeth. *Let Me Be a Woman.* Wheaton, Ill.: Tyndale, 1976.
Eims, LeRoy. *Be the Leader You Were Meant to Be.* Wheaton: Victor, 1975.
Engstrom, Ted W. *The Making of a Christian Leader.* Grand Rapids: Zondervan, 1976.
Gangel, Kenneth O. *Competent to Lead.* Chicago: Moody, 1974.
Geist, Harold. *The Psychological Aspect of Retirement.* Springfield, Ill.: Charles C. Thomas, 1968.

Godfrey, Geoffrey, and Stanley Parker. *Leisure Studies and Services: An Overview.* Philadelphia: W. B. Saundiers, 1976.

Graendorf, Werner C., ed. *Introduction to Biblical Christian Education.* Chicago: Moody, 1981.

Graubard, Stephen R., and Gerald Holton, eds. *Excellence and Leadership in a Democracy.* New York: Columbia U., 1962.

Harbin, Elvin O. *The Recreation Leader.* New York: Abingdon, 1952.

Havighurst, Robert J. *Social Roles of the Middle-Age Person.* Chicago: Center for the Study of Liberal Education for Adults, 1953.

Holbert, Joe. *Word Banquet and Party Book.* Waco, Tex.: Word, 1975.

Hocking, David L. *Be a Leader People Follow.* Glendale, Calif.: Regal, 1979.

Hugen, M. D. *The Church's Ministry to the Older Unmarried.* Grand Rapids: Eerdmans, 1960.

Jacobsen, Marion. *Good Times for God's People.* Grand Rapids: Zondervan, 1952.

Jackson, Edgar H. *When Someone Dies.* Philadelphia: Fortress, 1971.

Knowles, Malcolm S. *The Leader Looks at Self-Development.* Washington, D.C.: Leadership Resources, 1961.

Kraus, Richard. *Recreation Today: Program Planning and Leadership.* New York: Appleton-Century-Crofts, 1966.

Kubler-Ross, Elizabeth. *Death: The Final Stage of Growth.* Englewood Cliffs, N.J.: Prentice-Hall, 1975.

Levinson, David J. *The Seasons of a Man's Life.* New York: Alfred Knopf, 1978.

McFarland, Dalton E. *Management Principles and Practices.* New York: MacMillan, 1958.

McKenzie, Leon. *The Religious Education of Adults.* Birmingham, Ala.: Religious Education, 1982.

Page, Richard, ed. *Beyond Death's Door.* Port Washington, N.Y.: Ashley, 1979.

Perry, Lloyd. *Getting the Church on Target.* Chicago: Moody, 1977.

Rawlings, Maurice. *Life Wish: Reincarnation, Reality or Hoax?* Nashville: Nelson, 1981.

Rehfeldt, Richard. *The Pastor's Role in Educational Ministry.* Philadelphia: Fortress, 1974.

Richards, Lawrence O., and Clyde Holdtke. *A Theology of Church Leadership.* Grand Rapids: Zondervan, 1981.

———. *Youth Ministry.* Grand Rapids: Zondervan, 1972.

Rood, Wayne R. *Understanding Christian Education.* Nashville: Abingdon, 1970.

———. *On Nurturing Christians.* Nashville: Abingdon, 1972.

Ross, Murray, and Charles E. Hendry. *New Understanding of Leadership.* New York: Association, 1957.

Selznick, Phillip. *Leadership and Administration.* New York: Harper & Row, 1957.

Shawchuck, Norman, and Lloyd M. Perry. *Revitalizing the Twentieth Century Church.* Chicago: Moody, 1982.

Smith, Frank Hart. *Social Recreation and the Church.* Nashville: Convention, 1977.

Smith, JoAnn Kelly. *Free Fall.* Valley Forge, Pa.: Judson, 1975.

Weinstock, R. *The Graying of the Campus.* New York: Educational Facilities Laboratories, 1978.

FAMILY MINISTRY

Adams, Jay. *Christian Living in the Home.* Grand Rapids: Baker, 1979.

Bustanoby, André. *But I Didn't Want a Divorce.* Grand Rapids: Zondervan, 1978.

Chapman, Gary. *Toward a Growing Marriage.* Chicago: Moody, 1979.

Christenson, Larry. *The Christian Family.* Minneapolis: Bethany, 1970.

Conway, Jim. *Men in Mid-Life Crisis.* Elgin, Ill.: Cook, 1978.

Dobson, James. *Hide or Seek: How to Build Self-Esteem in Your Child.* Old Tappan, N.J.: Revell, 1979.

Duvall, Evelyn Millis, David R. Mace, and Paul Popenoe. *The Church Looks at Family Life.* Nashville: Broadman, 1964.

————. *Faith in Families.* Nashville: Abingdon, 1970.

Goode, William J. *After Divorce.* Glencoe, Ill.: Free Press, 1956.

Hyatt, I. Ralph. *Before You Marry . . . Again.* New York: Random House, 1977.

Johnson, O. R. *Who Needs the Family?* Downers Grove, Ill.: InterVarsity, 1979.

Johnson, Rex. *At Home with Sex.* Wheaton, Ill.: Victor, 1979.

Kirkendall, Lester A. *Premarital Intercourse and Interpersonal Relations.* New York: Julian, 1970.

Knox, David. *Exploring Marriage and the Family.* Glenview, Ill.: Scott, Foresman, 1979.

Meier, Paul D. *Christian Child-Rearing and Personality Development.* Grand Rapids: Baker, 1977.

Mace, David and Vera. *How to Have a Happy Marriage.* Nashville: Abingdon, 1977.

Petersen, J. Allan, ed. *The Marriage Affair.* Wheaton, Ill.: Tyndale, 1971.

Pinson, William M., Jr. *The Biblical View of the Family.* Nashville: Convention, 1981.

Renich, Jill. *To Have and to Hold.* Grand Rapids: Zondervan, 1976.

Schulz, David A. *The Changing Family.* Englewood Cliffs, N.J.: Prentice-Hall, 1972.

Sell, Charles M. *Family Ministry.* Grand Rapids: Zondervan, 1982.

Sheeny, Gail. *Passages.* New York: Bantam, 1976.

Shorter, Edward. *The Making of the Modern Family.* New York: Basic Books, 1975.

Small, Dwight Harvey. *How Should I Love You?* San Francisco: Harper & Row, 1979.

Strauss, Richard L. *Marriage Is for Love.* Wheaton, Ill.: Tyndale, 1973.

Swindoll, Charles R. *Strike the Original Match.* Portland: Multnomah, 1980.

Udry, J. Richard. *The Social Context of Marriage.* Philadelphia: J. B. Lippincott, 1974.

Vigeveno, H. S., and Ann Claire. *Divorce and Children.* Glendale, Calif.: Regal, 1979.

Wahlroos, Sven. *Family Communication: A Guide to Emotional Health.* New York: New American Library, 1974.

Wright, Norman H. *The Family That Listens.* Wheaton, Ill.: Victor, 1979.

———. *The Pillars of Marriage.* Ventura, Calif.: Regal, 1979.

General Index